S0-AFY-590

DOWNLOADING GOD

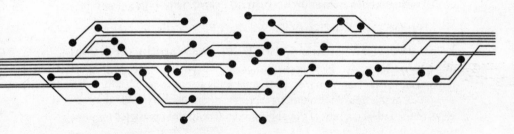

JACK ALAN LEVINE

Downloading God

By Jack Alan Levine

Published by Great Hope Publishing LLC, Coconut Creek, Florida

Cover Design & Layout By Scott Wolf

www.JackAlanLevine.com
www.Don'tBlowItWithGod.com
www.LifeSolutionSeminars.com

Email: Jack@JackAlanLevine.com

Copyright 2017 Jack Alan Levine. All rights reserved. Printed in the United States of America. Excerpt as permitted under United States copyright act of 1976, no part of this publication may be reproduced or distributed in any form, or by any means, or stored in a database retrieval system, without the prior written permission of the copyright holder, except by a reviewer, who may quote brief passages in review.

Neither the Publisher nor the author is engaged in rendering advice or services to the individual reader. Neither the authors nor the publisher shall be liable or responsible for any loss, injury, or damage allegedly arising from any information or suggestion in this book. The opinions expressed in this book represent the personal views of the author and not of the publisher, and are for informational purposes only.

Many of the various stories of people in this book draw from real life experience, at certain points involving a composite of stories. In some instances, people's names have been changed in the stories to protect privacy.

ISBN 978-0-9904097-0-0 – Paperback
ISBN 978-0-9904097-1-7 – E-Pub

Library of Congress control number: 2016957664

Scripture taken from The Holy Bible, New International Version Copyright 1973, 1978 1984 Biblica. Used by permission of Zondervan. All rights reserved.

Scripture taken from the New King James version. Copyright 1982 by Thomas Nelson, Inc. Used by permission. All rights reserved.

Scripture taken from The Message. Copyright 1993, 1994, 1995, 1996, 2000, 2001, 2002. Used by permission of NavPress Publishing Group.

Downloading GOD

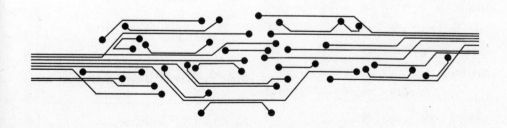

TABLE OF CONTENTS

Section 1
Boot It Up

Section 2
Operating System Analysis

Section 3
Configuring Your Hard Drive

Section 4
Installing Virus Protection

Section 5

Copy & Paste His Power & Promise

Section 6

Remote Access To The Kingdom

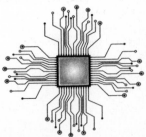

PRAISE FOR DOWNLOADING GOD

""Downloading God" is the file of information that today's generation needs to click on more than ever. Jack Levine's authentic and transparent self-disclosure rings through in his passionate devotion to his Lord and Savior Jesus Christ. His simple, straightforward, trademark writing style as in his previous books allows the reader to easily absorb, appropriate and apply the word and truth of God in a realistic, revolutionary and redemptive way. 'Downloading God' has short chapters all themed around a clever computer technology motif which makes the timeless truths of God both real and relevant to contemporary culture.

In 'Downloading God' Jack addresses many of the most important issues we all face in life. Jack's message is clear, bold, exciting, invigorating and life-giving. His words pack a punch and a purpose and speak a radiant lightning bolt of truth into the pervasive darkness of our corrupt culture. I pray you read and internalize them as they will electrify your connection to, service for and relationship with God. Start 'Downloading God' now and update and program your life for Kingdom success!"

Dr. Jared Pingleton

Vice-President, American Association of Christian Counselors.
Clinical Psychologist, Credentialed Minister

Author of 'Making Magnificent Marriages,'
Co-author of 'Be Strong and Surrender: A 30 Day Recovery Guide,'
'Praying With Jesus: Reset Your Prayer Life',
'Christian Perspectives on Human Development'
Editor of 'The Struggle is Real: How to Minister to Mental and Relational Needs in the Church.'

INTRODUCTION

We live in a technological age. We have seen revolutionary and breakthrough computer and communication technology that has changed the world. Internet access, high-speed transmission, virtual reality and a host of other innovations have made the world in the twenty-first century a digital age, futuristic reality, come true.

Everyone under twenty years old today (and many under thirty) communicate by digital communication in one form or another - phones, iPads and computers. Thus, information is no longer studied or memorized, but it is usually just downloaded and stored somewhere in a digital memory bank for quick, easy access. Anything, anywhere, anytime.

Flying cars, drones delivering packages the same day, 3-D printing... it really seems the technology keeps coming faster and faster. Most would agree it's making the world better. Regardless of your thoughts on that, you would have to agree it is certainly changing our world dramatically and making it a faster world.

However, I want to remind you with this book that it is imperative for you to have the most revolutionary information of all. The most critical, life-saving, life-giving information is the truth about God. By Downloading God, you can have access to Him instantly, now and forever. It is my hope that you will download the information in this book into the memory sensors of your brain and the information and truths about God will stick not only to your brain, but also to your heart. I pray it will impact and change your life for the better and forever as it brings you closer and closer to God. "Come closer to me and I will come closer to you," promises the Lord.

You'll notice the section titles in the book reference your computer, downloading information and technology, that's because we now live in a super-paced, highly-charged technological world. Yet many people wrongly view God as old-fashioned, ancient, or worse, as just a historical figure. Quite the opposite, God is alive today as He always has been. He's the same yesterday, today, tomorrow and forever. He is the Alpha and Omega, the beginning and the end, and He has written a perfect plan for each and every person's life. My desire is to see no one misses this plan. I pray that you don't miss the blessing of the greatest truth of all, which is the Truth of God, and its revolutionary impact and life changing power.

So, regardless of the means you use to access God - whether it's old-fashioned memory, studying printed books, or accessing files on your computer electronically - the data and Truth remain the same. Technology has only changed how we exchange the information.

I was speaking at a meeting of the Christian Harness Horseman's Association at a horse farm in central Florida in June of 2016. A few friends of mine came with me. There was an old rotary payphone there. The one where you used to drop coins in to make a call. When I was a kid, they were on every street corner. One of my thirty-year-old friends looked at it quizzically, turned to me, and said, "What's that?" As if it were an ancient, foreign piece in a museum or something from outer space. And to her it was. Yet to anyone under 25 the Internet is not an amazing invention, and computers are not amazing, revolutionary inventions that changed the world. Rather they are as commonplace and as nondescript as the refrigerator in your kitchen. Something that's always been there since they were born and not looked at by them as revolutionary and game changing at all.

Yet those of us who are older see the world a little differently based on its changing technology. The leaps and bounds we have made in healthcare technology have been astounding and amazing. Stem cells, replacing human organs with animal parts or new 3-D printed parts, robotic surgery, revolutionary new medical lasers... all add up to better medicine and a better life. But regardless of your perception on the pace, advancement and capacity of the amazing changes that occurred in your own individual lifetime, your heart and your mind can still change as you are exposed to and learn Truth.

Apple, Facebook, Yahoo, Google, Microsoft and a host of other companies have led the way in fueling this great technological revolution. Yet the greatest programmer of all, God, the One who created and designed the most intricate, complicated and greatest code ever written, has hardwired you in the most effective and efficient way possible. Your software is incomparable and unduplicatable. It is also interactive with your Creator so He can constantly upgrade it for your benefit. You have a battery source (the Holy Spirit) that never runs out or needs charging. He is eternal.

Now our computers today have extensive memory capacity so we can download all the stuff we need and want (as well as some stuff we don't.) Use the infinite memory capacity of your brain and make it a priority to download this information about God.

My prayer today is that your heart and mind and soul would be open to the Truth and Word of God. I promise the change that takes place in your life will be far greater than any technological change you have witnessed in your entire lifetime. Don't miss it.

So what are you waiting for? Start downloading. You'll have all the information you'll ever need.

Wishing you all of God's best blessings.
Jack

Section 1

BOOT IT UP

Turning On Your Spirit's Operating System

To boot up a computer is to turn it on. This process involves loading the startup instructions from the computer's ROM, followed by loading the operating system from the current boot disk. Once the operating system software is loaded, the boot process is complete and the computer it is ready to be used.

During this process if any of the internal system was not working properly and initialization was not done to verify there was functionality, other parts of the computer would fail.

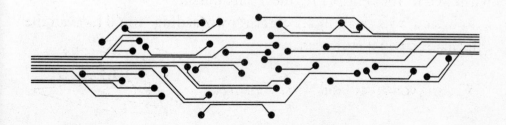

Stressed Out

God gave me a startling perspective change. This one will apply to every single person reading this book. Like most of you, occasionally I have an issue in life. I know you've probably had one yourself — health, finance, relationship, children, job, future, anything. I've had a couple and I was thinking about them. I was asking God for answers to specific issues and situations in my own life. In the midst of worrying about the outcome of these situations, I think I was worrying about them a little too much, and I was getting stressed out. I could feel the stress physically and emotionally getting to me.

When I went for my annual doctor's checkup, he said, "All of your blood levels are high. Your cholesterol is high, and this level is high and that level is high."

I said, "No way, my stuff is usually never high." It's always great.

My friends have teased me all my life in envy, "How can you eat like you do and not have high cholesterol or blood pressure."

I said, "Because of my metabolism. It's good." So this time I thought, well, wait a minute. It's got to be stress related. I'm not eating any differently. It must be stress related. And of course I hoped that was the case and there was not some other serious physical issues.

Anyway, I went to God with these questions, my questions, as I'm sure you go to God with your own questions, issues, problems and prayers. The individual and specific issues that were causing my stress are not relevant to the story or point, so just plug in your own stuff that you're worrying about, going to God about, praying about, and stressing out about. As I was lying there one night talking and praying to God, I sensed in my spirit God asking me two very specific questions. He impressed on my heart very strongly, they're the only questions that matter. If you ask yourself these two questions, as I found out, I promise they will apply to and change your perspective on every single situation you are facing in your life today.

Here's the first question the Holy Spirit of God asked me to ask myself that night. While not audibly, God was speaking directly to my spirit very loudly. He said, "Ask yourself this question. Does God love you?"

I asked myself that question. "Does God love me?" I thought about it. Clearly the answer is yes. There's not even a doubt in my mind, 100 percent. I was saved at thirty-three years old. It's twenty-five years later, and there's not one of those days since March 10, 1991 that I would tell you I didn't know and think for sure that God loves me. I definitely believe God loves me. That answer was yes.

God said, "Then there's just one more question. One more simple question. Last question. Ask yourself, Jack, is God in control?"

I said, "Is God in control?" I thought about it again. I tried to come up with a reasonable way I could possibly say God was not in control. Somehow, even in the slightest way. I could not. My answer was yes. God is in control! There's not even a single doubt in my mind. There's not even a possibility in my mind it could be otherwise. I believe 100 percent that God is in control of my life, of your life, of the world, of the past, of the present, of the future, and of eternity.

I believe he made the heavens and the Earth. He is the Alpha and the Omega, always has been, always will be, the same yesterday, today, tomorrow. Absolutely, God is in control. Then what is the problem? There was no more problem! Oh the issues were still the same, the things that before had stressed me out were still a part of my life — worries, concerns, pressures, obligations, desires — but my perspective on all of them and life had changed dramatically. If God loves me and God is in control, what do I have to worry about?

That was a great perspective shift for me and I hope for you. Does God love me and is God in control? Apply that to every single question, issue, concern, and area of your life. I believe God will speak abundantly to your heart through that as He did to mine.

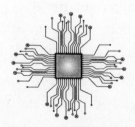

You're Already Dead

Another perspective change, here's an interesting one for you. This may shock you in a good way. If I asked you when you were born, you'd give me a date. My wife Beth would say March 9. I won't say the year (don't want to get divorced... Smile!) But you get the picture. You'd give me a date and a year that you have referred to as your birthday all your life.

Well, let's see what God says. God says in Ephesians 1:4, "He chose us in Him before the foundation of the world that we would be holy and blameless before Him."

God had created you before your physical birth. I know you physically came out of your mother's womb on a certain day and you marked that and refer to that as your birthday, but that's not when you were born. God created you before the foundation of the Earth. In Psalm 139:15, it says, "My frame was not hidden from you when I was made in secret and skillfully wrought in the lowest parts of the Earth. Your eyes saw my substance being yet unformed and in your book they were all written. The days fashioned for me when as yet there were none of them." What's that? Before anything happened, before the foundation of the world was created, you saw me, Lord? You formed me? Let me get this right. You had already written out my days? They were already written, but yet they really hadn't even happened yet? Even before there were days, they had already been established.

God says, "That's exactly right."

That's your proof. God has a perfect plan for your life. God has a plan for every life. He said it to Jeremiah and he is saying it to you and me today. In Jeremiah 1:5 He said, "Before you were born I set you apart. I appointed you as a prophet to the nations." God had a plan for Jeremiah's life. He had a plan for Jesus' life. He had a plan for every life we see written about in His gospel, and He has a plan for every single one of our lives. We're to fulfill this perfect plan by just loving God, by just reflecting God and by just living our lives for the glory of God and the benefit of the kingdom of God.

Now if I said, "Well, when did you die?"

You'd say, "Well, Jack, don't be crazy. I'm sitting here reading your book, so I don't know yet. I certainly hope it's not today."

"Well, wrong on both."

"What do you mean?"

You were born before the beginning of the world, so when did you die? You say, "Well, I haven't died yet."

"Yes, you have. You're making a big mistake. You have died."

Let's, again, go to the word of God. He says in Romans 6:4, "We were, therefore, buried with Him through baptism into death in order that just as Christ was raised from the dead through the glory of the Father, we too may live a new life." You died with Jesus on the cross! You're dead already to the things of this world. Let me ask you something. Why would you possibly fear something that's already happened? How could you fear death? You died already.

Can you just imagine if I came into church this morning and said, "Listen, I couldn't sleep last night and I'm really, really nervous."

You say, "Why?"

I say "Hurricane Matthew. Oh man, this thing is going to kick the crap out of us. No, no, no really. I've got to go home and I've got to protect my house from the storm. I'm just going to live like this, in fear of hurricane Matthew, every day for the rest of my life."

You would laugh. You would say, "Jack, you're either insane or delusional. You're wrong."

"What do you mean I'm wrong?"

"Well, Hurricane Matthew has passed. We escaped unscathed. It's passed. It's over."

Yes, and you have already died with Christ. You have already risen to live with Him forever and ever. It's happened already! It's over.

This part of the story, our lives on Earth, are just us fulfilling God's purpose for our lives here. What do I possibly have to fear? What do I possibly have to fear about death if I've already died? That's the perspective God wants you to have. There are too many Christians worried about death. No, we're living forever with God. We died already. Physical death can't hurt us. Jesus took care of that already. In 1 Thessalonians 5:10 we read, "Christ died for us so whether we are awake or asleep we will live together with Him." The Apostle Paul confirmed it in Galatians 2:20. He said, "I have been crucified with Christ. It's no longer I who live, but Christ lives in me and the life which I now live in the flesh I live by faith in the Son of God who loved me and gave Himself up for me."

I've been crucified with Christ. I've died on the cross with Christ. I no longer live, but Christ lives in me. That's what we miss. We just miss it. We just think so selfishly, just living for ourselves all of the time. God has told us and said, "Listen, be ready. Be sober. Be alert. The thief comes at an hour you don't expect. I need you to be alert and ready and live lives that glorify me so you're prepared, so I can bless you with all of my blessings. That's the perspective God wants you to have on life and death. So download that and make sure to save it!

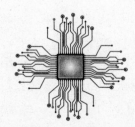

Time Moves Too Fast

My buddy Douglas Cooper also gave me a new perspective the other day. Doug and I were talking before church. I said, "Doug, it seems the older I get the faster time is moving. Time is really moving fast."

Doug looked at me without missing a beat and he said in a kind voice as if I were a child in kindergarten and he was the teacher, "Jack, Jesus is coming back soon and we're going to reign with Him forever. We should be looking forward to it."

He's right. What's the difference if time seems to be going faster or not? Time doesn't matter. Doug was saying time is irrelevant in regard to how fast we perceive it to be moving. The only thing that was relevant and that I should be focused on, as Doug properly was, is that Jesus is coming back soon and we're going to reign with Him forever and ever. We need to be looking forward to it. We should not worry about how fast our earthly life is passing by but excitedly looking forward to the beginning of our eternity in heaven! That is the perspective a true believer in Jesus should have. Notice I said true believer because in order to really have that perspective you must truly believe.

You Get To Do It

Two weeks ago I went to an Ironmen of God men's conference. There was a guest speaker, a guy named Heath Ritenour. He's forty years old and the CEO of an insurance company. I thought it was going to be a boring business talk, but it was a great talk. He talked about how he got testicular cancer at forty years old. That's not the great part. He has a wife and kids, and his whole perspective on life changed because he thought he was going to die. He went through all of this chemo and radiation for a year and it was horrible. They had to remove one of his testicles and fortunately he lived. He's healthy at the moment. Through the ordeal he said his whole perspective changed.

He said, "All of these things I used to complain that I had to do. I can't believe I have to do this. I can't believe I have to do that. I have to take my kids to school, have to go to work, have to mow the lawn, etc. No, no, no. That was all wrong. I now see that I GET TO do them. It's a blessing and a privilege. I get to take my kids to school. I get to go to work. I get to love my wife. I get to mow the lawn. I get to do these wonderful things."

His whole perspective has changed. The situation hadn't changed, but his whole perspective had. That's what God wants from us. God wants our perspective to change to one of gratitude for the blessings and gifts of God.

Don't Lose Heart

Here's the bottom line to everything. This is it. It's Psalm 27:13, and this is the greatest thing ever. I pray that God would speak to you through this passage now. David wrote this Psalm. He's being chased by Saul at this time in his life, probably the darkest hour of his life up to that point. He's running, being chased and hiding. He said this, "I would have lost heart." What's that David? You would have lost heart. You would have quit. You would have given up. You would have killed myself. You wouldn't have gone on? That's exactly what he was saying. But there's more. Here's the end of the verse "I would've lost heart UNLESS I had believed that I would see the goodness of the Lord in the land of the living."

How amazing is that? He would've lost heart, but he didn't because he knew something better was coming. Maybe you're in that situation today. Maybe something's got you — maybe it's cancer, maybe it's finances, maybe it's a relationship, maybe it's kids, maybe it's life, maybe it's fear of a terrorist attack, maybe it's whose running the government. I don't know, maybe just a lot of things.

Maybe you're suffering from depression. Maybe you're struggling with addiction. Maybe you have anger that you can't get rid of and you know you should. Maybe there's lack of forgiveness in your heart for people you know you should forgive, but you don't want to. "I would have lost heart, unless..." There's an "unless." "...unless I had believed that I would see the goodness of the Lord in the land of the living." God has promised each and every one of us that we will see His goodness in the land of the living. We will see it in heaven for all eternity and we get a deposit right now with the Holy Spirit in our hearts in this life. You and I have already died and are going to live forever because we died with Christ on the cross. We have that same hope, that same assurance, and that same certainty. We should never lose heart.

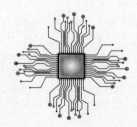

Make God Laugh

It's was just Father's Day. For the believer in Jesus Christ, every day is Father's Day because we get to worship our Lord each and every single day — not only in this life but in the life to come. The certainty of that brings us such great joy and peace and happiness. We love that.

If you want to know how to make God laugh on Father's Day, just tell Him your plans. That'll do it. That'll get Him laughing. I met with some guys the other day. We were sitting around in a Bible study, and the topic came up. The leader of the group said, "Let's talk about fathers. Tell me about your fathers."

I was excited to talk about mine because I have a great father, a wonderful dad who has treated me so well all my life, sacrificed all my life so my brother and I would have a better life. My mother has the same attitude, so I know that wonderful love of parents, that sacrificial giving loving. I can relate to it so much. It was easy for me to accept Jesus Christ as a loving Father when I saw how much my parents loved me.

As we went around the room, there were a couple of guys in the room who didn't have such a good experience. One said, "My father ran out on us when we were little kids." Another said, "I never knew my father. So I have no good memories to share. I have no inspirational quotes. No great lessons that my father taught me. As a matter of fact, I had a father who birthed me, but I didn't know him. I had no relationship with him."

I thought how sad but yet how wonderful that these brothers had still come to know Jesus Christ as their true Father, that even though an earthly father may fail, our heavenly Father will never fail us.

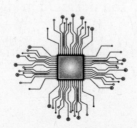

The Luckiest Son In The World

Last week we were out to dinner up in Orlando and met a businessman who was a friend of our pastor. There were twelve of us sitting at dinner and the businessman was there with his twenty-year-old son. The kid had no interest in being there. It was a dinner of adults. He didn't want to be there, but he was sitting there politely. He was built like a rock, so I asked him, "Tommy, what's your future like? What do you think life is going to be for you, kid?"

He looked at me and said, "I don't know."

I said, "Oh, are you going to go to school? Are you going to work?"

He said, "Oh, we'll see."

His father, the businessman, interrupted and put his hands on his shoulder. He said, "He's in no rush. I'm right here. I'm not going anywhere. He's in no rush."

I thought man, what a great picture of God's love. By the world's standards it would be, "All right, kid. You're twenty. What are you going to do with your life? What are your plans? Come on." But the father's going, "No, no, no. You have all of my resources at your hand. You're not in a rush. You take your time. You decide. I'm right here. I'm behind you no matter what." I believe God wants to remind you and me today that He's behind us no matter what. That's the exact same attitude God has for us.

Character Witness

I was reading the newspaper the other day and saw an article about Paul Betlyn, owner of a heating and AC repair shop in Pennsylvania. He got a call late at night from a woman named Bridget, it was in the middle of winter her heater had blown. He walked her through the steps to fix the heater on the phone, but it didn't work. An hour later he got in his car, drove over, and fixed her heater. It took him another hour and a half to fix it. The lady was a mother whose husband was deployed overseas,. the wife of a serviceman with a little baby. She said, "I was really worried about the bill and nervous about what it was going to cost."

He handed her a bill and it said, "Deployment discount, total due $1.00." The job would have been hundreds. When asked why he did it he said, "They're the real heroes. I'm not the hero. Her husband is the hero. He's the one overseas serving."

You say, "What does that matter?" Here's how it matters. Paul Betlyn had a model in his life and that was his grandfather. Listen to what Betlyn told ABC news, "My grandfather was a milkman during the Great Depression. Many times he'd go to the door and the women didn't have any money for milk, but the baby was crying in the background." He'd put the milk right on the table. When I heard about Bridget with her husband being deployed, I put the milk on the table." Here's a guy modeling what he saw his grandfather do.

My question for you and me today is, "What kind of models are we?" What kind of models are our friends, our coworkers, our kids, our family seeing? What kind of models are we?

I was so inspired by the story that I sent him a couple of my books and CDs in the hopes they would bless him. I got back a hand written thank you note. Not a surprise based on his character. The kind of character I hope you and I would have.

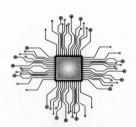

You're A Dog!

I was sitting there on the porch the other day and thinking about my own struggles, my own issues and what I would define as problems. Such as the bank has decided they don't want to give me a mortgage for our new house because I don't have the income they wanted. I said, "Well that's particularly annoying."

We have a business we're planning to start up in Orlando, a drug and alcohol rehab business. It's just not starting according to the pace I want. I'm thinking, "I've got young kids, a family whose future I have to prepare for," and just wondering how this is all going to come together. A little bit of it has been stressful.

I was outside on the porch and my eight-year-old dog, Skasha, a German Shepherd/Husky/Lab mix, sweetest dog in the world, was at my feet. God spoke to my heart in the Spirit and said, "Look at the dog."

"What do you mean, God? Look at the dog? I've looked at the dog for eight years. Big deal, God. There's the dog at my feet. The dog's always at my feet."

God said, "No, no, no. Look at the dog. Is the dog worried?"

I said, "No, the dog's not worried."

"Do you feed the dog every day?"

I said, "Not only do I feed that dog, I love that dog. I take care of that dog. My family takes care of that dog. That dog has the greatest life ever and she's also the greatest dog. She's always at my feet. She listens to everything I say." She's not there nervously scratching and worried, "Daddy, are you going to feed me tonight? Dad, are we okay?" We have a fence in place to protect her. She can go out but not past the fence. Why? Because then she wouldn't be where we can see her, take care of her, and provide for her. That dog has nothing to worry about and she knows it.

God said, "You're the dog! You have nothing to worry about and you need to know it."

I said, "Okay. I get it."

Usually we (I) always pray, "God, here's what I need. Here's what I want. Fix this. Fix that. You love me. Fix this. Fix that." I think we miss something sometimes. I think we miss listening to God. I want to qualify this by saying, of course we are to pray to God. Of course we are to pray continually, to pray without ceasing, that's how we communicate with God, but it's also supposed to be intimate time with God. It's not supposed to be, "Here's my list and fix my stuff."

I just want to suggest to you as it's been suggested to me that before I pray perhaps, just perhaps, I may want to meditate on the greatness of God. Perhaps I may want to focus on who God is, what God's done, His majesty, His splendor, His sacrifice, His throne, His greatness, His goodness, His love, His mercy, His peace, His grace, His righteousness, His forgiveness, everything — who He is, the beginning, the end, the Alpha, the Omega, the Creator, the Healer, everything that God is. Then when I'm focused on Him and in worship with Him, absolutely I would make my prayers known to him. I'll bet at that point it would sound a lot different than, "God, here's my list. I need this. If you'd just give me these four things (mine usually consists of financial security, success, health, respectful kids, etc. and once in a while I throw in a closer walk with God... Smile) God, that would be good and you'd have done good. You'd be a good God."

God says, "No. No, I want you to love Me and focus on Me. I'll take care of everything. You're the dog! I have everything taken care of. What do you think? You're not going to have a house? You're not going to have food? No, no. You're going to have all of that. You just don't know how it's going to happen. Oh, so that's your problem, Jack. You know it's going to happen because you have faith and trust in Me. You just don't know how it will happen and how I will work it out, and you're particularly annoyed and even worried about that."

I said, "Exactly." And that's my problem. The answer is we need to focus on God, His greatness and His mercy.

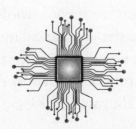

Well Connected

A buddy of mine who I met up in Orlando was telling a story about when he was a young kid. He used to ride his bicycle into his father's office all of the time. Day in and day out he'd just ride into his dad's office, share stuff with him, and talk to him. He always had access to his dad, which sounds pretty cool to me and I hope pretty cool to you.

It may not sound like such a big deal, except that his father at the time was a top general in the South African Army. He was a very busy man. You couldn't have access to him without an appointment, a meeting, or without a high security clearance. It never dawned on my buddy as he was growing up that this was an issue, that having access to his father was a big deal because he had it all the time.

I want to remind you today that we have that same access to God. We're that little kid riding our bicycle in to see God, no matter how busy God is, no matter how high on the throne He is. He loves us so much. We're His kids. He always wants to know what's going on in our lives. He always wants to know what's going on in our hearts. He always wants to know our thoughts, our concerns, our cares, our hopes, our dreams, our problems, our issues because He is with us, and He always has time for us. If you ever doubt that or you're not sure, just look at the cross and Jesus' death and blood shed on the cross for you and his body broken on the cross for you. You'll know for certain that you matter to God and God always has time for you.

Broken Heart

I know a twenty-year-old. He's a great kid, and he's had this girlfriend for over a year. She came from another state to live near him. They're very, very close. He loved her very, very much. Then she broke up with him. She had threatened to about a month or two ago, and he was devastated. She didn't, and he was so happy, but this time it was for real. She packed up her stuff and left.

We were sitting in church last week, and he was a row in front of me. He had some friends with him and he was sitting. Everybody else was standing for worship, but he was sitting. He couldn't even stand up. He was so upset. He was so distraught because the love of his life had left. He was sitting there with his head in his hands., crying. His friends lovingly had their arms on him.

In my mind God showed me this picture of his future. I saw him married with all these wonderful kids. He's twenty years old now, but I saw him married with children, happy and with a wife who loves him (and it wasn't the same girl who broke up with him). I saw God had His hand on this kid, and he was just going to have the greatest life ever. Yet at that moment in time, he was the most miserable person in the world. Nothing could console him.

Get this right. In his perception of the moment of what was happening to him, he was miserable, upset, defeated. He thought life as he knew it was over. This was the worst thing that could ever happen. I was looking at the situation going, "This is the greatest thing that ever happened to you. You are so lucky. If you could only see what was ahead, you wouldn't be crying. You'd be cheering." God spoke to my heart and He said, "Don't you do that same thing, Jack?"

Don't we do that same thing in life sometimes? We look at situations, and we get so upset by what we see, what we think, and what we feel, we don't believe God when He said things like, "I know the plans I have for you, plans to give you a hope and a future, to prosper you and not to harm you. All things are working together for your good. I have a perfect plan for you. Before you were formed in your mother's womb, I knew you."

God has all these great promises for us, and yet sometimes we live like they're not true. We get so caught up in that moment and our perception of what is good or bad, in our belief of what we think we need, thus making ourselves out to be God instead of trusting God.

How ironic. Can you imagine? The best thing that could happen to this kid, and he was just miserable. I'm not saying he'd ever kill himself, but he was probably thinking, "My life is ruined," because he was so upset. He couldn't see it. You and I can only see it when we see it through God's eyes, when we're communing with God, when we're praying, talking and walking with God. So how about we download and use "God's version" of life!

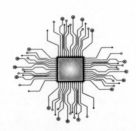

Keys To The Kingdom

God's been putting something on my heart lately. I believe, for me, it's the key to life. You might discover it's the key to life for you as well.

Here's how it started. God was burning a specific verse in my heart. Matthew 6:33. You're probably familiar with the verse. "Seek first the kingdom of God and His righteousness and all these other things will be added to you."

I was a little surprised when I felt the Lord's spirit impressing that verse upon my heart. I said, "God, maybe you made a mistake. I know that verse very well. Matthew 6:33 is a life verse for me." You might have heard people use that term. Christians often use that term. A "life verse" is a verse that has a lot of meaning to them. It has rallied them all of their life.

Matthew 6:33 came to me almost twenty-two years ago directly from God at a desperate time in my life.

I said, "I get it, Lord." I turned my life and my drug addiction over to God. Everything got tremendously better after that point. I've been riding that verse for twenty-two years; that's how it became a life verse.

I said, "God, why would you possibly need to share that verse with me? I know that verse."

I felt the Lord's spirit answer me, "No. I want you to focus on the second part of the verse."

The first half of the verse reads, "Seek first the kingdom

of God." The part I knew I needed to focus on was the next phrase: "...and His righteousness."

"All right," I told the Lord. "I'm going to listen to what you're telling me. I'm going to find out what we're talking about here."

That's what you should do, too. When the Holy Spirit of God speaks to you, you should dig deep to see what He's talking about. Seek Him and He will answer. He'll talk to you in sermons, He'll talk to you through Christian music, He'll talk to you through other believers, but the time He will speak loudest without a doubt is when you are individually studying His word. The Holy Spirit will take that Word, shine a light on it, and explode it in your heart. He will explain it as well. God says the Holy Spirit will teach you all things.

For the next week or two, after God put that on my heart, I began searching the scriptures and reading my Bible with that verse in mind. Like 3D or a neon sign, all of these verses on righteousness and the righteousness of God began popping out to me. I knew God wanted me to go deeper, even though these were verses I'd read a hundred times.

I believe God wants you to go deeper as well. If God wants us to go deeper, why don't we try it and see what happens?

First of all, what is our definition of righteous? The dictionary definition of righteous is "acting in accord with divine or moral law." We would agree with that. Somebody's righteous if they do the right thing, if they're morally right, if they're spiritually right. It's also defined as being free from guilt or sin. Why would you be free from guilt or sin according to the dictionary? Because you acted in accordance with divine law; therefore, you are free. That's our definition of righteousness by the world's standards.

The Hebrew definition from the Old Testament was pretty similar. It talked about being upright, just, straight, innocent, true, and sincere. In the book of Job, Job is introduced to us as having perfect righteousness. Clearly, he was living a righteous life. He was just. He was straight. He was true. He was sincere. That's the same requirement we would use for ourselves. We would consider ourselves righteous if we behaved like that—with sincerity, justice, and honesty.

How about God's righteousness? What is God's righteousness? We know from the Bible that righteousness is a key attribute of God. It's used also in a legal sense; the guilty are judged, but the guiltless are deemed righteous. The concept of righteousness concerns ethical conduct. It also concerns legal conduct. God is described as a righteous savior as well as our deliverer in Isaiah 61. We are told in the book of Psalms that the righteous are those who trust they will be vindicated by the Lord. We're considered righteous if we trust in the Lord's vindication.

What happens in the New Testament in regard to righteousness? Jesus asserts the importance of righteousness by saying in Matthew 5:20, "For I tell you that, unless your righteousness surpasses that of the Pharisees and the teachers of the law, you will certainly not enter the kingdom of heaven." Righteousness was a critical requirement to enter the kingdom of heaven. Righteousness that exceeded the Pharisees and the teachers of the law — that was a tall order.

What's our definition of righteousness? Here's the best one I know of and what I hope and pray your Christian definition of righteousness is: "God the Father is righteous. He is just. Jesus Christ, His Son, is the righteous one. The Father, through the Son and in the Spirit, gives the gift of righteousness to repentant sinners for salvation, believing sinners are declared righteous by the Father through the Son. They are made righteous by the Holy Spirit working in them and they will be holy/righteous in the age to come.

They are and will be righteous because they are in a covenant relationship with the living God who is the God of all grace and mercy and will bring to completion what has begun in them by declaring them righteous for Christ's sake."

That's the great promise of God. That's the hallelujah and amen moment. You and I are righteous in the eyes of God, but not by our own righteousness. Our righteousness is but filthy rags before the Lord. We know that. We're all descendants of Adam, born with sin in our blood. We could never be righteous if the standard were our own perfection. We can do righteous things, we can do some good things, but we can't be righteous all of the time. We're not perfect according to God's standard, so God sent His Son to die for us that whoever believe in Him should have eternal life, should be declared righteous, holy, blameless, and above reproach. We are clothed in the righteousness of Jesus Christ. What a wonderful thing. Make sure you download that!

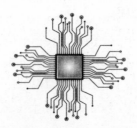

Seven-Year-Old Kid Impacts The World

At New Year's, we make resolutions. It's what we do. Much of the time, we promptly break them. It rarely takes me much time to break my New Year's resolutions. I'm so thankful as we're reminded, in Lamentations, of God's assurance. He tells us His mercies are new every morning.

For the child of God, every day is New Year's day. We can have a new beginning, a clean slate each and every day.

I read a story in the newspaper in September of 2015. It was about a kid who lived in a small town in Canada with only fifteen hundred residents. His name was Evan Leversage, and he died at seven years old. The town knew he was going to die. The doctor knew he wasn't going to make it to Christmas, so he told the boy's family, "You may want to celebrate Christmas a little early this year."

The whole town of St. George gathered together in October, and they strung the town full of lights. They celebrated Christmas in October and had a great parade. People came from all over and eight thousand people showed up that day in St. George for the parade. Little Evan brought the spirit of life to the city that day and his story spread around the globe.

Why did eight thousand people make the sacrifice for this seven-year-old kid who many of them didn't even know? Because it started to be about other people. The love of God swept through that town; it swept through the world through this kid. The Internet lit up like a pinball machine and love and blessings came from around the world for Evan and his family.

Did this seven-year-old kid's life matter? Yes. It mattered in a big way. We can see it in his life and the difference that was made through him. The good news is that our lives matter. God wants to use our lives to matter for the kingdom in the way He chooses. No one could've known how God would use seven-year-old Evan's sickness and cancer to spread the message of God, but God did.

God wants to use you and me to spread His message in the way we live our lives and impact other people. Make sure to download that!

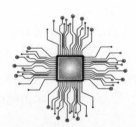

You Can't Kill Me

My prayer is that we would live like we really believe Jesus, like we really believe we're going to heaven. My prayer is that we'd not wait until we die to experience all that God has for us. There is still a lot of evil in the world today. We see so much of it that perhaps we're getting numb to it at this point. There are so many killings and so many shootings and so much bad going on. But we're reminded in God's word that no weapon formed against us will prosper. God is in control. God knows what's going on.

There are too many killings. It grieves my heart. One in particular hit me hard this year. It took place at Oregon Community College. A gunman walked on campus and killed ten people. The gunman's name was Christopher Harper Mercer, and he claimed that he was a warrior of Satan and wanted to earn points in hell by killing people. He approached people and asked them if they were Christians. Those who responded yes, he said, "Get ready. You're going to see your God in about one second." And he killed them. He was right about one thing. They definitely met God the next second. They went to their reward, to live forever and be with God for all eternity.

In the book of James, he talks to people who are not believers and says, "You believe there is one God. Good. Even the demons believe that and shudder." This evil shooter knew when a Christian died, they were going to be with

God. You and I have that same certainty. We should be so thankful we know for certain where we're going when our time on Earth is up.

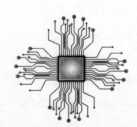

No Greater Love

How do you know somebody loves you? I could say I love you, but does that mean I really love you? I think, if I said I loved you, you would know if I really loved you or not. You would know it by my actions. But is there more to love than that?

What if I demonstrated my love to you in action? What if I picked you up at work? What if I loaned you money? What if I gave you gifts? What if I cleaned your house? Wouldn't that all demonstrate love? If I do those things, doesn't it show you that I love you? Not necessarily.

It's not because I do these things that you know you are loved. How, then, can we know? I know because I can feel it. I know in every fiber of my being if someone loves me or not. It really doesn't matter what you say or what you do. It really matters what you feel and how you know.

That's how it is with God. That's how it is with salvation. You could love somebody and not see them for years, but you still know they love you very much. Even if you're not around them, you still know they love you very much. You've experienced it. You've felt it. When you feel something, you experience it.

I know I'm forgiven. I believe God wants to bring me closer to Him so I can feel and experience His love even more. I believe this is an important reminder for every Christian. We're all the same. We all struggle with our flesh, with our hearts, with our minds, with the enemy. We're all human. But we've all experienced the love of God.

I was sitting in church the other day, and I saw in my mind an image of Jesus weeping over me because I wasn't getting it. I wasn't basking in His forgiveness; I was still suffering in my mind and heart. I would cry for my children Ricky, Jackson, and Talia if they weren't getting it. If they didn't understand that I loved them, it would grieve me. Why? Because I love them so much, all I want is for them to get it and understand my love. All I want is for them to have every blessing they could possibly have. It would break my heart if they did not understand that.

I know the bible verse well. "Whom the Son sets free is free indeed" (John 8:36). But I realized I needed to actually accept God's forgiveness. The problem is that my plumb line—my goal—is perfection. I judge myself guilty when I don't measure up. Well, if I use that measuring stick, I can never win.

I was sitting there realizing, "You know what, Satan? You tricked me. You almost had me going back and putting myself under the Old Testament Law, thinking there are things I have to do and accomplish in order to be loved by God." If I don't do this, I'm not a good husband. If I don't do this, I'm not a good father. If I don't do this, I'm not a good businessman. If I don't do this, I'm not a good person. If I do this, I am. I could've done ninety-nine things right and one thing wrong, and I'd condemn myself and say, "I did that wrong." If my guide is always perfection, I'm going to judge myself guilty every time I fail.

All the while, God is saying, "Wait a minute. I've forgiven you. I died on the cross so that you don't feel that way." We need to remember to walk in, live in, and accept the grace of God and love of Jesus pouring out on us. Satan can trick us. He can trap us. God is our refuge and our fortress, Psalm 91 assures us, but Satan can trick us into coming out of that protection, into trying to go it alone and stepping out from under the protection of God.

That was what I felt the Lord showing me. Have you been doing the same thing? If you have, you need to get back under the grace, mercy and forgiveness of God. That's what it's all about.

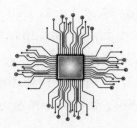

How Much Is Enough To Give?

God says in Malachi 1:14,

"Cursed is the cheat who has an acceptable male in his flock and vows to give it, but then sacrifices a blemished animal to the Lord."

God calls him cursed who has a good offering to give and doesn't give it or gives a substandard/lame offering instead.

Do we have a good offering to give to the Lord? Of course we do! We have our lives, the most fragrant offering we could give to God. When we don't give that to God, God asks, "Why would you hold this back from me? I gave it to you. I control in my hand every breath you take, everything you do. I gave it to you." Every hair on your head is numbered. You're worth more than sparrows who fall from the tree. You are the ones God loves. God ordained that you would be adopted into the kingdom of God. God ordained that you would be an heir to the throne of heaven. We are the King's kids.

God says He will curse those who have a better sacrifice and don't offer it. I pray this would not be a reflection of our Christian service to God. I pray that when God sees our hearts, He will see dedication and love. I pray that we are going to hear, "Well, done, good and faithful servant," for the attitude of our heart. Not only for the accomplishments of our lives but more importantly the attitudes of our hearts.

What we don't want to hear is, "Depart from me. I do not know you." God's word says there are people who will come to God face to face on Judgment Day and they'll hear, "Depart from me. I did not know you."

They'll say, "But wait a minute. We mourned in the streets. We played the flute for you and you didn't dance. What do you mean, 'Depart from me. I didn't know you?'"

It would be like us saying today, "Lord, I read my Bible. I came to church. I donated money."

Those are very good things, but they are not the requirements for salvation. That requirement is accepting Jesus Christ. There are also requirements for living a life that is pleasing to God. What is it that pleases God? What is our reasonable service? Paul makes it very clear in this passage:

"Therefore, I urge you, brothers and sisters, in view of God's mercy, to offer your bodies as a living sacrifice, holy and pleasing to God—this is your true and proper worship" (Romans 12:1). A living sacrifice is what God calls us to be. Not to lay before Him half-baked commitments or half-lived lives. No. He wants us to give Him ourselves out of a heart of love. That is the life He will honor.

What honor is due to God? Our very lives. I pray we will honor God with all our lives, and in that way give Him the honor that He alone deserves. Our plans are futile without the Lord, but with Him, purposes and plans are established and fulfilled, and potential is realized. Blessings flow and life has meaning.

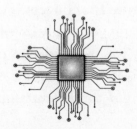

How Can Wrong Be Right?

By their fruit you will recognize them (Matthew 7:16).

My wife and I have a friend. He is a great guy, an on-fire Christian. We have a little bit of a difference in theology. He believes you can lose your salvation, which is impossible. We don't believe that. That's the whole basis of the grace of God. His approach is a little more works oriented.

He and I were talking for three hours one day, trying to solve this great theological issue. Finally, I come to the conclusion that we're both saying the same thing. He was saying it in words that I would never allow and would never be acceptable. To this day I say, "You cannot lose your salvation" because it's an irrevocable gift. God says His gift and call are irrevocable. You can't lose it. It's a gift from God. You didn't earn it. You can't take it away. It's impossible. That's God's gift. But when I drilled down deep, I found that he agreed on that point—you can't lose your salvation.

What he was really saying was if you were saved, if you were really saved, you wouldn't behave in a way that doesn't honor and glorify God. I'm thinking, "How do I argue with that?" Because it's true. The concept is true, if you really have been saved by God and you really love Jesus Christ.

God's word says we see evidence of a tree by its fruit *(Matthew 7:16). If you are saved, we should see the glory of God in you. We should see the gratitude of God in you. We should see the Holy Spirit coming out of you.*

That doesn't mean you won't have a bad day. We all have bad days. We're only human. That's why Jesus had to die for us on the cross because we're not perfect. We know there is not one righteous, not one.

But it does mean that there really is no excuse and no apology for someone who has been transformed by the word of God, whose mind has been renewed, who is a new creation in Christ, to not live a life that reflects and glorifies God. And it is not unreasonable or wrong for people who see so-called professed or self-declared Christians not living that way to question their salvation. Of course we know only God is the judge of someone's salvation, as it is between them and God, but you would think and God's word clearly says we would see evidence of a tree by its fruit. May there never be any question about where you and I stand. May the evidence of our lives speak loudly for who we are, what we are and whose we are! To God be the glory.

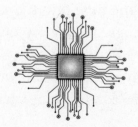

Can't Have One Without The Other

Check out Malachi 3:7

"Ever since the time of your ancestors you have turned away from my decrees and have not kept them. Return to me, and I will return to you," says the Lord Almighty. But you ask, "How are we to return?" Will a mere mortal rob God? Yet you rob me. But you ask, "How are we robbing you?"

You know the famous verse that comes next. This is the "tithing" verse.

"Bring the whole tithe into the storehouse, that there may be food in my house. Test me in this," says the Lord Almighty, "and see if I will not throw open the floodgates of heaven and pour out so much blessing that there will not be room enough to store it."

That verse does not apply only to tithing. It applies to all of life. Here's the example. In order to get B, you have to do A. First, you bring the tithe into the storehouse. Then God pours out the blessings of heaven so much that you won't be able to store them.

It's the same with our lives. First, we're obedient to God. Then we get these amazing blessings that God promised. I do the same with my kids. I'm like, "Hey, I need you to do this, that, and that. If you do those things and behave accordingly, I can bless you abundantly and exceedingly more than you can ask or imagine. If you don't listen to me and instead do what you want, ignoring your responsibilities and what I need you to do, I can't bless you. It doesn't mean I love you any less. It just means no bicycle, no extra time to watch TV, no ice cream, no anything else that you might like and think is good.

Sometimes that's our attitude with God. In order to get B, if we want to see the floodgates of heaven open and see a blessing poured out that there won't be enough room to store it, first we have to do A—bring the tithe into the storehouse. First, we need to honor God with every area of our lives. I believe God is testing our faith. In Luke 12:48, He says, "For everyone who has been given much, much will be demanded. From the one who has been entrusted with much, much more will be asked."

Do you trust God with your money and your life? I get that you trust Him with your salvation. You know you can't get salvation on your own. If God doesn't give it to you, it's certainly not going to happen. But we tend to say, "Okay, God, I'll trust you with my salvation. The other things I think I might have some control over—like my money, my life, the way I behave—I'm going to control that, God."

I don't think He's happy with that attitude. God says, "Listen. I'm giving you instructions on how I want you to do this, and I want to bless you." Remember, "he who is faithful with little will be faithful with much." Don't you think God is telling the truth when He says, "I'm testing you. I'm going to test you to see that you'll be faithful. If I can trust you in the little things, I can trust you with much. If I can trust you with your finances, with your marriage, with the way you speak to people and act around people, I can trust you with much"? God wants us to be trusted with much. After all we are His children and His representatives here on Earth. You would think we would act like it and live up to the calling we've obtained!

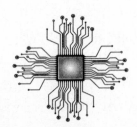

Heart Surgery

Consider the promise God gives in Ezekiel 36:26-28:

I will give you a new heart and put a new spirit within you. I will remove your heart of stone and give you a heart of flesh. I will place my spirit within you and cause you to follow my statutes and carefully observe my ordinances. Then you will live in the land that I gave your fathers. You will be my people, and I will be your God.

Could the Old Testament prophecy be any clearer? It has come true. We don't need anybody to interpret that. It has come true because of Christ Jesus. God has placed His spirit in us. He has removed our heart of stone and replaced it with a heart of flesh, a godly heart.

Jesus Christ has come. The Lord says, in Ezekiel 33:11, "As I live ... I take no pleasure in the death of the wicked..." It is not God's desire for anyone to perish. God came so that all would be saved. God doesn't send people to hell. People choose to go to hell by rejecting Jesus Christ. Many Old Testament kings chose not to follow the ways of God and they paid the consequences swiftly, usually with their lives or the loss of their kingdoms. God tells us that we, too, have consequences on our actions and our behavior, but God takes no pleasure in the death of the wicked. The scripture continues, "...but rather that the wicked person should turn from his way and live. Repent of your evil ways!" God is asking us to repent. Could He be any clearer on this subject?

The passage goes on to say:

"Now, son of man, say to your people: The righteousness of the righteous person will not save him on the day of his transgression; neither will the wickedness of the wicked person cause him to stumble on the day he turns from his wickedness. When I tell the righteous person he will surely live but he trusts in his righteousness and commits iniquity, then none of his righteousness will be remembered, and he will die because of the iniquity he has committed" (Ezekiel 33:12-13).

The Lord says the righteous person won't be able to survive by his righteousness on the day he sins. Then God brings in a contrast.

Now when I tell the wicked person, "You will surely die," but he repents of his sin and does what is just and right, he returns collateral, makes restitution for what he has stolen, and walks in the statutes of life without practicing iniquity, he will certainly live; he will not die. None of the sins he committed will be held against him. He has done what is just and right; he will certainly live (Ezekiel 33:14-16).

God is saying that the righteous who commit iniquity will die. The wicked who turn from sin and do the right thing will live. Verse 17 says, "But your people say, 'The Lord's way isn't fair,' even though it is their own way that isn't fair." How often do kids say, "It's not fair that we get punished," even if they're being punished for doing something they knew was wrong.

You were speeding. It's not fair you get a speeding ticket? You rob a bank. It's not fair you go to jail? What you did wasn't fair. It's not the punishment that isn't fair. It's what you did that isn't fair. Our sin, our iniquity, is what keeps us from receiving the full blessing of God, not God's love. You have God's love no matter what.

We sin and then we justify it and say, "God, I can do this. It's okay. You understand."

God says, "No, I don't understand. I don't understand why you wouldn't live a sold-out life for me. I don't understand what part of "the cross" you don't understand. I sacrificed my life. I gave everything for you so you could live and you're greedy with your time, your money, your life, as if you control it, as if you actually had something to do with it." It doesn't work like that.

But Lamentations 3:22-24 leaves us with a promise:

Because of the Lord's great love, we are not consumed, for His compassions never fail. They are new every morning. Great is your faithfulness. I say to myself, "The Lord is my portion. Therefore, I will wait for Him."

I recently attended a men's conference, and the main speaker said even if you never saw God deliver a single promise on this Earth, even if you lived a life of suffering and misery, it would have been worth it waiting for God because your citizenship is in heaven. Whatever is happening in your life should be used for the glory of God. We should be thankful for everything, even when we don't understand it.

A later verse in that same chapter of Lamentations says, "For no one is cast off by the Lord forever. Though He brings grief, He will show compassion, so great is His unfailing love. For He does not willingly bring affliction or grief to anyone" (Lamentations 3:31 - 32). God does not willingly bring affliction or grief to anyone, but you can certainly willingly bring it upon yourself by being disobedient to God. You can bring it upon yourself, just as an unbeliever can reject

Jesus Christ and bring upon himself spending eternity in hell separated from Jesus. That's a choice. The choice is ours. We also have a choice to make with how we live our lives. That choice is ours as well.

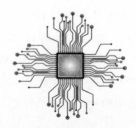

Worthless Life

Here is a warning from God, something that we can apply to our own life today:

They will throw their silver into the streets, and their gold will seem like something filthy. Their silver and gold will be unable to save them in the day of the Lord's wrath. They will not satisfy their appetites or fill their stomachs, for these were the stumbling blocks that brought about their iniquity (Ezekiel 7:19).

Our flesh, our appetite, our stomach, the things of this world, God says, are stumbling blocks, which bring about our iniquity. It's like Judas throwing back the thirty pieces of silver he thought was so valuable that he would betray Jesus for it. The next day, he went and hanged himself because he couldn't live with it anymore. God says these things of the world will rust, decay, and be consumed by moths. They're worthless. Only the things of the spirit and the things of God are worthwhile.

I came to the point, one day, where I couldn't bear the thought of not seeing what God could do with my surrendered life. I was getting older, in my forties, and I reached the point where I said, "I'm going to die one day, and I can't live with the thought of not seeing what God could do if I give Him my whole life.

If I'm a believer, I've got to trust. I've got to have faith.

I'm far from perfect. I have sin in my life. I struggle with it. I give it to God. I try to walk with God as best I can. It's about progress, not perfection. Only Jesus was perfect. We're to be like Him and imitate Him.

I can imitate a basketball player by trying to make baskets. I can copy a guitar player by playing the same notes he plays on my guitar. I might not be as good as they are, but I can do what they do. How can we expect the Lord's blessings when we don't do what God said to do? God is telling us to turn and repent. To listen to his voice and his Holy Spirit. Why should we do so? Because we are treasured by God. Like Daniel in the days of old, God loves us, He treasures us, He calls us His own. We should do all we can to give Him glory in pure gratitude and gratefulness for His love for us. Whatever you do, don't forget the download that!

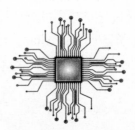

Treasure Map

For the grace of God that brings salvation has appeared to all men, teaching us that denying ungodliness and worldly lusts, we should live soberly, righteously, and Godly in the present age, looking for the blessed hope and glorious appearing of our great God and Savior, Jesus Christ, who gave Himself for us, that He might redeem us from every lawless deed and purify for Himself His own special people, zealous for good works. (Titus 2:11-14).

That's you and me. We are to live with purpose, on a mission from God. We're the special people, zealous for good works. I was lost for thirty-three years before I came to know Jesus as Lord. Jesus died for my sins and died for all the sins of every man. He came that all might be saved. When we know Jesus, when we come to Him, we are God's special people, zealous for His good works.

Look into your heart and ask yourself this question, "Am I zealous for the good works of God?" Zealous means you can't wait to do it. Hey, I'm zealous for a Bruce Springsteen concert. I'm zealous for a Dolphins game. I'm zealous for good pizza. Am I zealous for the works of God? Is that the priority of my life? We should be set apart for a godly life. Separated and identified just as is a person serving in the military.

Here's the map to what a separate life looks like. It consists of four things.

First: Confession.

First, you have to confess Jesus is Lord. You acknowledge Him as your Savior. He comes into your heart. He takes out your old heart. He puts in a new heart. You're born again of the spirit of God, a one-time transaction, an irrevocable transaction between you and God. You can never lose your salvation. You confessed Christ as Lord.

Second: Transformation.

Next, we should see a transformation. You're different. You're not who you were in the old man. You're the new man. What does that look like? Check out this passage: "And He died for all, that those who live should no longer live for themselves but for Him who died for them and rose again ... Therefore, if anyone is in Christ, he is a new creation; old things have passed away; behold, all things have become new" (2 Corinthians 5:15, 17).

We're a new creation in Christ. That's the transformation. When I put my bread in the toaster, it went in as white bread. It comes out as toast. There's a transformation. There's no question. All you have to do is look at it and see. It was white bread. It's now toast. People should be able to see the transformation in our lives. Wasn't saved. Was of the world. Is saved. Is of God. Black and white. Clear as day. This fact should exude and radiate from everything we say and do.

In Romans 12:2, the apostle Paul says "And do not be conformed to this world, but be transformed by the renewing of your mind, that you may prove what is the good and acceptable and perfect will of God." Our minds are to be transformed by God, by the Holy Spirit, by the Word, by our relationship with God. It should be evident that we have been transformed by God.

That's what the world is supposed to see. As we are told in Colossians 3:10 to "Put on the new man who is renewed in knowledge according to the image of Him who created him."

Third: Preparation.

Next, we should see preparation on your part, demonstrated through study of the word of God. We want to be prepared. God says we are to be prepared to preach in season and out of season. God says that we're to put on the full armor of God in Ephesians 6, and that the sword is the word of God. We need to know it so we can deflect and defend against the treacherous darts and schemes of the evil one who wants to destroy us and sift us like wheat.

God says be prepared. God says be sober. "Be alert. You don't know the hour at which I come. Be prepared. Be ready." That's our obligation. If we want to get ready for the hurricane, we put our shutters up. If we want to get ready for Thanksgiving dinner, it's a good idea to go buy some turkey and other food. If you've got a lot of people coming over, it'd be embarrassing to just have a loaf of stale Italian bread. You knew they were coming. Why didn't you get ready?

I don't want to be standing before God and God saying to me, "Why didn't you get ready? Why didn't you do what I told you to do? Why didn't you live like I told you to live?" So we should see preparation in your life.

Last: Demonstration.

After confession, transformation, and preparation, we should see a demonstration of God in your life. God says we know a tree by its fruit. God tells us to live a life that glorifies God. Be salt to that tasteless generation and light to a world of darkness.

Our confession, our transformation and our preparation is demonstrated by how we live our lives. The Lord tells us, "Be holy, for I am holy" (1 Peter 1:16). You can't demonstrate God any more than that. Just be holy. Just do the right thing. Live a life that glorifies God. You'll be demonstrating God really well.

Romans 13:14 says, "But put on the Lord Jesus Christ, and make no provision for the flesh, to fulfill its lusts." It didn't say you wouldn't have lusts of the flesh. It says you're not to make provision for them. You're not to feed the lust of the flesh. We are not to indulge in that. We are not to prepare to sin. We are to prepare for God and to be transformed. That's the life God wants.

Why should we be separate? Why should we confess? Why should we be transformed? Why should we demonstrate Christ to a lost world? Because we believe and love God. It's that simple. "Yet for us there is but one God, the Father, from whom all things came and for whom we live; and there is but one Lord, Jesus Christ, through whom all things came and through whom we live" (1 Corinthians 8:6). For us, there is one Father, one God through whom we live. We live for Him and through Him.

He wants our hearts to know the hope, the riches, and the great power of God (Ephesians 1:18). If you don't know those three things, you're missing it. You're doing something wrong because it's God's desire that you know His hope, you know His riches, and you know His great power — the same power that raised Jesus from the dead. That is power.

What of those who ignore God's provisions, God's purpose, and God's power? What happens to them? What of those who choose the possessions and pleasures of this world? What happens to them? In Luke 12:15, Jesus said to them, "Watch out!" It's always a good idea to pay attention when Jesus says, "Watch out!"

Jesus is not fooling around. He says, "Watch out! Be on your guard against all kinds of greed; life does not consist in an abundance of possessions." He goes on to tell the parable of a rich man who had an abundant harvest and he thought to himself, "What should I do? There is no place to store my crops. I know what I'll do. I'll tear down the old barns. I'll build bigger barns. I'll put everything in there. Then I'll say, 'Eat, drink, and be merry. You've got nothing to worry about. Take life easy.'"

God says to the rich fool in verse 20, "You fool! This very night your life will be demanded from you. Then who will get what you have prepared for yourself?" The next verse gets to the heart of the matter. I believe God wants us to be familiar with this warning in today's world: "This is how it will be with whoever stores up things for themselves but is not rich toward God."

God says the same thing to you and me. This is how it will be if you store things up for yourself but are not rich toward God. But if we choose to be zealous for God, His redeeming power will shine in our hearts and out through our lives. We will be prepared, and we will help others be prepared too. When that final day comes, we will not be seen as the foolish rich man, but as the wise who knew their God and lived accordingly. I would call that being smart and responsible. God would call it being obedient and faithful. No matter what you call it, it's the right thing and the smart thing to do!

Where There's Smoke

I used to go to Denny's to eat a couple of times a week, along with a pastor buddy of mine, as we worked on a project together. A young waiter worked there — thirty years or younger. As time went by and we interacted with him, I could tell he was a Christian kid.

We got to talk with him a lot and were sharing about God a little bit back and forth. He started to tell me about his father one day. He said, "A lot of people would consider my father fanatical. Some people say he's crazy."

I said, "Well, why is that? What does he do?"

He said, "His name is Smokey, and he's up in Port St. Lucie, Florida. Everybody in Port St. Lucie knows him. He's out on Federal Highway in Port St. Lucie with a big huge cross every single day and has been for eighteen straight years."

That is this man's individual mission. I'm not telling you to go on Federal Highway with a cross to glorify God. That's between you and God. The Lord will tell you what He wants you to do. This guy — Smokey Barber — responds to the spirit of God in that way. To this day (as of 2016 when I finished this book), he's out on Federal Highway in Port St. Lucie with a big cross glorifying the gospel of God and doing street ministry in God's name.

I haven't met Smokey yet, but it's my desire to go up there and meet him. I love his kid. He's clearly a Christian kid. Smokey has done a good job raising him. I've got to see the man behind this kid. That's what fascinated me about him. This kid's own light so fascinated me that I wanted to know about his family.

So let's say it's Judgment Day. I'm up before God pleading my case and there's Smokey Barber. Man, he doesn't have to say a word, does he? His actions spoke louder than his words ever could because he lived a life sold out to God. He sacrificed for God. There's not a question about it. There's not a question in the eyes of the world and certainly not in the eyes of God.

The question we need to ask ourselves today is: What would prevent me from living a life sold out for God? What are we afraid of? God's word says, "This is how love is made complete among us so that we will have confidence on the Day of Judgment: In this world we are like Jesus. There is no fear in love. But perfect love drives out fear because fear has to do with punishment. The one who fears is not made perfect in love" (1 John 4:17-18). I want to have confidence on the Day of Judgment. I assume you want to have confidence on the Day of Judgment. We want to be in Smokey Barber's position where there is no question what we're going to hear from God when we step over that great divide. We want to hear Him say, "Well done, good and faithful servant. Come and share your master's happiness. You have been faithful with little. I will trust you with much."

How do we do that? The above scripture says, "In this world, we are like Jesus." That's what we're supposed to be. We are to be salt to a tasteless generation and light to a world of darkness. We do that by being like Jesus, not just once in a while, not just when it's convenient, not just when we feel like it. No. All the time.

Can you imagine our military only fighting when they felt like it, when it was convenient, when they wanted to? No.

They're under military command. They're focused on the task at hand. That's what they do. Thank God for that. God says we're supposed to do the same thing. We are soldiers of God.

The apostle Paul says, "Who serving in the military focuses on civilian things?" Who, when they're in the middle of the Super Bowl, goes out and calls their wife on a cell phone during a play? There's a time and place for that. It's not when you're focused on the game and the play is at hand.

You might not be called to the same ministry as Smokey, but you are called to live for Christ. And if you have no idea where to start, you might begin by looking at where you are right now, at the gifts and talents He has bestowed on you. Seek God and His will for your life, His direction for your service to Him, and He will show you. You will please Him and He will be pleased to fill your life with righteousness, peace, and joy.

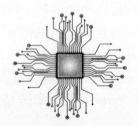

Whole Hearted

The psalmist says, "Give me understanding, and I shall keep your law." What are you asking God to give you? Are you asking God for health, money, and power? Or are you asking for God's will to be done in your life regardless of what you can do to serve Him and bless Him? What are you asking God for in your life?

The psalmist asked for understanding. Solomon asked for wisdom, and God gave him more wisdom than he could ever imagine and everything else to boot. This same concept is found in Matthew 6:33: "Seek first the kingdom of God, and all these other things will come."

King David says, "Indeed, I shall observe it with my whole heart" (Psalm 119:34). The Lord says, "You'll find me when you seek me with all your heart" (Jeremiah 29:13). What are you observing with your whole heart? Is it the world? Is it politicians? Is it sport stars, musicians, comedians, or businessmen? What are we following and focusing our whole heart on?

Psalm 119:35 says, "Make me walk in the path of your commandments. For I delight in it." What do you delight in? It should be a joy to follow the Lord. I can tell you personally — I was saved at thirty-three years old. I was brought up Jewish. No one ever handed me a Bible and said, "Jack, you need to come to church." It was Jesus Himself knocking on my heart. I sought God, and I accepted God.

It's twenty-five years later now, and my life has gotten better every day since then. I'm preaching because I want to, not because I have to. I go church because I want to, not because I have to. We do Bible studies and open the Word of the Lord, and it is a joy. I spend time in the Word with God in the morning because I want to not because I have to. It's the greatest thing ever. I want more of it. It's like pizza. It tastes so good.

The next part of the Psalmists prayer says, "Incline my heart to your testimonies and not to covetousness." This is so critical and necessary. As we know, the heart is deceitful above all things. Here his prayer is, "Incline my heart to your testimonies. Make my heart want more of those. Not to covet. Not to want for the things of the world." Then he says, "Turn away my eyes from looking at worthless things."

He knows the things of the world are worthless. He realizes they'll rust and decay. He knows you can't take them with you; they have nothing to do with your spiritual reward in heaven.

Have you turned your eyes away from worthless things, or do you have a place in your life for them, the place where Satan lives and plays and rules, a place you think is separate from the place you have for God? It's not, as long as you have both of them. Remember bad company corrupts good character. You're polluting the place of God in your life when you give a place to the devil. You say, "Well, Jack, I love God. I wouldn't give a place to the devil." Anything that doesn't glorify God is the devil's place.

Perhaps, as you read, you realize that the prayer of your heart is not quite in line with the prayer of the psalmist. That's okay. Simply realizing it is the first step toward renewing your heart and soul in God. All you have to do is begin with the prayer, *"Create in me a clean heart, Lord, and renew a right spirit with me" (Psalm 51:10).*

If you pray that with your whole heart and open your life to what God has for you, He will work within your heart and life. He will renew you. He will open your eyes to the things that last forever. He will allow you to see the truth — that His word is more precious than thousands of coins of gold and silver.

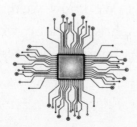

Do You Want Survival Or Revival?

Revive me in your righteousness (Psalm 119:40).

Revive me. Let that be our prayer. "Shake me up, Lord. Wake me up. Shock me. Give life to this dead mind and body. Revive me so that I may be like you, Lord."

Have you asked God to revive you according to His righteousness, His way, or His word? Or are you not interested in a spiritual revival? Are you satisfied with the Earthly life you live and the fleshly benefits you receive, knowing you're going to heaven but not concerned enough about God and the kingdom to live sold out 100 percent for God?

I believe that's the toughest question you can ever ask yourself. Are you interested in spiritual revival or are you satisfied with your life the way it is? That's the toughest question I could ever ask you.

Psalm 119 contains this prayer: "Establish your word to your servant." It is asking of God, "Build in me a foundation. Establish it. Create it, Lord. Turn away my reproach, which I dread. Revive me in your righteousness." It is a cry for righteousness. We know we're righteous in God's eyes through Jesus Christ because we're clothed in the righteousness of Jesus Christ. God sees us holy, blameless, and above reproach.

But are we righteous in men's sight glorifying God? We're righteous in God's sight because He looks at us clothed in the righteousness of Christ. But are we righteous in the eyes of other men? Are we representative of God to other men? Do they look at us and say, "There is a likeness of Jesus. This guy, this girl, is what Jesus must be like"? Kind, loving, considerate, righteous, truthful, merciful, graceful, forgiving, long-suffering — all the wonderful fruits of the spirit. Is that what our lives look like? That's exactly what we're supposed to look like.

The Psalmist says, "Revive me, O Lord, according to your word" (Psalm 119:107). In Joel, the prophet tells us to be fasting. Call the assembly. Gather the elders and cry out to the Lord for mercy and forgiveness that He might relent and bring us blessing. We're to cry out.

When was the last time you cried out to the Lord for revival in your heart? Not for a loved one who is dying. We cry out to the Lord then. Not for money when you lose all your money in the stock market, real estate market, or something similar. We all cry out to the Lord then. I get that. Not when we're sick and need healing. When was the last time you truly cried out to God for revival in your heart? When was the prayer of your heart that His will would truly be done in your life, that you would be a vessel He can use on Earth here to truly glorify Himself and His kingdom? When did you last sincerely believe that if you did that in obedience, you would be blessed abundantly and exceedingly, as He promises, more than you could ask or imagine?

The writer of Psalms says, "I rise before the dawning of the morning and cry for help" (Psalm 119:147). Do you do that, or do you sleep late? You can pray to God at night, during the day, or both. It's not necessary to rise early in the morning, but that's a good time. It shows another level of commitment and dedication to the things of God.

"I hope in your word" (Psalm 119:147). Not in the stock market. Not in some TV or radio talk show host. Not in my boss. Not in my relationships. "I hope in your word. Revive me according to your word. Revive me according to your judgments. Revive me according to your loving kindness. Revive me for your name's sake. Revive me so I may live for your name's sake, for Christ's sake. For Christ's sake, revive me."

In Psalm 19, the psalmist asks this. And I hope this is the prayer of your heart. Only pray it if you mean it. He says, "But who can discern their own errors? Forgive my hidden faults. Keep your servant also from willful sins. May they not rule over me. Then I will be blameless, innocent of great transgression."

God has forgiven any sin you confess. In 1 John 1:9, He says, "If we confess our sins, he is faithful and just to forgive us our sins, and to cleanse us from all unrighteousness." God promises, "As far as the east is from the west, I'll remember your sins no more" (Psalm 103:12).

The psalmist prays, "Keep your servant also from willful sins. May they not rule over me. Then I will be blameless, innocent of great transgression." If we're sinning willfully, we are not innocent.

First, he is saying, "Lord, take away the sins I don't even know about." Then he's saying, "And keep me from the ones I want to do." That's spirit over flesh.

Who is going to rule your life — your flesh or your spirit? It's easy to sin. We know sin is tempting. We know the devil is tempting us with sin. It looks good. It's like that candy criminals hand out to your kids when they want to steal them away and rob them and hurt them. "Hey, come here, kid. Look, here's some free candy for you." Free until you take it, and then you're trapped like a rat, soon to die.

May God revive our spirits so that we can live our lives for Him and Him alone.

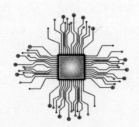

Skating On Thin Ice

A few years ago when my kids were still young (ten and eight), our family went ice skating. The kids and I were out on the ice, and my wife Beth was watching from the sidelines. We were going around, and it was an open skate. We skated around for an hour. Jackson and Talia were hanging on to the walls as they slowly moved around the rink. They were just learning how to ice skate. I was standing close to Jackson the whole way because I didn't want him to fall and hurt himself. A couple of times, I grabbed him before he fell and I thought, "I'm doing a great job of being a dad. Look at me protecting my kids." I'd skate over to Talia and do the same for her as well.

The first hour ended, and we got off so the ice could be cleaned. Then we went back on for another hour. Soon the entire second hour was almost up. There were maybe five minutes left. For an hour and fifty-five minutes I shadowed my kids, grabbing them to keep them from falling. Jackson had taken his hand off the ledge, growing in confidence. He started skating around and was coming around the last time. I saw him starting to fall backward. I immediately rushed in to grab him, but it was too late. I saw his head hit the ice. He started crying hysterically. I stood over him, really nervous, scared, in fact.

"So, are you all right? Are you all right?"

He looked up at me without missing a beat, crying hysterically because he's hurt, and he said, "No, daddy, I'm not all right. You stepped on my finger!" Luckily, he had gloves on. I picked him up and rushed him off the ice to first aid.

The lady there said, "You're lucky he had his glove on because you would've severed his finger." We didn't know then if it was broken or not, but later we learned it wasn't. That was very good news.

We were driving home in the car, and I was silent. By then, Jackson was feeling a little better, but I was somewhat in shock. I was talking to God silently. "God, two hours. For two hours I stood there, so close to protect my kids, to do everything I could to make sure they would have a good time and be protected, and I was the one who wound up hurting him."

God reminded me that we do the best we can, but our kids and our lives are in God's hands. We need God to protect them. We can't do it. As much as we want to and as much as we try, we can't do it all the time. We need God to protect them. If you are a parent, it is your job to do the best you can. Yet also just as important, you've got to be on your knees in prayer for your kids, because only God can protect them from everything, as I learned the hard way.

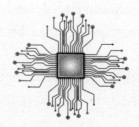

Who Cares What The Manufacturer's Instructions Say

Here is the call I sometimes get from friends and family who don't know the Lord when they're in trouble. You probably get it too. I get it because people know I love Jesus Christ. They say, "Hey, could you do me a favor?"

"What's that?"

"Well, I'm sick," or, "Somebody's dying," or, "I have this financial crisis. Could you pray for me?" Now that everything they've put their faith in and depended on in the world has proven to be useless, can't get them what they want, and can't save them, they want prayer? Yes, of course, I'll pray for them. I'd be happy to. But they don't need me to do it. They can do it themselves. Every person on Earth has the same access to God I have.

You have the same access to Jesus I have. You just need to take it, believe it and then of course use it.

Paul says, "I determined not to know anything among you except Jesus Christ and Him crucified" (1 Corinthians 2:2). That's pretty simple. That's not rocket science. Paul is saying, "I don't know anything except Jesus Christ and Him crucified. That I know. That's all I'm going to tell you. I didn't preach with power or persuasive words so that you would think I had any power. No. I preached simply so that you would know it was the power of God speaking through me. It was the word of God speaking through me. That's all I know, Jesus Christ and Christ crucified." That's all you and

I should know too. The Bible tells us not to go past what is written. Just believe God's word.

The other day, I had a patch of brown grass on my lawn. The lawn guy told me some bugs had been eating it. It was a good size patch. I said, "All right, I'm going to go to Home Depot, and I'm going to buy bug killer, and I'm going to kill those bugs."

I went to Home Depot and bought stuff and I read the directions. They said to use a cup of the bug killer, mix it with water, and spray it. I said, "Not enough for these bugs. I'm going to get these guys." So I put four times the amount in. I wound up killing all the grass...yes, the entire lawn! Now the grass is gone and I have to put new grass in.

I went above what was written. All I had to do was follow the instructions and everything would have been fine. But, no, in my thinking, I assumed even though the instructions said one thing, I knew better than the makers of the product. I paid the price in a comical way. (Although not too comically as it cost me financially. Re-sodding an entire lawn is expensive!) But we don't want to pay the price in a spiritual way with God.

When God said don't go beyond what is written, it wasn't to punish us. It was to bless us. It was to instruct us so that we would get the right result from this life we live, so we get this tremendous blessing and joy and peace as we live our lives, the abundant life now. Jesus said, "I've come that they have life abundant" (John 10:10). That comes from the joy of the Holy Spirit inside of you, exploding in you. That's what the world should see in you and me.

It should never be about where we work or what we do for a living. Corporate executive, IT guy, teacher, bus driver, entrepreneur, housewife — it doesn't matter what your profession is. I hope it's one you love and enjoy, and I'm sure

God's desire is for you to use your natural talents. If you can get paid for those, it's a wonderful thing. But beyond that, all that matters is that you glorify God wherever you are, whether you're in joy or hardship.

The apostle Paul was chained, beaten, robbed, and stoned ... and he was joyful. He knew what his purpose was. He said, "I understand I've got to go through all this. By the way, I'm not particularly enjoying it. But I know why I'm here. Jesus told me, 'Do this for me. Glorify me.' I am going to run the race. I am going to get the prize. I'm going to have the crown of righteousness." There was no doubt in Paul's mind.

Is there any doubt in our minds? God doesn't want there to be doubt. I can't give you certainty in your heart. That can only come from Jesus Christ. I know what it's like to feel the certainty. I remember it like it was yesterday — the day I felt the certainty of God in my life when I accepted Jesus into my heart March 10, 1991. My life has only gotten better and better since then.

If you're not sure, ask God. Tell Him about your doubts. Say, "Lord, I'm not sure. Reveal yourself." When I want to learn something new, I spend time studying it, whether it's a business thing, a new sport or anything. Also if I want to learn something new that I don't know about, I do research on the subject. If you want to learn about God, spend time with Him. Spend time in the word of God. Do some research yourself, and see if He doesn't explode in your heart.

Let us not think that we're so wise that we say, "God, I know what to do with my life. Give me my life," just like me with that bottle of bug spray on my lawn. "Give me that. I know what to do. I'm going to put this much and do this much." It turned out I was wrong. The manufacturer/maker of the product knew more about how to use it than I did. So the grass was burned and destroyed and I wondered, "How did I do this? How stupid was I not to have listened?"

I don't want that to be our regret when we go home to meet God. We want it to be, "Lord, we listened. We were faithful. We understood. We did what you told us." Either God is a liar, or He is Lord. If He is not a liar and He is Lord, why wouldn't we do everything He said?

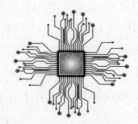

Who Am I To Stand In God's Way?

Acts 11 has what I call Peter's great revelation. It's the same revelation for you and me today. One of Peter's greatest revelations was when he realized that Jesus was God. Jesus said to him, "Peter, who do you think I am?" He said, "Thou art the Christ." That was an amazing revelation. You and I have that same revelation. It has been revealed to us by the spirit of God.

But check out this other revelation from Peter. "The apostles and the believers throughout Judea heard that the Gentiles also had received the word of God ... Starting from the beginning, Peter told them the whole story." Peter had a vision from God of wild beasts spread out on a sheet and God saying, "Kill and eat them, Peter."

Peter is saying, "Oh, no, Lord. I would never eat them and kill them because I can't eat anything unclean." They were wild beasts with blood in them. That would be unclean according to Old Testament law.

God spoke to Peter the second time and the voice said, "Do not call anything impure that God has made clean." Peter realized through divine revelation that God was talking about the spirit of God and the salvation of God coming to the Gentiles as well as the Jews. Even though the Gentiles had previously been declared unclean and seen as unclean by the Jews, God made clear to Peter that the gift is available to all. There is no person unclean when God makes them clean.

This was an unbelievable realization for Peter! It would be like us discovering life on Mars or when past generations discovered the world wasn't flat, but round. It is life-changing. Peter says of the Gentiles to whom he was talking, "As I began to speak, the Holy Spirit came on them as he had come on us at the beginning." Then Peter said, "Then I remembered what the Lord had said: 'John baptized with water, but you will be baptized with the Holy Spirit.' So if God gave them the same gift he gave us who believed in the Lord Jesus Christ, who was I to think that I could stand in God's way?" [See Acts 11:1-17.]

I believe that's the revelation God wants us to have. Who are we to think we can stand in God's way? God is the creator of the universe, the maker of everything. Believe me, God's will is going to be accomplished. God is God. He can do anything. With or without you, He'll have his will accomplished.

You can't stand in God's way. You can ruin your life. You can go with the flesh, the world, the devil but you can't stand in God's way. Peter says, "Who am I to think I could stand in God's way?"

Are you standing in God's way today? Is there an area of your life in which you are standing in God's way? Does God want to give you freedom from addiction? Does God want to give you freedom from anger, from jealousy, from rage, from malice, from envy? Does God want to give you greater mercy, greater grace? Does God want to see you forgiving someone you haven't forgiven? The answer is yes, yes, yes, and yes. Are you standing in God's way? Is there some sin? Is there some thought pattern? Is there some disbelief? Is there some disobedience by which you're standing in God's way?

The New King James Version says, "Who was I that I could withstand God?" We cannot possibly withstand anything that comes from God. Is anything different today than it was then? In Acts 4:2 it says the Sadducees came to Peter when they were speaking to the people, and "they were greatly disturbed because the apostles were teaching the people, proclaiming in Jesus the resurrection of the dead." It sounds like the world today. Everybody seems greatly disturbed that the people of God are out there proclaiming Jesus and the resurrection of the dead. Everybody seems greatly disturbed, so much so that they want to take away your right to say it.

In Acts 4:6, the rulers, elders, and teachers of the law met in Jerusalem. The high priest was there. They had Peter and John brought before them, and they began to question them, "By what power or what name did you do this?" Referencing when Peter and John healed the lame beggar. Scripture tells us, "Peter, filled with the Holy Spirit, said to them, 'Rulers and elders of the people! If we are being called to account today for an act of kindness shown to a man who was lame and are being asked how he was healed, then know this, you and all the people of Israel: It is by the name of Jesus Christ of Nazareth, whom you crucified but whom God raised from the dead, that this man stands before you healed.'" By the power of God. To God be the glory for all things; all things are possible with God. John and Peter made it clear it was Jesus' power.

In verses 12 and 13, Peter goes on to state, "Salvation is found in no one else, for there is no other name under heaven given to mankind by which we must be saved. When they saw the courage of Peter and John and realized they were unschooled, ordinary men, they were astonished and they took note that these men had been with Jesus." Ordinary, unschooled men astonished the leaders of their time, and they took note. Clearly, these guys have been with God.

The same thing should be said about us. It's not about education. It's not about how many years of college you attended. It's about a love for the things of God, a desire for the knowledge and wisdom that God gives freely to all who seek it. John and Peter were unschooled, ordinary men, but they loved God. They followed God completely. They sacrificed all. They lived completely sold-out lives for God. The same should be said of you and me today. Our spirits should reflect God's spirit. Our obedience should come out of joy and gratitude for what God has done.

The word of God goes on to say, "Then they called them in again and commanded them not to speak or teach at all in the name of Jesus. But Peter and John replied, 'Which is right in God's eyes: to listen to you, or to him? You be the judges! As for us, we cannot help speaking about what we have seen and heard.'" We cannot help it. We have to talk about it.

I pray that the same would be our attitude in the body of Christ today. We wonder, "Where's the revival? Where's the spirit of God sweeping the nation?" Where's the power of God? It's in our hearts. That's where it is! How could it be that we have time to speak about the things of the world but not about the creator of it? The majority of my life should be talking about God and Jesus Christ, not those things that pass away. Hey, it's okay to enjoy your life. God didn't say you had to reject everything in world. He just said he is to be our focus and priority. We are filled with the Holy Spirit upon salvation. The question is, do we speak the word of God boldly? Acts 4:31 says, "And they were all filled with the Holy Spirit and spoke the word of God boldly." All were filled with the Holy Spirit. All spoke the word of God boldly. What is our excuse? We can't say we're not filled with the Holy Spirit; if we know Christ, we have the Holy Spirit upon salvation. God put His spirit in our hearts. He took out our old hearts and put in new hearts. We have the Holy Spirit of God living in us. God says, "Apart from me you can do nothing," and yet we constantly challenge that. We test Him. Then we come back to God on our knees, and God loves us, forgives us and continues to bless us.

Acts 5:12 reads, "The apostles performed many signs and wonders among the people. And all the believers used to meet together in Solomon's Colonnade." It was a happening meeting place at the time.

The Church was growing because people were talking about God. Then it says, "When the high priest and his associates arrived, they called together the Sanhedrin," the governing body at the time, "the full assembly of the elders of Israel, and sent to the jail for the apostles." They had put them in jail.

Verse 27 tells us, "The apostles were brought in and made to appear before the Sanhedrin to be questioned by the high priest. 'We gave you strict orders not to teach in the name of Jesus,' he said. 'Yet you have filled Jerusalem with your teaching and are determined to make us guilty of this man's blood.' Peter and the other apostles replied: 'We must obey God rather than human beings!'"

What's our response to God today? Is it we must obey God rather than human beings? If we just obeyed God in that way, we would see revival spread in our church, in our town, in our city, in our country, in the world like a forest fire out of control. It would happen if we just obeyed God rather than people, obeyed our spirit rather than our flesh.

Consider this amazing promise from God: "Therefore, my friends, I want you to know that through Jesus the forgiveness of sins is proclaimed to you. Through Him everyone who believes is set free from every sin, a justification you were not able to obtain under the Law of Moses" (Acts 13:38).

In the Old Testament, you couldn't be set free from every sin unless you followed every law and commandment perfectly and consistently. In the New Testament based on Jesus death, his blood sacrificed in your place, everyone who believes is set free from every sin. God is saying the same thing to you today. Whatever Satan is accusing you of, God has said, "You're innocent." God has paid the price for your freedom. You are set free. Live like it. Don't live like a prisoner. We should be so grateful, have so much gratitude that we wouldn't be able to contain our love, our gratitude, our joy, our excitement at what God has done for us.

Let us not stand in God's way.

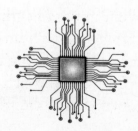

What Do I Do Now?

Life is hard sometimes. Really. I'm in a business situation where I am at my wits' end. I have no idea how to make it work. I'm completely frustrated. Everything I've tried has failed. I have no clue what to do. From a human perspective, I am very frustrated. Yet, from a godly perspective, I'm laughing. I'm not enjoying it, by the way. Still, I am laughing in my heart because I can look back on my life, and I can see the hand of the Lord on my life in every single instance. I know God is in control. I can stand on Hebrews 12 where God says we have this great cloud of witnesses, this great inheritance of faith. I've seen it in my own life, and I know God will complete what He has begun.

God is not fooled. According to my plan, this isn't working at all. I don't know what's going on. But I know that God's plan is working perfectly. God has me exactly where He wants me. The place where I realize I can do nothing of my own and I have no choice but to say, "God, this is all in your hands." I freely admit I can do nothing of my own. I've tried everything I can do.

God said, "Got anything left you want to try?"

I said, "I don't think so. Not at the moment."

I just want to have faith in God. I know that whatever God has in store for my future is what is supposed to happen. That is exciting to me. It is exciting that my fate and your fate are in God's hands. That's exactly where it should be.

So in this difficult business situation, I said to God, "Well, God, what do you want me to do in the meantime? I'm waiting on you. I'm supposed to wait, right? Okay, I'm waiting. I'm supposed to stay focused, right? Okay, I'm focused. What would you like me to do in the meantime while you're cooking all this stuff in the pot of my life? What am I supposed to do?"

God answered. He said to me — and I believe He is saying to you — "Be a minister." It doesn't mean from the pulpit. It wasn't a "preach on Sunday" commandment. It was, "Be a minister with your life. Minister to other people. Jesus said, 'I came to serve.' That's what you should do. While you're waiting for me, Jack, to do what you think I'm supposed to do in your life on Earth, be a minister of my love to other people, and you will be doing exactly what I'd like you to do."

I believe that's what God wants each of us to do. He said we're to love one another as we love ourselves. In Isaiah 43:25, He says, "I am He who blots out your transgressions for my own sake and will not remember your sins." God did it for His sake. He forgave our sins for His sake so that He could have a relationship with us because He loves us so much.

God reminds us of our purpose and His promise in Isaiah 43:10: "You are my witnesses, says the Lord, and my servant whom I have chosen that you may know and believe me." We are God's witnesses. God has chosen every single believer to be a witness and to know Him as a father knows a son, as a mother knows a daughter, to know that individual love God has for us. He says in Isaiah 43:21, "There is no one who can deliver out of my hand. These people I formed for myself. They shall declare my praise."

That's my job and your job no matter what situation we're in our lives — good, bad, happy, sad. We are to declare His praise. The apostle Paul said, "I've learned to be content in all situations, whether I have plenty or I have nothing." Why? Because he trusted God. He said, "Leap and rejoice, for our salvation is assured." He believed God. That's why he was singing at midnight in jail. He believed God. "These people I have formed for myself. They shall declare my praise." That's your purpose.

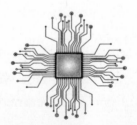

Are You Really My Kid?

We are the King's kids. We are heirs to the throne of heaven and brothers and sisters of Jesus Christ. That is your birthright and title. Now, you don't have to accept it. You can say, "I'm not worthy of it. I didn't deserve it. I didn't earn it." And you would be right on all three counts. I didn't earn it either. I'm not worthy of it. I don't deserve it. My young children, Jackson and Talia, can say they are not the son and daughter of Jack and Beth Levine. They can go and tell that to all their friends. They could change their name legally under the court system if they wanted to and say, "I deny that as my birthright," but it doesn't change the fact that they are who they are. They are the children of my wife and me.

Satan would like nothing better than to convince you and me that we don't deserve heaven. We don't deserve to be heirs to the throne of Jesus and God based on our behavior and who we are. He's right on that account. But let's not stop there. Because this inheritance through Christ is a gift. It was given to us by our Father to be used as a blessing for our certainty as we walk through this life. It is so we can know, "Yes, you are my children. Yes, I love you. I have blessed you abundantly and exceedingly more than you can ask or imagine because I love you."

What a precious promise. What an incredible inheritance. Don't let anyone take that from you for any day, any minute, or even any second of your life. Don't let that serpent — that evil Satan who comes to steal, kill, and destroy — rob you of what your Father has for you.

Claim this abundant life today, this abundant inheritance into heaven.

If I showed up at your door and said, "Hey, I want to take you out for filet mignon, pizza, shrimp, lobster, and anything you could want, the best ever. It's all free," would you turn me down? How about front row tickets to your favorite band or musician. Or the very best seats in the house to see your favorite sports team play? Would you refuse to take it?

Would you say, "No, no. I don't deserve that"? That's right. You don't deserve it but I want to give it to you as a gift. It's free. It's a gift. I'll bet you'd not only take my gift, but you'd be grateful to me for giving it to you. And God's love is infinitely greater than any fleeting gift or experience we can have on this Earth.

God loves you. God desires that you have an abundant life.

I pray we would resolve to focus on God, to wait on God, to trust in God, to believe in God, and to — like Jonah — define God as great and merciful and of loving kindness. I pray we would know what we have is true, our inheritance is true, God's abundance, His love, His mercy, His grace, His spirit are for you and me. They are for today and every day of our lives.

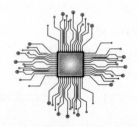

They Died As Heroes

A lot of things are going on in the world around us. On June 17, 2015 in Charleston, South Carolina, nine of our Christian brothers and sisters were senselessly murdered in a church. They were worshipping and praising God when a twenty-one-year-old man named Dylann Roof came in and shot them for the color of their skin. His complaint was that they were African American and not white.

Many Christians today are being shot and killed around the world for their religion, for what they believe and how they believe. Christians are being assassinated for their faith and we look on in horror. We say, "How could this be? This shouldn't happen. This is not the world as it is meant to be."

When I heard the tragic story of what happened in South Carolina, here's what I thought.

Our brothers and sisters in Charleston were faithful in doing exactly what they were supposed to do; they were glorifying God. They welcomed that twenty-one-year-old stranger into the church and into their Bible study. They shared the love of God with him. Amazingly enough, he later said they were so kind that he almost decided not to do it, not to kill them. Imagine that, an hour with a wonderful group of loving Christians and this evil, demon-possessed kid was almost changed by the love of God. Imagine if they got to spend a day or a week with him. God's power was at work. But our Charleston brothers and sisters were faithful to the calling. They shared the love of Christ with everyone they met, even this kid who killed them. Of course we are reminded that the body can be killed but the spirit cannot. So how do we respond to this? When we look to Jesus, to our Heavenly Father, I think we realize we can only respond one way. With the love of God in our hearts. We need to love, not to hate. We need to glorify God by exalting the qualities of God: love, mercy, grace, forgiveness, which we have been given in abundance.

God has lavished His grace on us and we are to do the same to other people. We know life is a gift from God. We know every hair is numbered, and no sparrow falls from a tree apart from the will of God. Neither does your life exist apart from the will of God.

If you died peacefully in your sleep at 104 years old, does that mean you were a good person? No. If you were murdered senselessly, tragically, does that mean you were a bad person? No, of course not. It's not about how you die. It's about how you live. We don't want to see our brothers and sisters die a tragic death. We know people will die, but the circumstances sometimes shock and horrify us. We tend to ask ourselves, "How could a God who loves us allow this to happen?"

God says, "My ways are higher than yours. I give you life. Life is a gift. Whatever time I've given you, you use for My glory. You use to build the Kingdom." God decides how much time we get.

Another difficult question comes to mind. "How can this kid do this to these innocent people? Why?" It should be no surprise that Satan, through deceitfulness of the flesh, through the sin of the mind and the desire of a heart gone astray, accomplishes his mission — which is to kill and destroy and separate us from the love of God, through a wayward soul who was trapped in Satan's darkness.

Everything that is against the gifts and the fruit of the spirit was in this kid. He was the product of a broken home. His parents had divorced at five years old. Where's his love? Love is always the answer for everything. That's what God said. He said, "I want you to love me with all of your heart and soul and love each other as you love yourself."

On Father's Day, I wanted one thing, one thing only. I wanted my wife's secret recipe coffee cake and I got it. My daughter baked it for me. All God wants is for you to love Him with all of your heart and love others as you love yourself. You give God that and you have given God the greatest gift you can give Him. It's the gift of faithful obedience. In this world we live in, this fallen world where Satan's minions run wild, our job is to be the light of Christ. That's our purpose here on Earth.

I had been witnessing to a friend in Delray Beach. He came up to me the other day, after this tragedy took place. He said, "I've got a tough one for you now, Jack. How could this Charleston tragedy happen?"

I said, "How? God's ways are higher than ours. Listen, we know the script. We know how the movie ends. You're surprised that the world's going to hell? I'm not surprised. You're surprised as these signs of end times are coming closer and closer? You're surprised at the recent Supreme Court decisions regarding abortion and marriage? You're surprise at the terror in the world? Don't be surprised. All these things are coming as signs that the end is near."

Joel 3:16 gives us this great promise. "The heavens and Earth will shake, but the Lord will be a shelter for His people." He will be our shelter in spite of the storm. He has a plan for us. All we need to do is follow that plan, stay within the shelter of His wings, His loving care, seek to love Him with all our hearts, and love our neighbor as ourselves.

Every breath is a gift from God. Each second, each minute, each hour, each day, each week, each year, we're not to take for granted. We're to appreciate this gift of life He has given us.

He told us we're to do something with our lives like the Parable of the Talents. We want to use our lives to glorify God, for Kingdom purposes. He's promised if we do that, if we invest our lives in Him, we can expect to be blessed more than we can ask or imagine in this life and in the life to come.

Our brothers and sisters in Charleston didn't die in vain. They died in glory. Their deaths, and the deaths of Christians since, will rally the world for Jesus. It's happening already. They were martyrs killed, but before their death, they loved this twenty-one-year-old kid who killed them with the love of Jesus. It's there in the news reports. They showed him love before; and afterward, the survivors spoke words of forgiveness. What a great reward in heaven! What blessings on their souls! Is there a better way to go than praising God?

I'm not saying God's calling you to a martyr's death, but I am telling you He's calling you to a Christian life. That's the purpose of our lives, to live a life that matters for God. Could we respond with hate and revenge? Of course we could, but we shouldn't. We could respond in our flesh, but then how would the scripture be fulfilled? We need to respond in the spirit of God with love and peace and mercy.

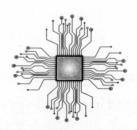

Maybe You Missed Something

About eight weeks ago, I was praying. I said, "God, how can I be more of a man of impact? I've known you, Lord, since I accepted Jesus in 1991. Now it's twenty-five years later." I'm very stubborn and slow, and it took me a long time to learn the things of God. I should have matured a lot quicker in my spiritual walk, yet God still blessed me and matured me. He was patient with me. I said, "God, I want to be more impactful with my life."

God spoke to my spirit and said, "Read the book of James."

I said, "God, what do you mean read the book of James? First of all, I've read the book of James probably a thousand times. I know James inside out. 'The prayer of a righteous man is effective. Consider it pure joy when you face trials and tribulations.' The book of James, I get it. Plus, I read it last week."

I felt Him say, "No. I want you to read it again." I went back and I read it again.

Here are the two verses that God spoke to my spirit about when I read James this time.

Religion that God, our Father, accepts as pure and faultless is this: to look after orphans and widows in their distress and to keep oneself from being polluted by the world (James 1:27).

Another version says, "keep yourself unstained or unspotted by the world." I said to myself, "Wait a minute. I am stained by the world. I'd like to really say I'm not, but I am."

Then I went on and I read James 3:16.

For where envy and self-seeking exists, confusion and every evil thing are there.

I said, "Wait a minute. I am self-seeking too." I'd like to tell you I'm not. I'd like to think I'm not, but everything I do is for myself. If it happens to help God, that's great, but I am self-seeking and polluted by the world.

God then spoke to my heart again and He said, "Meet me at the cross."

I said, "Jesus, what do you mean meet you at the cross? I've been saved twenty-five years. I know you died. You shed your blood for me. I completely get the cross. I fully understand the cross."

He said, "No. Meet me at the cross. If you're kneeling at the foot of the cross, looking up at me and seeing me dying for you, you'll never have a problem with those other things. You won't have any problem with being self-seeking. You won't have any problem with being stained by the world if you keep your eyes focused on the cross. This is why I told you just to keep your eyes on me, the author and perfecter of your faith and not yourself."

What's standing between you and living that life of impact for God?

It's not about going to Bible College. It's about glorifying God in everything that you do. I remember going on a mission trip with friends to St Louis. We went for eight days. We were on fire for God. We were like the guys from Men in Black. We were super agents for God, 24/7, for eight days in a row. It was amazing.

I got back home and God spoke to my heart. He said, "Let

me ask you a question, Jack."

"What's that, God? Wasn't that great? Wasn't it an amazing mission trip? Look at what we did for you."

I felt the spirit of the Lord say, "Yes, let me ask you a question. How come you're not like that all of the time? How come you're not like that to the people in the grocery when you go shopping or at the gas station or the dry cleaner or anywhere? How come you're so wrapped up in yourself all of the time? Isn't your life a mission trip?"

Yes, it is. It's supposed to be. God spoke to my heart that way and I hope He's speaking to your heart too.

God says in 1 Corinthians 2:9, "No eye has seen, no ear has heard, nor have entered into the heart of man the things which God has prepared for those who love Him, but God has revealed them to us through His spirit."

Jesus spoke these words in John 15:15: "No longer do I call you servants, for a servant does not know what his master is doing, but I have called you friends. For all things that I heard from my Father, I have made known to you." We are the friends of God. Jesus calls us His friends. What a privilege!

God loves you. God wants to bless you and has all of these things prepared for you. He wants you to have them now, not later when you die. Now. He wants you to live the abundant life, the one where rivers of joy are overflowing from you. He wants to give you peace that transcends all understanding. You can only get it from God. You can't get it from the world. You can only get it from God.

Psalm 4:3 tells us, "Know that the Lord has set apart the godly for Himself."

In 1 Corinthians 1:9, Paul puts it this way: "God has called us into fellowship with Himself."

God wants fellowship with you. God wants to walk side by side with you through life.

Psalm 91 speaks of being under the shadow of God's wings. We want to walk with God. That's the purpose of our lives, to walk with God. God doesn't want your ministry. He wants you. God tells us He counts it as a tragedy when we choose to simply watch life instead of living it.

Jesus described as "wicked" the person who leaves his talent unused. You can't put your life on hold. It moves forward with or without your approval. God help us to choose to move forward with Him, to decide that we will live a life of impact for Him.

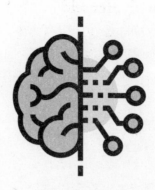

Section 2

OPERATING SYSTEM ANALYSIS

Communicating God's Promise in Your Life

The Operating System is the computer's software that communicates with the hardware and allows other programs to run. It is comprised of system software, or the fundamental files your computer needs to boot up and function. Without a computer operating system, a computer and software programs would be useless.

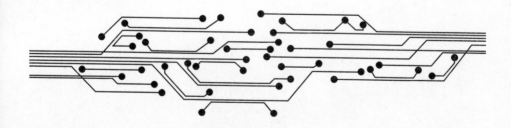

You Do It... I Don't Want To!

When Nicodemus approached Jesus, he came to see Him at night because he didn't want to be seen in the day. He was scared what people would think. But Jesus had a surprise for him. Nicodemus had studied the Torah, the first five books of the Bible from the time he was a kid. He was a religious leader of his day. Jesus said, "Nicodemus, none of that will get you into heaven. In order to see the kingdom of God, you need to be born again." It wasn't about accomplishments and stuff he had done. It was about a relationship with Jesus Christ, and Nicodemus did that, even though it cost him plenty in his day.

What has following Jesus Christ cost you? Has it cost you anything? Your friends may not like it. Your family may not like it. People may not like it. But God will like it. Who are we here to serve? Are we serving ourselves, or are we serving God? That's the question.

In Haggai 1:9, God says, "My house remains in ruin while each of you is busy with your own house." We need to consider that in our own lives. There is a lost generation out there that needs us to be faithful witnesses for Jesus Christ. I have a pastor buddy who is writing a book about why he told his people to stop inviting people to church. I was fascinated. I asked him, "Why did you tell people to stop inviting people to church? I'm inviting people to church. Why aren't you?" He said it was because he realized his congregation (and many others, he believes) were dependent on the church to save people.

In other words, the attitude of so many people in the church is, "Well, I don't have to do anything. I'll just invite people to church, and the pastor will save them. All I've got to do is get them there." Some churches preach that mentality. "Hey, just get them in, and we'll save them."

My friend said, "If I let them think they don't have to do anything, I'm not teaching them their responsibility. Why can't they tell their neighbor about Jesus Christ? Why can't they tell their friends what Jesus Christ has done in their lives? We need to have the faith to just tell somebody, 'Here is what the Lord has done for me. Here is my life before I got saved and here is what it's like now that I am a Christ follower.'"

Personally, my life before Jesus stank. I can't even tell you how bad it was. I had all the things of the world. I had money, power, jobs, and relationships. I had everything by the world's standards, but when my head hit the pillow at night, I would think, My life stinks. I was empty inside. There was a void. I didn't have peace. I didn't know why I was alive. I didn't have a purpose. I had all the things of the world, but they were meaningless.

Then Jesus came into my life when I was thirty-three years old. My life has gotten better every single day since then. I have an amazing walk with God. I am happy to tell people what Jesus Christ has done in my life. Here's how I was before. It stank. Here's how it is now. It's the greatest thing ever.

That's our job. Surely, you can tell somebody what Jesus Christ has done for you. It is the Great Commission.

Would You Tell Jesus To Leave?

In the region of the Gerasenes the demon-possessed man was acknowledging Jesus as God:

A large herd of pigs was feeding there on the hillside. The demons begged Jesus to let them go into the pigs, and he gave them permission. When the demons came out of the man, they went into the pigs, and the herd rushed down the steep bank into the lake and was drowned (Luke 8:32-33).

Can you imagine watching that? The demons come out of the man, go into the pigs, and the pigs drown themselves. Here's what the Bible says about the people's reaction:

Then all the people of the region of the Gerasenes asked Jesus to leave them, because they were overcome with fear. So He got into the boat and left.

What are you asking Jesus to do today? Are you asking Him to come in or to leave you alone? Do we ask Jesus to leave because we're afraid? Are we scared Jesus is too powerful, so we don't want anything to do with Him? If that's the case, you don't understand the cross; you don't understand Jesus' death and resurrection. You don't understand Jesus' love for His children, for sinners. You don't understand His word and His promises. You don't understand any of it because if you did, you'd be running to Jesus for your life.

I know how much I love my kids. It's more than any love I can imagine. I know how much I love my wife. It's more than any other love I can imagine. If you're afraid of Jesus, if you're afraid of what He'll do or what He'll ask you to do, you don't understand how much He loves you.

I may say some things my kids don't like. I may have them do some things they don't like. But I know it's because I love them so much. If you knew how much God loves you, you wouldn't be scared of God. Jesus' death on the cross was for you, personally and individually.

Do we sometimes think that? "Hey, God, I've got to push you away a little because you might ask me for something that's important to me. You might want my pig, my car, my job, my heart, or something. I've got to hold on to everything I have for as long as I can." Good luck with that. I've yet to meet the man who can hang on to everything he has for more than the mortal time he's been allotted on this Earth. God says, "What does it profit a man to gain the whole world if you forfeit your soul?"

So they were scared of God, what God would require, and what God would do. We've got to look into our own hearts and say, "Is this message for us today? Does this relate to any of us today? Are we in that same spot?"

Here is the scariest part of all. At the end of the chapter, Jesus got into the boat and left. They asked Him to leave, and Jesus left. Luke 8:37, "Then all the people of the region of the Gerasenes asked Jesus to leave them, because they were overcome with fear. So He got into the boat and left." Uh-oh. Let me get this right. If you ask Jesus to leave, He'll leave? Absolutely. You have to choose God. You have to invite Him in. It's God's desire that all come to salvation, that all come to know Him, to have a relationship with Him, as he is father to all. That's God's desire.

John 3:16 says, "For God so loved the world that He gave His only begotten Son that whosoever shall call on Him shall have eternal life." In the book of Joel, it tells us, "All who call upon the name of the Lord shall be saved." Timothy tells us it's God's desire that every man be saved. That's God's desire. However, if you tell Jesus to leave, He will leave. What are we telling Jesus by the actions of our life? Are we telling Him to leave?

The man who was freed from demonic powers said to Jesus, "I want to follow you. I want to go with you." You would think we would have that same reaction to Jesus Christ. "You just gave me salvation? You mean physical death can't touch me? I'm going to live forever with you?" Yes. Yes. Yes. It's all true!

I would think there would be a parade every day. Every day of our lives we should be going, "This is amazing. This is the greatest thing. I can't believe how great this is." We'd never shut up about it. Well, that was the attitude of this guy. He knew Jesus had just changed his life figuratively, spiritually, and physically. He had experienced the demon in his life, and it was gone. You and I have experienced the demon of death in our lives, and it is gone. Jesus has crushed Satan at the cross. Physical death can't hurt us. It is gone.

But the story doesn't end there:

The man from whom the demons had gone out begged to go with him, but Jesus sent him away, saying, 'Return home and tell how much God has done for you.' So the man went away and told all over town how much Jesus had done for him (Luke 8:38-39).

What about me? What about you? "Go and tell what Jesus has done for you." How dare we live a life of silence, of quiet enjoyment of the things of this world without living a life that glorifies Him? It's not just about giving praise internally to our Father. We are to "go and tell these great things that Jesus has done for you."

Go and tell.

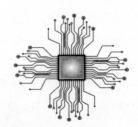

Have You Been Healed Any Less?

Our discussion on Luke Chapter from the last chapter isn't over. Not until we answer one last question today, and I believe this is the question the e Holy Spirit of God wants to ask you today. Have you been healed any less than that man? Than that demon-possessed man, in chains, naked, foaming, possessed by a legion of demons and God healed him completely and cast those demons out and, in essence, saved his life? Have you been healed any less? The response of the demon-possessed man: "Jesus, can I come with you? Can I follow you? You obviously are God. I've seen it. I believe it. I know it. You're obviously God. I want to come with you and follow you."

Is that our response? Have we been healed any less? Has God not promised us eternal life and abundant life? Is the Holy Spirit not living inside of your heart? Have we not been saved from eternity in hell? Have we not been saved from all the penalty of our sins by the grace and mercy and love and blood of Jesus on the cross? Is our response, "God, I want to come with you. I want to follow you"?

What does Jesus say to the guy? He says, "No. Don't come, but there is something I want you to do. Go and tell everybody about the great things I have done for you." I believe God says the same thing to you and me. I believe that's our purpose and mission here on Earth, that people know what we stand for, that people know who we represent, that we see in our lives representing Jesus.

One Wish

Here is critical piece of evidence, a vital piece of the puzzle, as we ask what the Mighty One has done for us. Jesus is eating at the house of one of the Pharisees:

When one of the Pharisees invited Jesus to have dinner with him, he went to the Pharisee's house and reclined at the table. A woman in that town who lived a sinful life learned that Jesus was eating at the Pharisee's house, so she came there with an alabaster jar of perfume. As she stood behind him at his feet weeping, she began to wet his feet with her tears. Then she wiped them with her hair, kissed them and poured perfume on them.

When the Pharisee who had invited him saw this, he said to himself, *"If this man were a prophet, he would know who is touching him and what kind of woman she is—that she is a sinner" (Luke 7:36-39).*

This woman had lived a sinful life. She stood at Jesus' feet. She's weeping. Overcome by her own sins and Jesus' forgiveness, she wet His feet with her tears. She wiped them with her hair. She kissed them and poured perfume on them.

The Pharisee was mad. What on Earth was Jesus doing, allowing this kind of behavior from this obviously sinful woman? He didn't ask Jesus the question, but Jesus knew what was going on in the man's heart.

Jesus speaks to his self-righteous perspective with a parable, and I believe He's asking this same question to you and me today.

Jesus answered him, "Simon, I have something to tell you."

"Tell me, teacher," he said.

"Two people owed money to a certain moneylender. One owed him five hundred denarii, and the other fifty. Neither of them had the money to pay him back, so he forgave the debts of both. Now which of them will love him more?"

Simon replied, "I suppose the one who had the bigger debt forgiven."

"You have judged correctly," Jesus said.

Then he turned toward the woman and said to Simon, *"Do you see this woman? I came into your house. You did not give me any water for my feet, but she wet my feet with her tears and wiped them with her hair. You did not give me a kiss, but this woman, from the time I entered, has not stopped kissing my feet. You did not put oil on my head, but she has poured perfume on my feet. Therefore, I tell you, her many sins have been forgiven—as her great love has shown. But whoever has been forgiven little loves little"* (Luke 7:40-47).

There is only one question for us that really counts. How much have you been forgiven? If you have been forgiven much, your heart will know it, and your life will show it. If you know you have been forgiven much, you will love much. You will love Jesus Christ with all your heart and your life will portray that love. It will show in a life lived for Him, no matter what.

In First Peter (1:3-16), God calls us to be obedient to Jesus Christ. He calls us to do that in many places throughout the Bible. He calls us to live an obedient life.

Why does the Lord ask that of us? Does He need us to be like robots, obedient to him? No. It's for the same reason I want my kids to be obedient. I love them. I want the best for them. I want to be able to bless them beyond their wildest dreams. In order to do that, I need them to be obedient because I know what's in their best interest right now. I know stuff a little child can't know because I have experience. I'm an adult.

God says the same thing about us. He says, "You're my children. I love you. I'm telling you what to do because I love you, because I want you to have my best blessings."

Sometimes we say, "No, God. You don't know what I should do. I know what I should do." God says there's a way that seems right to a man, but in the end it leads to death. It's not about our way or our thoughts. It's about God's way and His thoughts. We're to live a life of surrender to God, of sacrifice to God, out of love and gratitude for what God has done for us on the cross. Jesus' death on the cross guaranteed each and every believer a place in heaven, eternal life, the one thing you'd wish for.

Well God I answered the one wish everyone has. Yes, that one big one... you know it!

"I want to live forever."

"Okay." God says, "Here. You have that, and you can have abundant life now." He gives us blessing after blessing. Forgiveness, love, mercy, grace, peace, joy, to name a few.

His love is the greatest blessing He has given us. He has done great things for us. If we understand that great gift and that wondrous blessing, we will respond with words of glory and praise to Him. Our souls will magnify the Lord and our hearts will delight in our Savior.

Don't forget to download that!

Would You Mind If I Gave You $100,000?

In Orlando there is a church called Mosaic Church. We only know it because some friends of ours go there. We were introduced to the people of the church, and I was amazed by all the people talking about the impact of Mosaic Church in their life.

I was amazed at what I saw happening in that church and I was thinking, "Wow, this must be a great church. They're really having a lot of impact on people."

I attended a small Bible study with ten guys, and many were from that church. Having just moved to the area in September 2015. I really didn't know many people. One of the guys there is the father of the pastor at Mosaic Church. He's a South African man named Marius, and he has an amazing story. He was a general in the South African Army for twenty-six years, a high-ranking general. There were some political changes and problems, and he was forced out of his country. Can you imagine working twenty-six years, having a pension as a high-ranking government official, and you're forced to leave the country with nothing? They came to America, they started businesses, but none of them worked out. Eight years passed.

One day, Marius was talking with his neighbor, Jim. He said, "We're going back to South Africa. It has been eight years. The climate has changed. We can go back now. We have nothing here, we aren't able to survive financially in

America."

The neighbor said to this South African former general, "I'm going to go smoke a cigarette." He came back five minutes later and handed Marius a check. He said, "This is a gift. We need more people like you in America." The check was made out for $100,000. Marius and his wife were blown away. They accepted the gift after much urging from their neighbor, Jim.

Marius went on to start a security company. It grew from just one person, him, to a thousand employees. He was rolling in the cash and was able to finance his son (Pastor Renault) to start Mosaic Church. Mosaic blossomed and grew and did unbelievable things, which continues to this day.

I heard that story and to me, it was an amazing testimony of the Church of God in action. When I heard the testimony, I sat there saying to myself, "Let me get this right. This guy, Jim, was obedient to the spirit of God and he gave Marius and his wife $100,000 and helped them stay in the United States. Marius was also obedient and used his financial blessing to further advance God's kingdom by funding the birth of Mosaic Church in Orlando.

Think about the impact this guy Jim had on the kingdom of heaven simply because he was obedient to God. God did everything through him. When Jim gave his neighbor the money, he didn't know what was going to happen. All he knew was the Holy Spirit told him to help somebody, and he listened.

That's all we have to do in our lives, whether it's just to pray for somebody, encourage them, encourage our family, or share with a stranger. Wherever we are, we are to listen for and respond to the Holy Spirit of God. God will ensure the increase takes place. God will do the job of multiplying and blessing. Our job is to be faithful and obedient.

I'm thinking of Abraham when he is told he is going to be the father of many nations. He's wondering, "How is that going to happen? I have no kids." Hundreds of years later, Romans 4:19-21 records this fact about Abraham's faith:

In faith, he did not consider his own body, already dead (since he was about a hundred years old), and the deadness of Sarah's womb. He did not waver at the promise of God through unbelief, but was strengthened in faith, giving glory to God, and being fully convinced that what God had promised God was able to perform.

Believing God, it was credited to Abraham as righteousness. Abraham refused to consider anything contrary to the promise of God's word. How is it that we are willing to consider everything contrary to the promise of God's word — our flesh, our spirit, Satan, the world? We tell ourselves, "Maybe God's word wasn't right. Maybe I need to rethink this position." No. We should have that same faith as Abraham. We should say it doesn't matter what our eyes see. We don't live by sight. We live by faith.

What is God's purpose for you? If you have Psalm 103, you have everything you will ever need for your life. Psalm 103:2 says, "Bless the Lord, Oh my soul." The next verse says, "And forget not all His benefits." What benefits? Well, let's see. The passage continues with this:

Who forgives all your iniquities, who heals all your diseases, who redeems your life from destruction, who crowns you with loving kindness and tender mercies, who satisfies your mouth with good things so that your youth is renewed like the eagle's. The Lord executes righteousness and justice for all who are oppressed.

If you were with all the saints in heaven today, would they say God has forgiven their iniquities? Would they say

God has healed their diseases? Would they say God has redeemed their lives from destruction? Would they say they were crowned with loving kindness and tender mercy? Would they say their mouths were satisfied with good things? Would they say their youth is renewed like an eagle? Would they say the Lord has executed righteousness for His people? Of course they would. We should do the same right now because we know that's the truth. God is merciful and gracious, slow to anger, and abounding in mercy.

You might tend to say, "That's Old Testament stuff. Big deal. I'm alive today. That was then. This is now." That's a legitimate argument; however, look at verse 17 of that same chapter. It says, "The mercy of the Lord is from everlasting to everlasting on those who fear Him." That word "fear" is meant as "love Him." It is not a fear that worries, "Oh, I'm going to get in big trouble." It is more a fear of, "I don't want to miss the blessings that you have in store for me, Lord, because I'm just in such awe and wonder of everything you've done, and I don't want to miss any of it. I want more of it." God's promise to you is that His mercy is forever. As far as the east is from the west is the distance He has removed our sins from us.

Sometimes He shows His love for us and His plan for us in big ways, like Marius, the man who received a $100,000-dollar check from his neighbor. Other times, we don't see such apparent or immediate signs of God's will for our lives. That doesn't mean it's not there or God is not working through us. It is there in His word, and all we have to do is seek Him, trust Him and love Him.

He forgives our iniquities. He heals our diseases. He fills our lives with good things. He renews our strength. Anything we do in return to the Lord is only our reasonable service, for He has given us all good things.

Give It All You've Got

First Peter 1:17 says, "Since you call on a father who judges each man's work impartially, live your lives as strangers here in reverent fear." Fear? Are we supposed to fear God? No, not fear God that He's going to hit you with a hammer or is waiting for you to do something wrong so He can punish you. It is not that kind of fear. It is the fear we discussed in the last chapter, fear that you would miss out on the blessings of God. Fear that you would miss everything God has in store for you. That's reverent fear.

It is the fear of knowing that God really is God. He truly has the power, as He says, to bless me abundantly, not just in this life but forever and ever eternally. He will base my eternal rewards on the choices and actions I make in this life. In all of this, the message coming through is God asking, "Where is my reverence? Where is my honor?"

God says in *Malachi 1:6, "It is you priests who show contempt for my name."*

You may be sitting there thinking, "I'm off the hook. I've got nothing to worry about. I'm not a priest. I'm not a pastor or a preacher or missionary or evangelist." No. You're not off the hook. God's word says in First Peter 2:4, "You, as living stones, are being built into a spiritual house, a holy priesthood to offer up spiritual sacrifices acceptable to God through Christ Jesus." Peter is talking to every believer, and God is talking to every believer today and saying, "You, as living stones, are being built into a spiritual house." You are a holy priesthood, offering up spiritual sacrifices acceptable to God through Christ Jesus.

When God says, "It is you priests who show contempt for my name," He is not talking only to those with the official title of priest. I love the next line in verse six. It says, "But you say, 'How have we shown contempt for your name?'" Once again, God says something and we say, "Well, God, I'm not sure that's what you mean. Can you prove that to me and then maybe I'll believe that's what you really mean?"

God answers. He says, "By offering defiled food on my altar. But you ask, 'How have we defiled you?'" I'm looking at my own life and I'm asking, "How have I defiled you, God?" because that's not what I want to do. I love God. I don't want to defile God.

God says, "Where is my honor? Are you defiling me with the crappy sacrifice of your life?" Again, I have to look at myself. I have to say, "Is my life a crappy sacrifice or a good sacrifice?" I should be able to look at and rightly judge that. I should be able to see. I should be able to take a look at my life and say, "Hey, is this life I'm living a fragrant offering to God?"

Will God take a breath of Jack Levine and go, "Oh, man, that smells like good stuff for Jesus," or will He say, "Get that away from me. That's not what I'm looking for"?

I think we all need to do that. We all need to take a look and see. It's not too late to change the things that aren't pleasing to God. God wants us to do that. It's never too late to come back to God. Like the prodigal son, we can always turn back to God. God says, "If you come closer to me, I'll come closer to you" (James 4:8). That's a promise. Any time you turn back to God, He's running right to you, like the father and the prodigal son, waiting to hug you and kiss you and love you.

Your sins are forgiven — past, present, and future. You don't need the darts of the enemy to condemn you. At the same time, we want to behave reasonably and follow the way the Lord would have us walk. We want to do what God would tell us and instruct us, as He wants to bless us and He loves us so much that He doesn't want us to miss out on the blessing.

We ask, "How have we defiled you?" *Malachi 1:7 goes on to say, "'By saying that the Lord's table is despicable or contemptible. When you offer blind animals for sacrifice, is that not wrong? When you sacrifice lame or diseased animals, is that not wrong? Try offering them to your governor! Would he be pleased with you? Would he accept you?' says the Lord Almighty."*

I love that line. God is saying, "Try giving an inferior sacrifice to somebody else. You try to pass off on me something you hope I'll accept but you know is crap. I'm God. You just throw something at me as, 'Well, God, I came. I gave a sacrifice.'" Like Cain, we're trying to give an unacceptable sacrifice, instead of being like Abel, giving our very, very best.

God as much as says, "Yeah, try that on your boss." Try in your eight-hour work day, giving your boss two hours a day of work and see how he likes that. See how long you'll be employed. Try giving your landlord half of the rent. You'd be out of there so fast your head would spin. Yet with God we take it for granted that it's okay and acceptable to give God sacrifices that aren't pleasing to Him.

God goes on to say in Malachi 1:10, "'Oh, that one of you would shut the temple doors, so that you would not light useless fires on my altar! I am not pleased with you,' says the Lord Almighty, 'and I will accept no offering from your hands.'" God is saying that crappy, lame, substandard offer is useless.

Remember the story in the life of Jesus, of the widow who put the two cents into the offering plate? Jesus said, *"Truly, she has given more than all those who are rich because she's given out of all that she has" (Mark 12:43-44)*. It's not about quantity. It's about the quality of your heart.

God is not sitting up in heaven with a high bar saying, "You need to do this, that, and that." But God is saying, "I want to see gratitude in your life for what I've done for you. I want to see a life that reflects the fact that I am truly Lord, that your salvation is truly assured, and that you're really grateful."

He wants you to get that He has a purpose and a perfect plan for your life. He has much to accomplish through you for the kingdom of heaven, for the glory of God, but you have to be moldable. He is the potter. We are the clay. We have to let Him mold us according to His will.

Then we say, "Well, God, what do you want me to do?"

He answers, "What part of my word don't you understand? I want you to love the Lord God with all your heart and love your neighbor as yourself. If you do that, you'll be fine."

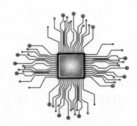

Love The One You're With

In Malachi 2:13, God is rattling off the list. It's like you got called into the principal's office, and He's telling you what you did wrong. He says, "Another thing you do: You flood the Lord's altar with tears. You weep and wail because He no longer looks with favor on your offerings or accepts them with pleasure from your hands. You ask, 'Why...'" Why, Lord, don't you look favorably on my offerings? Why don't you accept them with pleasure? God's word goes on to say, "It is because the Lord is the witness between you and the wife of your youth. You have been unfaithful to her, though she is your partner, the wife of your marriage covenant."

It would take far too long here to outline a husband's responsibility to a wife under God's marriage covenant and a wife's responsibility to her husband. But it's very clear and can be summed up succinctly. What part of "love your wife as God loved the Church" isn't clear? What part of "the two shall be joined together" as one flesh isn't clear? God loved the Church so much He gave His son's life for it and its people. That's how much He loved the Church. We're to love our wives the same way. Women are supposed to love their husbands, help them, respect them and lift them up in prayer. We know the obligations we have. How could it possibly be that 50 percent of Christian marriages end in divorce? How could that be when God has given us such clear instructions for how we are to operate in our marriages? With God in the center and us on the sides, it's a perfect triangle. We are to be obedient to God and look up to God.

Very simply, we're not listening to God. One hundred percent of the time, when I see Christian couples who are having problems in marriage and about to get divorced, it is because they have not followed God's instructions on marriage. Sometimes they don't want to. They don't like God's instructions. They think they have a better way. Then they wonder why they don't get the results. They wonder why they don't get the blessing.

My wife is a gift from God. She's a blessing to me from God. If God gave me a brand new house, I'd keep the trees and lawns cut regularly. I would decorate it beautifully and keep the inside and outside cleaned regularly so it looked great. I'd be saying, "Look at this. Jesus gave me this new house, man. Isn't this awesome?" The last thing I would do is let it go to hell in a hand basket. Jesus gave this to me. This is of tremendous value. I didn't pay anything for it. It was a gift from God. Yet sometimes we take for granted the people who love us the most, and we go out of our way to impress strangers who have no care or concern about us.

That's not the way it was meant to be. When God said the two shall be joined together as one flesh, He meant it. When He said we're to love our wives as Christ loved the Church, that's what He meant.

Look at how God finishes in verse 15: "'Has not the one God made you? You belong to him in body and spirit. And what does the one God seek? Godly offspring. So be on your guard, and do not be unfaithful to the wife of your youth. The man who hates and divorces his wife,' says the Lord, the God of Israel, 'does violence to the one he should protect. So be on your guard, and do not be unfaithful.'"

Wow. Can you imagine if David had slaughtered the sheep he was assigned to be the Sheppard of and eaten them? No, David was given those sheep to protect. Can you imagine if your pastor said to you, "We're going to go worship the God of the Muslims today or the Jehovah's Witnesses' God. Hey, could that ever sound like a good idea? After all, don't all roads lead to heaven?" Yet that would be ridiculous for Christians. Your pastor has a responsibility, a job, to protect, shepherd, and love you. We have a responsibility too. God says that if we divorce our wives, we do violence to the ones we should protect. May it never be said of us!

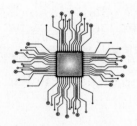

Do I Know You?

I ran into a guy at a Christian conference who had been a pastor for ten years. He was no longer in the ministry but is a nice guy. We were talking and he told me you didn't need to believe in Jesus to get to heaven.

I did a double take at that comment. "Excuse me?"

He replied, "See, all you have to do is do the things Jesus would have done." In essence, he has a works-based theology. You can work your way into heaven.

I said, "Well, wait a minute. All through the Bible and the word of God, God is clearly confirming that Jesus is the way to heaven. Jesus says, 'I am the way, the truth and the life. There is no other way to heaven, but through me.' How do you reconcile that verse?"

He told me, "Yes, but being like Jesus is enough."

I said, "No, you have to know Jesus and believe in Him as Lord and Savior. Trying to be like Him is not enough." I couldn't change his mind and I didn't try that hard. I left that between him and God, but I thought, Here's a guy who was a pastor for ten years. He left the ministry and now he has this delusional theology. It's scary but not that shocking.

God said in the last days, people would hear the things they want to hear and look for teachers to teach them the things they want to hear. I said to this guy, "What about the Bible?"

He said, "Oh, I don't believe the Bible because man wrote it."

I said, "But God inspired it." He wasn't going to buy it.

The reason I share this with you is to make sure you are sure of your faith. This man's comments didn't shake me. I didn't tell him, "Oh, well. Maybe you're right." I felt more like saying, "You're absolutely delusional, but I love you. I wish you the best. I can be friends with you. You don't have to think like I do to be my friend, but I know the truth and nothing can shake that truth out of my heart."

I pray that nothing can shake the truth out of your heart. The truth of God is in us. God's Holy Spirit is in us. No matter what the world says, no matter what other people's interpretation is, we go by the Holy Spirit. We match everything up to the Holy Spirit of God and that is the truth; that is what we need to pay attention to.

Then my heart was broken. I spoke at a Christian business conference, and I got to speak on how to eliminate stress and worry in your life. Of course, the answer is follow God and be obedient to God. You might be faced with stress and worry, but God will be with you through it so you'll go through it peacefully and God will use it to bless you (see James Chapter 1).

The talk ended and people came by and told me things like, "That was great." "God touched my heart."

One guy came up to me and said, "I've been saved for two years now." He looked to be about sixty-five years old.

I said, "Wow, that's great."

He then let me know, "Yes, but I grew up in church all of my life. As a matter of fact, I was baptized in church. I went to church as a little kid. I was a deacon in the church. I never knew Jesus Christ personally. I didn't know I was missing it. I didn't know. I was very religious. I knew the Bible inside out. I did everything I was supposed to do in the church, but I never knew Jesus Christ personally. Finally, I met Jesus two years ago." I could see the joy of the Lord radiating from his face. I was reminded of the saying that the farthest distance in the world is the eighteen inches between your head and your heart. He had all of the head knowledge in the world, but he didn't have Jesus in his heart.

Fred Smith is the current chairman of Federal Express. He's the founder of the company. He founded it over thirty years ago. Can you imagine going to work for Federal Express and saying, "Oh, well. I know Fred Smith. I work for Fred. Yes, I've been working for Fred for years. Fred puts money in my pension plan."

"Great, have you ever spent any time with him?"

"Well, no."

"Have you ever gone into his office?"

"Well, no."

"So you don't know him personally?"

"No, but I know him. I know who he is."

"Yes, but you don't know him personally."

Examine your heart. If you're in that situation, today's the day to find the Lord. I can tell you the difference in this guy's life in two short years. He didn't sit there and say, "I can't believe I never had the Lord before. How tragic." His reaction was the opposite. He said, "Thank God I found the Lord now. Thank God."

There are people sitting in churches who are Bible study teachers, deacons, and church members, yet are not saved. When I say not saved, I mean they don't have a personal, one-on-one relationship with Jesus Christ. Take a look inside your heart today and make sure that's not you.

No matter what decisions you have made in your past or what choices others who have affected your life have made, one choice you can make will make all the difference. Accept that God's grace, through Jesus Christ, is enough to bridge the gap between us and heaven. You can know Him personally and it will make all the difference.

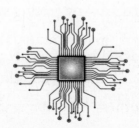

You Mean There's A Formula That Guarantees Success

We are living stones. We're being built up into a spiritual house, a holy priesthood. Our purpose is to offer up spiritual sacrifices acceptable to God (1 Peter 2:5). You ask, "How do I do that? If I'm being built up in a spiritual house, a holy priesthood, what does that look like? How do I do it?" God gave us the greatest mathematical formula of all time that will guarantee success. It is found in Second Peter, chapter one. It begins like this:

Simon Peter, a bondservant and apostle of Jesus Christ, to those who have obtained like precious faith with us by the righteousness of our God and Savior Jesus Christ...

Understand this. Peter is talking, and he addresses his letter "To those who have obtained like precious faith with us by the righteousness of our God and Savior Jesus Christ." That's you and me. That's every single believer. We've obtained that same precious faith by the righteousness of God.

Peter is talking directly to you and me and he then says, "Grace and peace be multiplied to you in the knowledge of God and of Jesus our Lord..." How is that for math? You want more of God's grace and peace? Peter says you can multiply it. Here is how you do it—by getting knowledge of God and our Lord Jesus Christ.

If I told you, "Hey, I can multiply your money. Give me a thousand dollars. I'll make it a million," you'd be camping at my feet. How do I do that, Jack? How do I multiply my money, Jack? I'd love to turn a thousand into a million. We should want the grace and peace of God even more. And it can be overflowing on you and multiplied in your life. Peter says you get that by knowledge of God and Jesus.

Second Peter chapter 1 goes on to say in verse 3, "...as His divine power has given to us all things that pertain to life and godliness..." Not some things. Not a few. Not most. All things. How do we get those? Through God's power. How do we access God's power? Through knowledge of God and Jesus Christ.

The passage continues, "...through the knowledge of Him who called us by glory and virtue, by which have been given to us exceedingly great and precious promises..." Get this right. Grace and peace are multiplied to you through the knowledge of God. You get His divine power, which has given you all the things you need for life and godliness through the knowledge of God who called us by glory and virtue. He's given you these exceedingly great and precious promises.

Why has He given them to you? The next verse says: "...that through these you may be partakers of the divine nature..." Through the promises, knowledge, and wisdom of God, we may now partake of the exact nature of God.

It goes on to say: "...having escaped the corruption that is in the world through lust." When we hang on and understand and claim these great and precious promises of God, through which we're partakers of the exact nature of God, we escape the corruption that is in the world. We escape the corruption of our flesh and live a life for the spirit.

That is what it's all about. That's how you get the abundant Christian life.

It doesn't stop there, though. In verse 5, Peter goes on to say, "But also for this very reason..." What reason? The reason he just told us — that grace and peace are multiplied to you, that His divine power has given you all things through knowledge of Him, and you get these exceedingly great and precious promises through this knowledge so that you may be partakers of the divine nature and escape the corruption that is in the world and the flesh. For that very reason, he goes on to say, "Giving all diligence, add to your faith virtue."

We're still in this math equation. God said grace and peace are multiplied to you in the knowledge of God and Jesus Christ. Now he's saying add to that. Add to your faith virtue.

What does virtue mean? Virtue means doing the right thing. Then he says add to virtue knowledge. Get more knowledge, and add to knowledge self-control. Develop the ability to control yourself. Be able to control yourself for what you believe in and act on what you believe in. You want to add virtue to your faith. You want to add knowledge to virtue. You want to add self-control to knowledge.

He then says add perseverance to self-control. That means you don't give up. You run the race. You keep playing until the clock ticks zero.

You then add godliness to perseverance. What does it mean to add godliness? It means to imitate God, to be like God. You add that.

To godliness, you add brotherly kindness. You're kind to your brothers and sisters in Christ. You're kind to those in the world and careful to reflect the love of Christ. You're considerate. You're merciful. You're forgiving. You're joyful. You're graceful. That's what it means.

Finally, Peter says to brotherly kindness, add love. Add love. Love others! Don't be about yourself all the time. Be about others and love others.

He goes on to say in verse 8, "If these things are yours..." What things? Virtue, faith, knowledge, self-control, perseverance, godliness, brotherly kindness, and love.

"For if these things are yours and abound..." Abound means you've got a lot of it. If I'm abounding in money, I've got a lot of it. If I'm abounding in laughter, I'm laughing all the time.

"If these things are yours and you abound in them, you will be neither barren nor unfruitful in the knowledge of our Lord Jesus Christ." It's a guarantee from God. If you'll do this, you will neither be barren — which means bare, have nothing — or unfruitful in the knowledge of our Lord Jesus Christ.

Verse 9 lays out a warning, "For he who lacks these things," the one who didn't do these things, the one who didn't think they were important, "...is shortsighted, even to blindness." If you don't do this, if you don't listen to this, you're like a blind man. You can't see. "And has forgotten that he was cleansed from his old sins." He equates this to blindness. You refuse to see the truth, and you have forgotten that you've been cleansed of your sins.

If you didn't forget you were cleansed of your sins, you'd want more knowledge of God. You'd want grace and peace multiplied to you. You'd want to make sure you're abounding in these things to guarantee you would neither be barren nor unfruitful in the knowledge of our Lord Jesus Christ. You know knowledge multiplies God's grace and peace in your life, and you want more of it.

In Verse 10 Peter writes, "Therefore, brethren, be even more diligent to make your call and election sure, for if you do these things you will never stumble." If you do that, you will never stumble. That's a promise from God, a guarantee from God. He says, "If you do these things you will never stumble; for so an entrance will be supplied to you abundantly into the everlasting kingdom of our Lord and Savior Jesus Christ."

An entrance will be supplied to you abundantly into God's kingdom. You will hear, "Well done, good and faithful servant." That's the greatest math equation I ever heard. Make sure to download that... And never erase it!

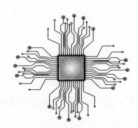

What Are You Scared Of?

The word of God says, "There is no fear in love. But perfect love drives out fear because fear has to do with punishment. The one who fears is not made perfect in love."

What are we scared of? I was doing a Bible study this week, and I was asking some friends in my Bible study group that same question. I was amazed at some of the responses I got. First of all, they're not scared of dying because every one of them was a believer. They know when they die they're going to go to heaven to be with Jesus Christ. However, some were scared of how they were going to die. Was it going to be a slow, painful death? Was it going to be a drawn-out affliction of cancer? Was it going to be Alzheimer's? Were they going to suffer? I get that. It's something we tend to think about. But in the end, we all know we're going to die and be with Jesus in heaven.

Some were scared of rejection. They said, "I want to do more for God, but I'm just..." This is a very transparent Bible study group. They were saying things like, "I'm scared of being rejected. I'm scared people are not going to accept what I say, and they'll reject me."

One response I heard broke my heart. One guy said, "I'm not sure I'm good enough." Coming from a Christian believer that's frightening. I'm not sure I'm good enough! If you're wondering if you're good enough or not, just look at the cross. That's how good you are. Jesus made you good.

Yes, you're not good enough and I'm not good enough, but by and because of Jesus' shed blood, we are good enough. We are now holy, blameless, and above reproach, clothed in the righteousness of Jesus Christ.

Romans 14:7 tells us the kingdom of God is not about eating and drinking. It is about righteousness, peace, and joy in the Holy Spirit. If you serve that way, you're pleasing to God, and you'll receive human approval.

When people look at us, do they see the righteousness, peace, and joy of the Holy Spirit in us? I'm not just talking about for two minutes at the checkout line. "Here's a tract for you. I invite you to church Sunday." No. God says if we see someone in need and we don't help their need, if we don't do the good we know to do, we're sinning. We need to be Christ-like all the time. It's easy to do it once in a while, but God wants us to be living for Him all of the time.

What if your kids listened to you once in a while? When they want something, they listen to you. When they don't want anything, they don't. Does it mean you love them any less? No, of course not. You couldn't love your kids any less if you wanted to, no matter what they do. But the blessings you give them are based on their obedience.

Determine that your life will be your testimony and that it will tell the greatest testimony — of a gracious and loving Savior who gave His life for mankind.

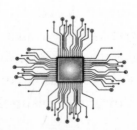

Can You Please Stop Loving Me So Much?

The Lord longs to be gracious to you. Therefore, He will rise up to show you compassion. The Lord is a God of justice. Blessed are all who wait on Him. How gracious He will be when you cry for help. As soon as He hears, He will answer you, although the Lord gives you the bread of adversity and the water of affliction... (Isaiah 30:18-20a).

What's that, God? You give me the bread of adversity and the water of affliction? What's that, God? You just likened adversity, trials, troubles, and tribulations to bread? You called physical, spiritual, financial, and emotional affliction "water"? Don't I need bread and water to live? Isn't that how I survive?

What's that, Lord? You're giving me these to nourish me? Hey, could you do me a favor and nourish me a little less?

God's answer to us is, "No, I love you too much. I love you too much to nourish you a little less." The passage goes on to say, "Although the Lord gives you the bread of adversity and the water of affliction, your teachers will be hidden no more. With your own eyes you will see them. Whether you turn to the right or to the left, your ears will hear a voice behind you saying, 'This is the way. Walk in it'" (Isaiah 30:20-21).

The Holy Spirit of God is available for every believer, telling you, "This is the way. Walk in it." Yes, we have trials and tribulations. We know they're for a short time so that our joy will be complete. God is molding and shaping us so we can be the men and women He wants us to be. He's letting those happen so we depend on Him, so He can teach us, so we can learn. The Holy Spirit speaks truth to our hearts and tells us all things.

In Isaiah 30:22, the Lord goes on to say, "Then you will deny the covering of your idols overlaid with silver and your images covered with gold, and you will throw them away like an unclean thing and say to them, 'Away with you.'" You're walking with God. You have the bread of affliction. You have the waters of adversity. Whether you turn to the left or the right, your teacher isn't hidden from you. You have the Holy Spirit telling you all things, guiding you in all things.

When you're walking with God and listening to the spirit of God, you will cast away all your images of gold and silver. That doesn't mean real gold and silver, although it can. It means anything on this Earth that's an idol to you, anything that's separating you from God, anything that's between you and God, anything that you value more than God — your money, your relationship, your family, your position, your power, your looks. Anything you would put in front of God is an idol for you.

He says you'll deny that idol of silver and image covered with gold. You'll throw them away like an unclean thing and you'll say, "Away with you." Isaiah 30:23 says after you do that — after you've walked with God, you've listened to the Holy Spirit, you've removed the things that are idols — He will send you rain for the seed you sow in the ground. He promises the food of the land will be rich and plentiful. What a great promise!

There is something required on our part. If you want to start your car, you've got to put the key in first. If you want to go anywhere, it's a good idea to put gas in the tank as well. You can have the car, but if you don't put the key in or put the gas in, you're not going anywhere.

"But I've got the car." I know. It still needs gas.

"But I've got Jesus." I know, but you still need to live His way and according to His plan for your life to receive all the blessings He has for you.

He will send you rain for the seed you sow in the ground. He promises the food of the land will be rich and plentiful. What a great promise!

There is something required on our part. If you want to start your car, you've got to put the key in first. If you want to go anywhere, it's a good idea to put gas in the tank as well. You can have the car, but if you don't put the key in or put the gas in, you're not going anywhere.

"But I've got the car." I know. It still needs gas.

"But I've got Jesus." I know, but you still need to live His way and according to His plan for your life to receive all the blessings He has for you.

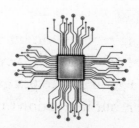

Open The Eyes Of My Heart, Lord

Look at the intent of the writer of Psalm 119. I pray this may truly be our prayer to God. This is intense, and it's good. It's from God so you know it's good. A lot of churches and pastors are praying for revival. If you have studied the word of God, you know history shows revival always starts with prayer. We don't need to wait for a church to wake up and have a revival. We don't need to wait for a city or a country for us to have an individual spiritual revival with God. It starts one person at a time.

Psalm 119:18 has the prayer, "Open my eyes that I may see wondrous things from your law." Open my eyes, Lord. Is that your prayer? Be careful what you pray for because God will answer. Before you ask God to open your eyes so you can see, be careful that's what you really, really want.

Consider the deep passion for God and the specific requests of the psalmists. They want more of God. My question is, do we want the same, or are we too busy and distracted by the world? Are we too selfish, too stubborn, or just don't care enough to live a life that glorifies and impacts the world for His kingdom? I know that's a scary question, but I think it's one we need to answer today. It could be a matter of life and death.

The psalmist goes on to pray, "Revive me according to your word." The word of God is the will of God. If you're asking God for revival according to His word, you're asking

Him to revive you according to His will. Not my will. Not what I want. What He wants. "Lord, use me. Take this piece of clay and use it for whatever you want. Don't let me sit there and be ineffective, a lump of nothing. Mold me into something. Revive me according to your word." May that be our prayer.

The psalmist goes on to ask God, in Psalm 119:26, "Teach me your statutes." Do you want God to teach you anything, or do you think you already know everything? By the way, this is the message God is giving me to look at my own life. This is the reason I am sharing it with you, only because God has asked this of me.

The next verse prays, "Make me understand the way of your precepts so shall I meditate on your wonderful works."

"Make me understand, Lord. Do whatever it takes, Lord. Mold me. Shape me. Do whatever it takes." Sometimes we're so stubborn. We're so macho. We try to be so tough. "No one makes me do anything. I'm my own man." What a disaster that mindset is. I want to be a slave to Jesus Christ, a servant of Christ like the apostle Paul said he was. He not only said it, but he lived it.

That's the definition I want to have. Lord, make me — whatever it takes — make me understand the ways of your precepts so I shall meditate on your wonderful works.

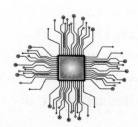

Show Me So I Can Understand

Give thanks to the Lord, for He is good! For His mercy endures forever. Oh, that men would give thanks to the Lord for His goodness and for His wonderful works to the children of men! For He satisfies the longing soul and fills the hungry soul with goodness (Psalm 107:8-9).

The longing soul can only be filled by God. You can only get satisfaction for your soul from Him. You can only be filled with goodness from God. I know. I've tried everything else in the world and so have you. It doesn't work. Money, sex, drugs, power, good looks, fame, fortune. None of it satisfies. It's nice for a little while, but it doesn't satisfy the longing of your soul.

Psalm 107:22 goes on to say, "Let them sacrifice the sacrifices of thanksgiving and declare His works with rejoicing. Whoever is wise will observe these things, and they will understand the loving kindness of the Lord."

What's that? Whoever is wise will observe these things? What things? Well, they'll sacrifice the sacrifices of thanksgiving. They'll declare His works with rejoicing. If I'm wise, I'll observe these things. If I observe these things, I'll understand the loving kindness of the Lord.

If you don't observe those things, you won't understand the loving kindness of the Lord. You won't want it, or live like it, if you don't understand it. If you want to understand computers, you ask somebody to show you. If you want to understand how to use the ATM machine at the bank, you ask somebody to show you. If you're lost, you ask somebody for directions.

"Show me so I can understand." The worst thing is not being able to accomplish anything because I don't understand how to do it. It's very frustrating. That's how life is when you're not living with the loving kindness of God. When the loving kindness of God isn't worth more to you than life, it's frustrating because that's not the way God intended to be. God intended for you to understand. Psalm 63:3 reminds us "God's loving kindness is better than life."

Why do so many Christians lack true joy, peace and rest? Because many have a hard time seeing themselves as God sees them. Lasting peace and joy come only when we believe deep down that we are who God says we are.

Here's who God says we are. In Colossians 3:3, He says, "You are dead, and your life is hidden with Christ in God. You are new in Christ." We're that new creation in God.

Here's what God has taught me throughout a month of reading the Psalms. God taught me I need to rejoice in who He created me to be — a unique individual, created by God to live for Him, to glorify Him. It is the same for you.

God knew me before I was formed in my mother's womb, God had a perfect plan for my life, and He says the same thing to you. "I knew you before you were formed in your mother's womb. I have a plan for your life. It's to prosper you, not to harm you," as He says in Jeremiah 29:11. He says, "I'll be with you always. I'll never leave you or forsake you. There is no condemnation for those in Christ Jesus."

We need to rejoice in who God created us to be. How could we be miserable? How could we want to be anybody else? We're supposed to rejoice in who we are, who God has created us to be for this life.

He's created me to be Jack Alan Levine. That's it, with all my flaws and imperfections. That's who God created me to be. I am to rejoice in that.

Christians should be the happiest people in the world, always. We will be if we rejoice in who God created us to be, and it's not too late to start doing that today.

Only Christ can satisfy the longing of our souls, and He will as we seek His face and turn our eyes to Him. Then, as the old hymn says, "The things of the world will grow strangely dim in the light of His glory and grace."

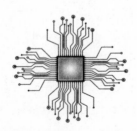

It Helps To Know How To Play The Game

If you're righteous, peaceful, and joyful, who is going to hate you? Can you just imagine your neighbor saying this about you? "I can't stand this guy. He mowed my lawn. This rotten [fill in your name here_____] took me and my mother to the hospital when I needed to go. I hate this guy." No, of course not. That's not going to be the response if your heart and life is filled with righteousness, peace, and joy.

There's a righteousness that God desires. We're to be holy because God is holy. God told us we're to be imitators of Jesus. We're to do what He did, as ambassadors, soldiers, and warriors here on Earth for Jesus.

Look at the great promise God makes for those who are righteous. It's found in Job 36:7. "He does not withdraw His eyes from the righteous, but they are on the throne with kings. For He has seated them forever and they are exalted." That's you and me. Let us not make it into heaven as one escaping from flames by the seat of our pants. No, let us enter as one welcome, joyful, hearing, "Well done good and faithful servant."

Here's the amazing news of the gospel for all who believe. "But now the righteousness of God apart from the law is revealed" (Romans 3:21). God has revealed His righteousness, not the one you get by following the law. No, the one you get through faith in Jesus Christ. The passage goes on to state:

For there is no difference. All have sinned and fallen short of the glory of God, being justified freely by His grace through the redemption that is in Christ Jesus whom God sent forth as a propitiation, as a sacrifice by His blood through faith to demonstrate His righteousness. Because in His forbearance, God has passed over the sins that were previously committed to demonstrate at the present time His righteousness that He might be just and the justifier of the one who has faith in Jesus (Romans 3:22-26).

Today, God is demonstrating His righteousness, His justice, and His Love to you. He wants you to accept it. He wants you to have this gift of life. Paul said it this way in Galatians 2:21. "I do not set aside the grace of God, for if righteousness could be gained through the law, then Christ died for nothing."

You can't earn the righteousness of God. It's a gift you have to get from God. God gives us His righteousness. He says, "Can you fulfill your purpose on Earth? Can you reflect my righteousness?"

Do you want proof that all you have to do is believe? It's found in Romans 4:3, which states, "For what does the scripture say? Abraham believed God and he was declared righteous for his faith in God." Verse 5 goes on to say, "But to him who does not work, but believes on Him who justifies the ungodly, his faith is accounted for righteousness." It's not about what you can do. It's about who we believe. All we must do is believe in Him who justifies the ungodly — that's Jesus. You believe in Jesus, and your faith is counted for righteousness. As it reads later in the passage, "Blessed are those whose lawless deeds are forgiven and whose sins are covered. Blessed is the man to whom the Lord shall not count his sin" (Romans 4:7-8).

Daniel understood. He prayed, "We do not make requests of you because we are righteous, but because of your great mercy." Daniel knew. We can't go before the Lord based on anything we did. We have no right to ask anything. We've earned nothing. We ask because of God's great mercy.

You don't become faithful in order to be loved by God and get into heaven. You're already loved by God. You're already in heaven for free. God paid your way in. That's why it's possible to be faithful and righteous, but you can't do it on your own. You have to do it through the strength of the Holy Spirit of God.

God says in Proverbs 8:17, "I love those who love Me and those who seek Me diligently will find Me." If you don't remember any other verse, remember that one. It's a promise from God to you. If you seek Me diligently, you'll find me. That's what it's about. It's about going deep into the word of God.

If you are an accountant, mechanic, engineer, doctor, or school teacher, you go deeply into what you're learning. You delve deeply into your subject matter because you want to know it, you want to be good at it, and you want to excel. You need to know it to be good at it.

It would be a good idea to know the things of God. It will make you much better at them. Imagine playing basketball and not knowing the boundaries of the court or where the basket is. You can't roll the ball down the court every time like it's a bowling ball. That would be stupid and it's not how you play the game and win. There are rules. If we compete within the rules, we can win the game. We need to know what the game is in order to know how to win.

I believe we know "the game" of our life for God. I pray the Holy Spirit of God is working in your heart and He's breathing into you the gift of understanding. Those who diligently seek Him will find Him. Stop whatever you're doing and download that right now!

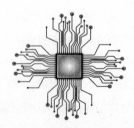

Can You Bet On God In Vegas?

Handicapping is a big thing in professional football and other sports. There's a point spread. Gamblers use it to bet. In sports leagues and football pools all over America, people are using it. They're handicapping who is going to win. It's not enough that the Miami Dolphins win or lose. They have to win or lose by a certain number of points. People handicap horse races. Well, I think this horse is going to win. I'll bet on him. Handicapping is a commonplace thing.

Handicapping happens in other places too. If you have any kind of investment or stock in a business, you've handicapped that stock. You've handicapped that business. What's handicapping? It's looking at past performances and trends to decide what will happen in the future.

If you married somebody, you "handicapped" your wife or husband. You made a bet on that wife or husband. How do I evaluate past performances when handicapping? If I see a horse has never won one race out of twenty previous races on this racecourse, I'm not thinking he's going to win today. If I have a team that lost ten games in a row, I'm not thinking they're winning today. If I have a woman who's been divorced four times, I'm not so confident she is staying with her fifth husband. If I have a company that was flying high and now is bankrupt — Enron, AIG, Lehman Brothers, or Bear Stearns — I'm not feeling too good about putting money in that company again. Why? Because history has shown me prior results. I've handicapped it. I've seen how it performs.

Why can't we "handicap" God? You can. Looking at Old Testament prophecy, you can see what happened. Did prophecy point to the birth of Jesus Christ, our Lord and Savior? Yes. Did it point to His resurrection and rebirth so that all who believed in God would be saved from sin and have a place in heaven? Absolutely. Does prophecy point to end times, to a Judgment Day? Aren't we seeing the signs of the handicappers of the past coming through? Aren't we seeing one-world currency soon to be? Aren't we seeing the Internet? Aren't we seeing anti-Christs coming and the big one certainly coming? Aren't we seeing the desolation and destruction that Jesus talked about almost at our doorstep? Nobody would be surprised if it happened in our lifetime.

If we can handicap that and we can see that, why do we so often bet against God? Your bet should be on God all the time. We see most Old Testament prophecy has come true already. We should be certain that the last bit will come true. The last bit, such as the actual Judgment Day in heaven, will come true, and we should live our lives as if we know it is coming true. We should be betting all we have on Jesus to win because He has won already. There is no gamble in that. He already won. That's how He wants us to live our lives.

I pray that we "handicap" His promises to us by remembering what He has done for us before and trusting He will do it again. He will always remain good on His word. Now that's my definition of a sure thing!

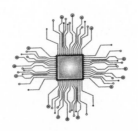

Don't Shut Up Just Because
People Don't Want To Listen

I was preaching at funeral a couple of weeks ago. There were 150 people there and I knew most of them were nonbelievers. The mother of the man who died said to me, "I want you to give the greatest salvation message of all time."

I said, "Well, it's the same message." Whenever it's given, Jesus is the salvation message of all time. I was looking out at 150 faces who didn't want to be there hearing about Jesus, yet I knew Jesus was their answer to salvation. And I spoke the salvation message. I understand that it's hard to go out and preach to people who don't believe. But we need to trust that we plant and God harvests. It's our job to get the Word out there. God does the rest.

I want to be obedient to God. We don't have to be intimidated by people's disbelief. They need to know the truth. The truth will set them free.

I love the message of Acts 2:24. "But God raised Him from the dead, freeing Him from the agony of death because it was impossible for death to keep its hold on Him." This is what David said about the Lord: "Therefore, my heart is glad, and my tongue rejoices. My body will also rest in hope because you will not abandon me in the realm of the dead. You will not let your holy one see decay. You have made known to me the paths of life. You will fill me with joy in your presence" (Psalm 16:9-11). That's the secret. The key to life is the joy of the Lord. You have it. You just have to focus on it to see it. It's in your heart, exactly where the Holy Spirit of God resides. The joy of the Lord is in the same place.

I pray that your prayer would be to speak boldly on behalf of God — that you would not be held back, intimidated by the reaction of the world or the rules of the world. My prayer is that you would be governed by the ruler of the kingdom of heaven, your God, your Father who loves you so much.

Every time you have the opportunity to share the Gospel, don't be afraid to give it out to all who come across your path. You are giving them the salvation message of all time.

I got a call a week later from the funeral home asking me if they could give my phone number to a girl who had attended the funeral and called. Of course I said yes. She called, scared and hesitant, but clearly she had been moved by the gospel message and the reality of the death of her friend. Scared but searching, she called to find out more about God. Thank you, Lord. You use our lives for Kingdom purposes. To God be the glory!

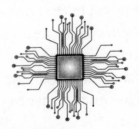

Can I Lose A Blessing?

I felt God saying something to me recently. It's a very personal lesson, but I believe it might be meaningful for you as well. It's from Joshua 13:1. "Now Joshua was old, advanced in years. And the Lord said to him, 'You are old, advanced in years, and there remains very much land yet to be possessed.'"

That's great news! There is more for us to do. You're not useless. You may be old and advanced in years, but there is more for you to do. There is more land to be possessed. God was dividing up the land in this particular story from the east of the Jordan to the west. Verse 12 says Moses had defeated and cast out the Geshurites and the Maachathites, but that "the children of Israel did not drive out the Geshurites or the Maachathites, but the Geshurites and the Maachathites dwell among the Israelites until this day." Moses had already driven these people out. God had wanted them driven out and told Moses to do it. The problem is that the Israelites didn't keep them driven out. They let them back in. What God had wanted out they let back in. How tragic is that?

Is there something in your life that God wanted out but you've let back in? And we wonder why we aren't receiving the full blessings of God in our lives. I must personally drive out the Geshurites and the Maachathites from my own life. One Bible commentary says the Israelites were at fault by not going on and perfecting the work that was begun by Moses. Another says, because they had not destroyed all as God commanded, what remained served as snares and pricks to hurt them. We've got to look at our lives and say, "Is there something we haven't cast out?"

You probably know the more popular story that says the same thing. It's about Saul and the Amalekites. Samuel the prophet goes to Saul and said, "The Lord told me to anoint you king over His people. Therefore, heed the voice of the Lord. I want you to go and attack Amalek. Utterly destroy all that they have. Do not spare them. Kill men, women, infant, child, ox, sheep, camel, and donkey" (1 Samuel 15:1-3).

Saul had very specific instructions to wipe them out. No question about it. Very specific instructions. Does Saul do that? No. The verse goes on to say in 1 Samuel 15:8, "Saul and the people spared Agag," who was the king, "and also spared the best of the sheep, the oxen, the lambs, and all that was good, and were unwilling to utterly destroy them." That is one of the scariest verses in the Bible. They were unwilling to do what God asked them to do. God told them what to do. There was no question, yet they were unwilling to do it.

Are we unwilling to do the things God tells us to do? I don't know about you, but I want to be sold out to the Lord. I fight the war with my flesh and with Satan and with my own heart, but I'm reminded that we're warriors. We're conquerors. We're champions for the Lord. The ground is no place for a champion. If you get knocked down, you get back up. You're a champion of God.

Clearly we see God was upset and disappointed with Saul. The word of the Lord came to Samuel and He said, "I greatly regret that I have made Saul king." Can you imagine God having a regret about your life regarding a blessing He gave you? Can you imagine God regretting a blessing He gave us because we weren't being obedient and using it for His glory?

Samuel says to Saul, "Why didn't you obey the voice of the Lord? Why did you swoop down on the spoil and do evil in the sight of the Lord? Why didn't you obey?" I pray that we don't give God reason to ask us that same question. Why didn't we obey? This is paraphrased, but Saul says to Samuel, "But I did obey the Lord. I did what God told me. I attacked the Amalekites. It was the people's fault. They spared Agag." Here's Saul trying to shift the blame when he was in charge. It was his responsibility.

Do we do that to God sometimes? "God, it's my wife's fault, my boss' fault, my kids' fault, these guys' fault, the world's fault. Lord, I'd be right if they would just..."

"What does that have to do with you?" the Lord will answer. "I told you what to do. I told you to live a life that glorifies me. Be fruitful. Live a life that glorifies me."

Saul blamed the people, and here's what God says in verse 22. Samuel is talking to Saul and he says, "Behold, to obey is better than sacrifice." It's not about sacrifice and tithes. That's a good thing, but it's about obedience to the Lord. Obedience is better than sacrifice. He then said, "For rebellion is as the sin of witchcraft." What? That's intense, but it is what God equated rebellion to. You're not going to listen? You're going to be disobedient? That's like being a witch and practicing witchcraft.

In verse 23 he then said, "Stubbornness is as iniquity and idolatry." Stubbornness is like idolatry. I know idolatry is bad, God, but I didn't think being a little stubborn was such a big deal. Exactly Saul... YOU DIDN'T THINK! We need to think! Samuel then said, "Because you have rejected the word of the Lord, God also has rejected you from being king." Saul lost a big blessing. God had blessings in store for

Saul. Saul lost a blessing. You and I don't want to lose the blessings that God has in store for us. By the way, Saul didn't lose God's love. But he lost a blessing.

In what ways do we need to obey God today? Saul wanted to make it right. He said, "Can't I just go back and say I'm sorry?"

God said, "Too late. Too late on this one. It doesn't mean I don't love you, but that blessing is gone. You're going to have to live with the consequences."

The important thing is that God tests us like He tested Saul. Psalm 66:10 says, "For you, O God, have tested us. You have refined us as silver is refined. You brought us into the net. You laid affliction on our backs." You mean I was walking around happy and carefree and you laid affliction on our backs? That's exactly right. God allowed these things.

He talks about it in the New Testament (James Chapter 1) when he says you're to consider it joy when you have trials and tribulations of many kinds. The Lord is going to use those to build your faith and perseverance so your joy will be complete. He also talks about it in 1 Peter when he says your faith, which is of greater worth than gold, is going to be tested so that it's proven genuine. Paul tells us that our light and momentary troubles are nothing compared to the glory that's going to be.

God's word says, "You brought us into the net and laid affliction on our backs." Then comes the greatest finish ever. "But you brought us out to rich fulfillment." You took us through these things, but you brought us out to rich fulfillment. That's a promise of God to you and me. We just need to be faithful, to stay the course, and God will bring us out to rich fulfillment. That's the hallelujah moment. That's holding firmly to the confidence you had at first so you share in the blessings of Jesus. It might not be in this life. You might not see rich fulfillment until you get to heaven. There, you're definitely going to see it. You may see some of it here, but you're going to see all of it there. What a great truth and promise from God. Thank you, Jesus!

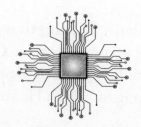

Don't Give Up Hope

It stinks to lose hope. The definition of losing hope is when you don't think tomorrow will be better than today and can't see how tomorrow could ever be better than today. It was tragic when comedian/actor Robin Williams took his own life. We say, "Hey, but that's not a Christian guy. But he's a guy who seemed to have everything by the world's standards. How could he do that?" He didn't believe tomorrow would ever be better than today.

As Christians, we should never lose hope. Here is God's message and reminder to us: *"Blessed be the God and Father of our Lord Jesus Christ, who according to His abundant mercy has begotten us again to a living hope through the resurrection of Jesus Christ from the dead to an inheritance incorruptible and undefiled and that does not fade away, reserved in heaven for you"* (1 Peter 1:3-4).

God is alive. Your hope in God is alive. So what do we do? What's the key to life? Set your hope fully on the grace to be given when Jesus Christ is revealed. That's what you do. You set your hope fully on the grace of Jesus Christ revealed, and you will live and have the abundant life God desired you to have.

God promises in Isaiah 55 that His word will not return to Him void. It shall accomplish what God pleases, and it shall prosper in the thing for which He sent it. God's word will prosper in the thing for which He sent it!

He sent you forth to be a royal priesthood. He sent you forth to bear fruit that would last. He sent you forth to do good works that He prepared in advance for you to do. God promises His word will not return void. It will accomplish His purpose. Not our purpose. His purpose.

I pray that our prayer will be, "God, accomplish your purpose through me." I pray we would rest in that and be satisfied in it, for that is the abundant Christian life. Trying to get anything else from the world is misery.

Colossians 4:17 urges us, *"Take heed to the ministry which you have received in the Lord, that you may fulfill it."* Your ministry is not from the pulpit. This is not a passage for preachers. This is a passage for Christians, for believers. God has called each of us to a ministry with our lives, wherever that may be.

Our only job is to glorify God with the way we live our lives.

What a shame and a tragedy it would be to not fulfill the ministry God has given us. What a greater shame to lose hope, when our God is alive and working in us every day.

I pray that we live for that hope of eternity and with that hope blazing in our hearts every single day we live our lives on fire for the Lord!

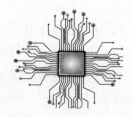

Most Awesome Bible Verse Ever

If I know a hurricane is coming, I act on it, and so do you. We go to the store for supplies. We board up. We do what we have to do. If I knew a thief was coming, I'd prepare and be ready for it, and so would you. We'd be ready. In the same manner, we should prepare, live our lives and be ready as if God is blessing us with His abundant love ... because He is! It's not something we have to think about. It's something that's really happening. Listen to how God describes Himself in Exodus 34:6, the passage that portrays the Lord passing by Moses. God describes Himself, saying, "The Lord, The Lord, merciful and gracious, slow to anger, and abundant in loving kindness and truth." Of course, if that's how God describes Himself, you and I would also be pretty smart to agree with God.

Do you want to know the most awesome verse ever? This should make you very happy. Its Psalm 68:19: "Blessed be the Lord who daily loads us with benefits." Why? Because He loves you so much. Hey, you know what? My wife and I feed, clothe, educate, teach, and take care of our kids daily. Why? Because we love them so much. We daily load them with benefits. You know what the problem is? Sometimes they don't perceive those as benefits. We act the same way toward God sometimes. God, who daily loves and loads us with benefits. He blesses us and works all things together for our good. Yet sometimes we forget to count our blessings or think we are smarter than God or know better for ourselves and consider the things of God not as blessings for us. That mentality makes us extremely foolish.

As I think about it, if someone is loading me up daily with benefits for my blessing, at very least I would be grateful. That's at very least!

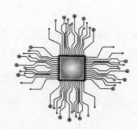

You're Full Of It

Let us see God's instruction and warning in Matthew 13:12: "For whoever has, to him more will be given, and he will have an abundance." It's a promise from God. "If you have, I'll give you more, and you'll have an abundance." The scripture continues, "But whoever does not have, even what he has will be taken away from him."

What does that mean? God doesn't want us to miss the blessing. What kind of blessing is God's word referring to here? It's a spiritual blessing. In case you're not sure, in case you think it's about money or health or relationships, Jesus says very specifically, in Luke 12:15, "Take heed and beware of covetousness. For one's life does not consist in the abundance of the things he possesses." It's not in the abundance of the things you possess. It's in the abundance of the spirit in your heart. That's what your life is comprised of. That's what God wants you to have. That's how you get rich in God. He provides us with a spiritual richness. You can't buy it. You can't earn it. It's from God. But you have to take it. You have to accept it. You have to plant that seed and let it grow. You have to water it. You have to give it life, not squash it.

John 1:16 is also an amazing promise for us: "And of His fullness we have all received." The spirit of God is in you. God has given it to you already. Jesus Christ is the same yesterday, today, and forever. God's spirit is in you. We have the full abundance of God.

Psalm 16:11 says, "You will show me the path of life. In your presence is fullness of joy. At your right hand are pleasures forever more." That's where the secret is. The answer is at God's right hand. Proverbs 3:5-6 urges us, "Trust in the Lord with all your heart. Lean not on your own understanding. In all your ways acknowledge Him. He will direct your paths." That's all you've got to do. You've got to trust Him and acknowledge Him.

Here is another of God's great promises, *Romans 5:17: "For if by one man's offense, death reigned through the one [Adam], much more those who receive abundance of grace, and the gift of righteousness will reign in life through the one, Jesus."* Here is God's beautiful promise given us through His Son's sacrifice. If we were convicted of sin by Adam, how much more through the abundance of grace and the gift of righteousness will we reign in life through Jesus Christ? The answer is a lot more! Thank you, Jesus!

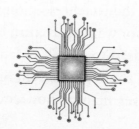

No Retreat No Surrender!

Then [Jesus] got into the boat and his disciples followed
him. Suddenly a furious storm came up on the lake, so that
the waves swept over the boat. But Jesus was sleeping. The
disciples went and woke him, saying, "Lord, save us! We're
going to drown!"

He replied, "You of little faith, why are you so afraid?"
Then he got up and rebuked the winds and the waves, and
it was completely calm (Matthew 8:23-26).

God tells us to be anxious for nothing, and I had been the
opposite of that regarding some big changes in my life. I had
been feeling anxious for everything.

I felt like I had hit that thunderstorm moment. That
moment where you're stuck in the storm. You're the pilot, and
you can't turn back. There is turbulence. There are passengers
screaming. But you're in the storm, and it's too late. You can
say, "Hey, I wish I never started this trip. I shouldn't have
gone," but right now you're in the thunderstorm. You can
only go forward. The only way out is to go forward.

Sometimes it's that way in our lives. We're in these
moments, and we look back. I'll tell you this. I will never
again make fun of the Israelites as long as I live. I will never
make fun of them for wanting to turn back, even after seeing
God's miracles. I used to think, "Man, those guys must be
idiots. How could they see the Red Sea parted, how could
they see God deliver manna, how could they see all these

miracles of God and yet doubt God for the next miracle?"

Now I understand. Even though I've seen miracles of God in my own life, as new threats came, they freaked me out. I get it. I get it firsthand. It's scary. But I trust God. I was tempted to turn back. I was tempted to look back at the old comforts my life had given me. You know what? I knew one thing for sure. I knew there was nothing in my past that had a hold over me anymore and that God was calling me to a new season in my life. I knew God had closed a chapter in my life and I needed to move forward with Him.

Proverbs 24:10 says, "If you faint in the day of adversity, your strength is small." Another version says, "If you falter in a time of trouble, how small is your strength?" God didn't say you wouldn't be scared. He didn't say you wouldn't face adversity. He just said don't panic. Don't quit. Don't drop out. If you faint in the day of adversity, your strength is small. It doesn't mean you're not scared. It just means you've got to keep going.

What should we do? The answer is in Proverbs 23:18: "There is surely a future hope for you, and your hope will not be cut off." That's a promise from God. God also promises in Jeremiah 29:11 , "I know the plans I have for you, plans to give you a hope and a future, not to harm you."

When we're fearful, what do we do? The answer is found in Joshua 4:19. God, in the story of Joshua, told Joshua to tell the people to take stones out of the river that He parted. They were to take twelve stones, each one to represent a tribe of Israel as a reminder of the miracles God did.

It's like a football team when they're down in the fourth quarter, and they're standing there saying, "Hey, you know what? Remember three weeks ago when we were down fourteen points in the fourth quarter, and we came back, and we scored twenty-one points in four minutes? We won the game, and we were amazing. We can do that again today. You know why? Because we've already done it. We can look back and see we've already done it."

Joshua 4:21 says, *"Then he spoke to the children of Israel, saying, 'When your children ask their fathers in time to come, saying, 'What are these stones?' then you shall let your children know, saying, 'Israel crossed over this Jordan on dry land,' for the Lord your God dried up the waters of the Jordan before you until you had crossed over, as the Lord your God did to the Red Sea, which He dried up before us until we had crossed over..."* God dried up the waters of Jordan. God dried up the waters of the Red Sea. He did it before, and He will do it again.

God controls your life and my life. God decides what happens. God has ordained the perfect plan for your life. In Ephesians 2:10 , God says, *"I created you to do the good works, which I have prepared in advance for you to do."* God did it. God did it for the Israelites. God did it for me. God is doing it for you. God is the same yesterday, today, tomorrow, and forever. He's alive. He's living. His power is real.

God says, "Before you were formed in your mother's womb, I knew you." Before you were formed in your mother's womb, God knew you and had a perfect plan for your life. God wants you to remember this fact. He wants you to look back in faith on the miracles that He's done as you look to the future when you are scared. You don't need to be anxious for anything. God wants you to trust that what He has done before, He will do again.

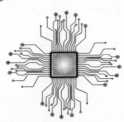

Section 3

CONFIGURING YOUR HARD DRIVE

Unlocking God's Treasure in Your Heart

A hard drive stores all of a computer's data. It houses the hard disk, where all files and folders are physically located. The data is stored on the hard drive magnetically, so it stays on the drive even after the power supply is turned off. A hard drive is a non-volatile memory hardware device that permanently stores and retrieves information.

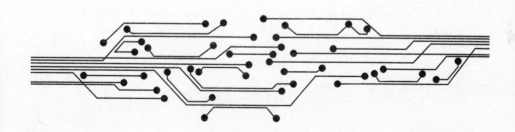

Are You Going In The Right Direction?

Here's a great example for all believers. Paul writes, "We conducted ourselves in the world in simplicity and godly sincerity, not with fleshly wisdom but by the grace of God" (2 Corinthians 1:12). That's all you and I need to do too.

Why should we live sacrificially for others? Second Corinthians 4:14 says, "Knowing that He who raised up the Lord Jesus will also raise us up with Jesus, for all things are for your sakes." This is Paul talking to the Corinthians and it is God talking to us today. God says you're already rich. You have all you want because you have the kingdom. Paul says, "For all things are for your sakes, that grace, having spread through the many, may cause thanksgiving to abound to the glory of God."

The purpose of God's grace is so the thanksgiving you have for this gift would abound to many and would spread to everyone you see, that people would see how grateful you are to God for His grace, for His mercy, for salvation, for His love, for His forgiveness, for His kindness. I could go on and list the attributes of God and never be finished. John said there weren't enough books in the world to record all the things Jesus did. There were too many to be described.

God's purpose is that His grace for you would spread and cause thanksgiving to abound to the glory of God. That's the bottom line. Either you get it or you don't. I sometimes fall off the horse (more than I care to admit). I have to pick myself up daily and remind myself what my purpose in life is. But it's well worth it.

Here is the question we need to ask ourselves. "Does my life reflect thanksgiving to God, or does it reflect concern and worry for self?" If it doesn't reflect thanksgiving to God, we need to change it.

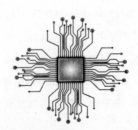

Life Or Death

God's word tells us we know when our Earthly houses — our bodies — are destroyed, we have an eternal building from God, a house not made with hands, waiting for us in heaven. We know God has prepared us for this very thing, and He has given us His spirit as a guarantee. For we walk by faith, not by sight. God's Holy Spirit is our guarantee, a piece of God is in each and every believer.

You get that when you accept Jesus Christ in your life. If you haven't accepted Jesus Christ as Lord and Savior, you wouldn't know what I'm talking about. You'd actually have to accept Jesus Christ as your Lord and Savior to have the Holy Spirit come and live inside of you. Again, that's a promise from God. He instantly puts the Holy Spirit inside you. We know that when our time on Earth is up, when our bodily tent is destroyed, we have a place in heaven. We have a home. God has prepared it for us. We walk by faith, not by sight; therefore, Paul tells us in 2 Corinthians 5:9, "Therefore we make it our aim, whether present or absent, to be well pleasing to Him." Why do I make it my aim to be well pleasing to God? The next verse reads, "For we must all appear before the judgment seat of Christ, that each one may receive the things done in the body, according to what he has done, whether good or bad."

That's the entire Gospel right there. It's yes or no, black or white, live or die. You either decide you will be appearing

before the judgment seat of God, and you live and act
accordingly, or you decide you won't. I believe Jesus Christ. I
believe I will be coming before the judgment seat of God on
Judgment Day. I believe He is going to ask me, "Jack, what
did you do with the gift of life I gave you?"

It is a gift, by the way. God gave it to you. You didn't create
yourself. God gave it to you. "What did you do with this
time I gave you?"

I want to be able to say, "I did what I could. I loved you
with all my heart, in spite of my flesh, in spite of my weakness,
in spite of my own heart being deceitful above all things, in
spite of the darts of Satan coming after me. In spite of that, I
stood fast, Lord. I was immovable in my faith because I know
you love me, and I know what you say is true. I believe you
not just for now, not just for what has already happened, but
for what's going to happen forever and ever. I don't want to
miss that. I want my part in it."

I hope and pray that you want your part in it.

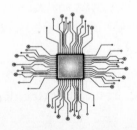

Fire Escape

Look at this awesome word from the God.

"Surely the day is coming; it will burn like a furnace. All the arrogant and every evildoer will be stubble, and the day that is coming will set them on fire," says the Lord Almighty. "Not a root or a branch will be left to them" (Malachi 4:1).

Thank God we're saved by the grace of God. No longer do our works — as it was in the old days — dictate whether we are good or bad, saved or not. Through the righteousness of Jesus Christ, His shed blood on the cross, our acceptance of that blood, our belief that God is God saves us. When God sees us, He sees us not in our own righteousness but clothed in the righteousness of Jesus Christ. We're very grateful for that.

And you're worried about evil guys or nonbelievers getting away with anything? You think it's better to not serve God or to cheat God or to not give God the offering He is due? Is God a liar or not? You decide.

Here is the promise of God. Malachi 4:2 says, *"But for you who revere my name, the sun of righteousness will rise with healing in its rays."* That's for you who believe in the name of Jesus. That's a hallelujah moment.

The next verse says, "And you will go out and frolic like well-fed calves." You're not going to be like the calves who aren't well-fed, who are starving to death from malnutrition. That's not going to be you. You're going to be the ones who are cared for, not the ones who are not cared for, who are left to roam in the wild, who the wolves are devouring and eating up and leaving their carcasses for vultures to eat. That's not you. You're safe. You're in the shepherd's pen. You're well-fed. You're the ones who frolic like Bambi. You're going to be the happiest people in the world.

That is the promise of God for you. "'Then you will trample on the wicked; they will be ashes under the soles of your feet on the day when I act,' says the Lord Almighty." That day when God will act is clearly a reference to Judgment Day. You have a guarantee from God of how and when the story ends and your place in it!

We can cry, laugh, anything we want because the Lord loves us so much. In this life He has given us, He didn't tell us not to feel the emotions we're having. He lets us feel each and every one. What He said is that every part of our lives we should give up to Him.

God didn't say we wouldn't have a lustful thought. He said that when it comes, we're to take it captive and give it over to Him. He said we're to lay our burdens down at His feet. He said we're to walk with Him.

You and I have already been declared righteous. We have already been declared clean by the blood of Jesus Christ. There is nothing you could do to make yourself clean. You can't wash yourself of sin any more than you can reach out and touch Mars or Jupiter. But Jesus' blood cleanses us. Your faith and acceptance in God brings you cleanliness. Your sins — past, present, and future — are forgiven. You're clean.

That should be a cause for "hallelujah." Thank God I'm not subject to this fire. I'm not going to have this test of judgment. Well, you were subject to it, but Jesus paid your price. Because of Jesus, you've passed the test. You're in on His blood, His sacrifice was your ticket into heaven. Now we need to look at our lives and determine that we don't want to miss the blessings in heaven, the one's that last for all eternity.

Jesus said His sheep know His name. They hear His voice. We hear His voice. I've been saved since 1991 and God is still searching out places in my life, seeking me, refining me, and making me better and better. I do it joyfully. I joyfully submit to God. I say, "God, look at me more. Examine me more." Even if I don't like what happens in my flesh and mind sometimes, I press on as I know I'm in this game for spiritual rewards.

I believe the word of the Lord. When He said heaven is for all eternity and I am to store my treasures up in heaven, that's what I'm supposed to do. I don't want to be standing there on Judgment Day looking God in the eye, and seeing Him shaking His head at me going, "Jack, why didn't you listen to me? Why didn't you listen to me, son? Didn't I tell you what to do?" God has told us what to do.

Second Timothy 3:16 — referring to New and Old Testament — says that all scripture is given by the inspiration of God, and all scripture is profitable for doctrine, for reproof, for correction, for instruction in righteousness that the man of God may be complete, thoroughly equipped for every good work. I believe that's the purpose of studying God's word, to know God and what God would have us to do.

May we joyfully respond in His name. I pray that would be the desire of every heart. We can know our sins are forgiven — past, present, and future. My prayer is that we would joyfully look to what we can do to glorify Him and be reminded it's not too late to do the right thing with God. It's not too late.

God's grace saves us, His love directs us, and His will for our lives guides us. What more could we want than that?

Stick 'Em Up

Every one of us, believer or nonbeliever, is going to appear before God on Judgment Day and God is going to judge us accordingly, based on what we've done, good or bad. For the nonbeliever their punishment is instant, it's eternity in hell separated from God, with the knowledge and reality of that, I believe, haunting them for all eternity. Just as the rich man knew he was separated from God by a great chasm in the story Jesus told (Luke 16:14-31) about Lazarus the poor beggar who was with God in heaven and the rich man spending eternity in hell. You have that option to be separated from God for all eternity or not, and none of us wants to be in that spot. What about the believer? We've just seen that we're going to be judged and rewarded based on our actions — good or bad. God loves us no matter what.

Malachi:7 contains these words from the Lord: "Since the days of your fathers, you have turned from My statutes; you have not kept them. Return to Me, and I will return to you." God says something similar in the book of James; come closer to me and I will come closer to you. God's saying return to me and I will return to you. This is a promise from God.

It's not too late to return to God. The next verse says, "But you ask: 'How can we return?'" That's a legitimate question. If I say, "Hey, you know, you can get to the moon," you'd ask, "How? How do I get there? What are the instructions?"

God asked this question in Malachi 3:8. The scripture

says, "Will a man rob God? Yet you are robbing Me! You ask: 'How do we rob You?' By not making the payments of the tenth and the contributions. You are suffering under a curse, yet you—the whole nation—are still robbing Me."

Tithing should be done out of maturity, not out of obligation. Tithing should be done from your heart out of gratitude for the blessing you've received from God. God gave you everything. God gave you a life. God gave you money. Everything you have comes from God. To give a tenth back to the storehouse, to the Church of God, so that God's work can be done, should be a blessing and a privilege. If you don't consider it that way, don't give. God doesn't want your money under those circumstances. God doesn't want your obligatory money. God doesn't need your money. If we love God, if we recognize what He has done for us, we should be so grateful for what He's done that it should be a joy for us to give, to help. God loves a cheerful giver. That's the heart and the attitude we're to have as we give to God.

Here's God saying, "Yet you rob Me." He then says, "Bring the full tenth into the storehouse so that there may be food in My house. Test Me in this way," says the Lord. "See if I will not open the floodgates of heaven and pour out a blessing for you without measure" (Malachi 3:9-10).

Tithing isn't the only way we rob God. We sometimes rob God with our time. We take our time away from God and we rob Him in that area. Other times, we rob Him of our friendship. We rob Him of our fellowship. We rob Him of the honor due to Him. We rob Him of the respect we owe Him. We rob Him of the responsibility that we're to fulfill for this great gift we've got — the gift of life.

How would you look at a policeman who went out and didn't do his job, who instead sat in a donut shop and ate donuts? You'd say, "Why are we paying that guy? We need a guy out there protecting us."

How would you look at a soldier who went to the battlefield and, instead of fighting the enemy, ran away and hid? You'd say, "What a coward. That's not the guy we want fighting for us. We need a guy who's going to get in there and fight."

How would you like a ballplayer who stops hustling and won't run out the ball when he hits it because he's given up already? He's defeated. You'd say, "He's a bum. We need a guy who's going to go in there and play to win."

God has given us victory. God wants us to fight like warriors, like soldiers, like the ambassadors we are. We're to fight on behalf of the kingdom of heaven and we fight with the life we lead.

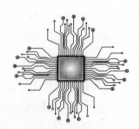

Love American Style

I have a friend who is about thirty years old. He and I were playing softball with a church team recently, and I told him how excited I was to get home after the game and play with my kids.

He looked at me and said, "Oh, I never had that."

I asked him, "What do you mean you never had that?"

He answered, "My parents got divorced when I was ten and I never had that. When I'd go to high school games, I'd be envious of my friends who had their family with them. Maybe my dad would be there, but he'd be on one side of the stands and my mom would be on the other. They never spoke." You could see that he'd been robbed of what God had intended for him to have — the blessing of a loving family and a family that supports him and loves him.

Divorce has a deep effect on the kids. It's usually a very negative and devastating effect. It may be okay for the wife; it may be okay for the husband but it's usually not okay for the kids.

My friend and his sisters are living with the ramifications of that. However, there's great news. No matter what we do, no matter how we sin, no matter who lets us down or who hurts us, God is there. God is in my friend's life, in your life, in my life, in your kids' life. If you've been divorced or your parents were divorced, God is there to give you the comfort that perhaps you didn't receive from your family. Just know that God loves you and His comfort is there. That is what I tried to share with my friend.

It was a reminder to me that divorce is not okay with God. I've been divorced (fortunately there were no kids involved in my first marriage). I know I made a mistake in that part of my life, not being obedient to God and loving my first wife as I loved myself. I repented of my sin and God has shown me the error of my ways. Six years later He blessed me with another wife (still married sixteen years later with three kids).

Thank you, Jesus!

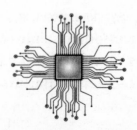

So What Does "Ask Anything" Mean?

Jesus says, "Ask anything in my name and you shall receive it" (1 John 3:21). God had just told me I'm to be like Jesus. I'm to live in love and not have fear because perfect love casts out fear. Now God says, "Ask anything in my name and you'll receive it."

Some people might respond, "Well, Jack, that sounds a lot like 'name it and claim it' to me. Can I ask for a car? Can I ask for a million dollars? Can I ask for a wife, a husband, a job? I can ask for anything in Jesus' name and I'll get it? It does say that in the Bible. It does say that." But that's only part of what it says. It's not "name it and claim it." I don't think that's what God said or intended. That doesn't mean God doesn't want you to be wealthy, healthy and happy. If God ordains that for you, great. There is nothing wrong with being wealthy. It's what you do with the money that counts. Anything you put before God and God's word and desire doesn't work.

Here's what the scripture actually says: "Dear friends, if our hearts do not condemn us, we have confidence before God and receive from Him anything we ask, because we keep His commands and do what pleases Him" (1 John 3:21). We receive from God anything we ask; some people just stop there with the conception that, "God's word says we receive from God anything we ask." No. It ends with these words: because we keep His commandments and do what pleases Him.

If you're walking in the will of God and you're doing what pleases God, you should know for sure you're going to get what you ask for. Your prayers are going to be answered. 1 John 5:14 says, "This is the confidence we have in approaching God: that if we ask anything according to His will, He hears us." That means if you ask anything not according to His will, He isn't listening. He hears you, but He isn't listening because He wants to hear the prayer that is according to His will. Only that prayer will ensure you and God are aligned on the same page. That's what God wants.

I don't want there to be any confusion with this concept. Many people think God's word says one thing when it says something completely different. In John 15:7, Jesus says, "If you remain in me and my words remain in you, ask whatever you wish, and it will be done for you." The problem is that some people stop right there. Some people cut the verse right there. There's another line after that. Here's what it says: "If you remain in me and my words remain in you, ask whatever you wish, and it will be done for you. This is to my Father's glory, that you bear much fruit, showing yourselves to be my disciples."

You ask anything you want for the glory of God, so that it bears fruit for the glory of God, so that you're walking as a disciple in the glory of God. You can rest assured if you ask anything you want, when you're operating like that, you'll get it from God. That's the difference. That's the attitude and the life God wants us to live.

Remember the miracle is not that you and I accepted Jesus Christ. That's not the miracle. That's not the amazing thing. The amazing thing is that Jesus Christ accepted you and me. That's the miracle. That's the amazing thing. And yes you can take that to the bank... And download it also while you're at it!

Orlando Tragedies

I had a buddy call me the other day. He's a longtime friend of mine since we were little kids. Great guy. Atheist guy. No spiritual background whatsoever. Brought up Jewish but no belief in God. I'm sure you guys are aware of the tragedies that went on in Orlando in 2016. My family and I had lived up in the Orlando area for almost a year when he called.

He said, "Hey, it's terrible what's going on in Orlando." Oh, yeah, it's terrible. Three tragedies in the span of a week. A young singer, a twenty-two-year-old girl, Christina Grimmie, got shot and was murdered by a fan in a meet-and-greet after a concert. The next day we had forty-nine people die in a nightclub shooting in Orlando. Then a couple of days later we had a little two-year-old boy eaten by an alligator at a local resort hotel as his parents stood nearby.

I said, "Yeah, yeah, it's all horrible." But he was talking specifically about the nightclub shooting of the forty-nine people. I said, "Yes, that was horrible."

He said, "It's funny how the world focuses on that. There are fourteen thousand murders per year in the country. That averages out to forty a day, but everybody just kind of focuses more when they all happen in one place at one time."

I said, "Well, okay, I kind of get that. I get what you're saying."

Then he shocked me and said, "Yeah, and most of the murders today are done by Christians."

I was like, "What? Excuse me?"

He said, "Yeah, most of the murders are committed by Christians."

I said, "I've got to just stop you there. I'm hearing everything else you're saying, but I've got to stop you there. First of all, I don't know any Christian who would ever commit murder. Now, I know there is a policeman in the line of duty or a soldier who is a Christian who, defending themselves, may have to kill an enemy. I understand that, but I'm talking about consciously setting out to murder. It is just contradictory to every single thing a Christian believes."

Yet my friend's perception of the world was quite different than yours and mine because he defines Christians as anybody who calls themselves a Christian. A lot of people out there call themselves Christians, yet are not behaving in Christian ways. I can't change that. You can't change that. My prayer for today for you and me is that the people who know us as Christians would just by knowing us be certain 100 percent that we could never engage in that kind of behavior. That is not the definition of Christian that we know. I just am amazed at how people give condemning stereotypes to certain people, groups and things without truly knowing the facts. It boggles my mind.

Here's the equivalent of how I look at that. Let's imagine you came to this gourmet meal, the best meal you ever had. It was delicious, great. Everything was wonderful, the steak, the potatoes. It was just this amazing gourmet meal. (Steak and potatoes is my definition of great food. You can substitute your own definition of a gourmet meal). Imagine you walked away from the greatest gourmet meal ever and I said, "Tell me about the food."

And you responded in a negative and demeaning way saying, "You know what? They used three toothpicks to hold the bread together instead of one. Those guys, whenever you go to their restaurant, you know what they do? They put three toothpicks in to hold the bread together. You know what else they do? They cut the bread vertically instead of horizontally. Can you believe that?"

That's what you're going to tell me about that your takeaway of the restaurant? You're going to focus on that minuscule detail and not tell me about the great food you enjoyed but comment on something obscure. And virtually irrelevant but that's how you define and stereotype an entire people, culture, religion, race, industry. That's ridiculous. It's like saying about the best-dressed guy in the world, "Yeah, but he wore rectangular cufflinks instead of square ones." Maybe he did, but you know what? He's the best-dressed guy in the world!

We, as Christians, are defined, generalized and stereotyped by the world as well. The nonbelieving world lumps all Christians together. So a born-again, loving follower and believer of Jesus Christ is classified the same as a lunatic person claiming to be a Christian murdering someone.

What can we do about it? Only one thing — just make sure that when you're out there representing Jesus Christ as His ambassador, as His son, as His representative, you are indeed representing the love and mercy of Jesus Christ first and foremost. That's what people remember about you and their encounter with you.

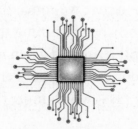

What Will He Find?

I believe God wants us to go further in our walk with Him. I believe He wants us to always seek to strengthen our connection with Him and deepen our understanding of Him.

Let's look at Paul's view of righteousness, something that might be vague to many people in the world today. I pray his view is ours. If it's not, I pray that we ask the Lord to change our hearts so that we understand what the righteousness of God truly is.

Romans 10:4 says, "Christ is the culmination of the law so that there may be righteousness for everyone who believes. He is the culmination of the law." In Philippians 3:7, Paul says, "Whatever was gained to me, I now consider a loss for the sake of Christ. What's more, I consider everything a loss because of the surpassing worth of knowing Jesus Christ, my Lord, for whose sake I have lost all things. I consider them garbage that I may gain Christ and be found in him. Not having a righteousness of my own that comes from the law, but that which is through faith in Christ."

Paul was very concerned about what spiritual condition Jesus would find him in. Are we concerned about how Jesus will find us? I am. God's been burning that question on my heart lately. "What will Jesus find when my life is over?"

How will you be found when Jesus comes to test us to see if our faith is genuine? Is it worth more than gold because it has proved genuine? God said when He tests our faith, that's what He's looking for. Genuine faith is worth more to Him than gold. What will be found in your life and mine? Will it be our own righteousness? Are we still striving by our own standards for righteousness, by what we think is good and bad? What we think we should or shouldn't do? Can we say, like Paul, that we consider all of that garbage?

If we are found having righteousness that comes from the law, it is meaningless. But if we are found having the righteousness of Christ that comes through faith in Jesus, it means everything.

Jeremiah 33:16 says, "The Lord is our righteousness." We understand this refers to us accepting the righteousness of God and not our own righteousness, which we know is a one-way ticket to hell. "For there's none righteous, not one" the word of God tells us in Romans 3:10. Only Jesus was righteous. Paul was willing to sacrifice everything for the righteousness of God. I felt the spirit of the Lord asking me if I'm willing to do the same. Are you?

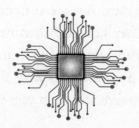

Can I Get An Amen?

My daughter and I were praying before we went to bed. I love to pray with my son, Jackson, and my daughter, Talia, before bed. They're in different rooms so I pray with them individually before they go to sleep. The other night, I was praying with Talia, and it was my turn to pray.

I finished and said amen. She looked at me and said, "Uh-huh."

I thought for a minute and I asked, "Don't I get an 'amen'?"
She answered, "I said uh-huh."

I said, "Well, you know what? That works. That's reaffirming the word of the Lord. I'll take 'uh-huh.'" Whether it's amen or uh-huh, it's all good. It means the same thing, as Talia taught me. Any affirmation of the word of God is a good thing.

I was reading in Isaiah 38 about King Hezekiah. Basically, the prophet Isaiah had come to Hezekiah and told him that he was going to die. His time was up. The Bible tells us in Isaiah 38:2 that Hezekiah turned his face toward the wall, and he prayed to the Lord. He said, "Remember now, O Lord, I pray, how I have walked before you in truth and with a loyal heart, and have done what is good in your sight."

In other words, here's Hezekiah saying to the Lord, "Isaiah just told me I'm going to die. Obviously, he's your prophet so he knows what he's talking about. But, Lord, would you remember how I walked before you in truth? Would you remember how my heart was loyal? Would you remember that I did good in your sight?" The Bible says that Hezekiah wept bitterly as he prayed to the Lord.

I want to ask this question: Can we say the same thing before the Lord today? Can we look at the Lord and say to Him, "Lord, remember how I walked before you in truth. Lord, look at my loyal heart. Lord, I've done what is good in your sight"?

I think it's imperative that we examine ourselves and be able to answer that question. If the answer is not yes, like Hezekiah, we need to change what we're doing so it is yes; that's the life we should be living to glorify God. That's a life that glorifies God.

Hezekiah is crying out to the Lord, and it makes me want to ask myself a question. If Isaiah came to me or Jesus came to me and said, "Your time is up today," and I said, "But Lord, I want you to extend my life," would God do it based on the way I'm living my life today? I'm not sure that answer is yes. I've got to examine myself. Would my life show choices and actions that give glory to God? I'm not sure.

God granted Hezekiah fifteen more years based on his prayer. "The word of the Lord came to Isaiah, saying, 'Go and tell Hezekiah, Thus says the Lord, the God of David your father: I have heard your prayer, I have seen your tears; surely I will add to your days fifteen years'" (Isaiah 38:5). I wondered if I made that same prayer would I get that same answer.

My answer to myself was that I need to change some things in my life because I really want to be able to say yes to that. I want to be able to stand before God and if I ask God for more time, He would say, "Absolutely. You're doing a great job. Of course. Here's fifteen more years for you. You deserve it, Jack." I think we need to look at ourselves and see if we can do that. Can we say that? How can we accomplish that?

I'm over fifty now, and I feel that I know what the Lord expects of me in my life. But it's not a matter of us being a certain age. You should be able to know what to do and how to live immediately upon knowing the Lord because the Lord tells you what to do. His Holy Spirit speaks to the hearts of those who know Him and seek after Him. It's not about age. It's about knowing the Lord.

I can't see the future, and the things I'm concerned and worry about, I can't possibly see how they're going to work out because, to me, it's a dark forest. I can't see through it. But the important factor is that I know God can. I can look back in my life at other times I felt the same way and didn't see the way out, didn't see how things would change or how it was going to get better. I realize that, all along, God knew. Everything always did work out. God wasn't lying in Romans 8:28 when He said all things work together for the good of those who love God. It's true. I love God. You love God. God is working everything out according to His will for our blessing.

You don't have to worry when you can't see the future. God sees the future. God is in control. All you have to do is believe.

"Uh-huh" and "Amen" to that!

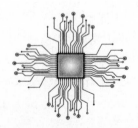

Raising Them Right

If you have kids, can you imagine not raising them to understand the difference between right and wrong, not making them understand where a life of crime is going to lead them and where they'll wind up versus a righteous life? "Oh, no, I won't make you understand. I'll just let you figure it out yourself. Then later in life when you're an adult, you'll yell at me for being a lousy parent." No. We want to make our children understand because it's important. I pray that would be the desire of our hearts. I pray that God would make us understand.

The word of God says this in Psalm 119:29... I love this, listen to this prayer made to God... "Remove from me the way of lying." Remove it. It is a vital prayer. "Take it away, Lord. Kick it out. Shake it out. Rip it out. Cut it out. Operate. Whatever you've got to do. Take away from me the way of lying. I don't want to lie, Lord. You said let your yes be your yes and let your no be your no. I want to be truth and righteousness and reflect you, Lord. Remove the way of lying from me."

That verse goes on to say, "And grant me your law graciously." We know that all things come from the Lord. A grant is something you usually get free from somebody. Charity organizations often receive grants. The psalmist is asking God to grant him the law graciously. Then he goes on to state in verse 30, "I have chosen the way of truth." What's that? Truth is a choice? That's right. Just like salvation, it's a choice. You can choose to have faith, or you can choose unbelief. It's one or the other. It's a choice. He says, "I've chosen the way of truth. Your judgments I have laid before me." My question is this: What have we chosen? You and I, what have we chosen? Truth or Lies?

It goes on to say, "I cling to your testimonies." You know what it means when something is clinging to you? You can't get it off. That's what the psalmist is saying. "I'm clinging to your testimony, Lord. There is no way you're shaking the word of God off of me." I hope that's how we live our life.

He goes on to say, "O Lord, do not put me to shame! I will run the course of your commandments. For you shall enlarge my heart." What are you running to? The apostle Paul says we're to run the race for Christ so as to win the prize, focused on the task at hand. The Apostle Peter tells us to be alert, sober, and vigilant. For our enemy the devil is prowling around like a lion looking to devour us (1 Peter 5:8).

We're to stand guard. We're to be ready for the Lord. We're to be in service for the Lord. "My life doesn't matter anymore, Lord. I want to live it for you. I have to have you." That's the prayer we need to have.

Psalm 119:33 goes on to say, "Teach me, O Lord, the way of your statutes, and I shall keep it to the end." What are you asking God to teach you? What ways are you keeping, the ways of the world and the flesh or the ways of God and the spirit?

What are we truly asking God to teach us? Do we have that commitment that can't be shaken? He says, "Teach me, O Lord, the ways of our statutes, and I shall keep it to the end."

In Hebrews 2:1, Paul says you need to pay careful attention to what you've heard so that you won't drift away. Here is a commitment the psalmist is making. "Teach me, Lord, and I'll keep it to the end." It's a promise. We know God has taught you and I. So what have we learned from the teachings and blessings our father has bestowed upon us? Will we teach it to our kids? Have we made that commitment to God? Do we live like that?

I know that's a lot of questions, but your answer to them may very well determine how you fulfill your purpose in this life and your rewards and in eternity.

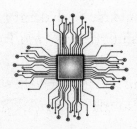

Handwritten

Having lived in New York until I was twenty-seven, I still get and read the New York Post. I kept a clipping from something I read on December 18, 2015. The title reads, "With a Loving Hand." It shows a picture of a boy and a hand. The headline of the article says, "Scared Colorado high school kid's note to family." It goes on to say the following:

A terrified teen, who thought he was going to die in last week's Colorado high school shooting, scribbled a heart-wrenching goodbye to his family on the only thing available at that time — his hand. He wrote in pen. Certain of impending death, Matt Bowers fumbled for a pen in his pocket as he cowered in a corner after hearing gunshots outside his classroom at the Arapahoe High School.

"That morning I didn't really tell my family I love them," Bowers, seventeen, told CCN. *"So I wrote, 'I love you,' on my hand just so that they knew I was thinking about them and I was praying for them. It said, 'Family, I love you all so much,' and I underlined 'so much' because I really meant it."* He also wrote on the same left hand, *"I'm here now,"* above a cross to tell his kin he was in heaven. *"That's where I genuinely thought I was headed if the gunman had happened to stumble into our classroom and actually end it for all of us."*

What great faith. A young man facing death knows he's going to heaven. I pray and hope you have that same blessing today. I know it. I hope you know it as well. When our time on Earth is up, we're going to heaven. If we know and believe Jesus, that is for certain. That seventeen-year-old was certain; he had no doubt where he was going and he wanted to take that moment to tell his family how much he loved them. I want to tell my family how much I love them. You want to tell your family the same thing. It's important to tell the people we love that we love them.

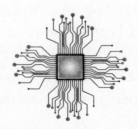

No Regrets Please

How do you make sure you get God's best blessing?

The answer is in Isaiah 66:2, which says, "But on this one will I look: On him who is poor and of a contrite spirit and who trembles at my word." This is the one I will look on. This is the one I'll have favor on, him who is poor and of contrite spirit and who trembles at my word.

God doesn't mean poor financially. He means broken. He means poor in spirit. "Contrite" means you have a humble heart toward God. You have godly repentance for the sin in your life.

What does it mean to be poor in spirit? We've all had sin issues that we've had to deal with. For many of us, it's not so much our sins we must deal with now as it is our natural abilities, our strengths, our ambitions, our desires, our independence, and our self-sufficiency. For some of us, it's our denominational doctrines and our self-wisdom. For many of us, these things must now die to the cross of God if we're to be able to move into a life of total abandonment to God. That's what God desires. When God said die to self, that's what He's talking about — a life of total abandonment to God.

Only those who become poor in spirit and who have learned not to trust in their ability — these are the ones God can fully use. Those who have learned to trust not in their abilities or their feelings or their desires or their personal plans or their self-will any longer, who have learned to be led by the spirit of God in everything, those are the ones I believe God references will be entrusted with high positions and many things in eternity forever and ever. God says he who is faithful with little will be faithful with much. Your life on Earth is the "little." That's the test of God. Will we be faithful with this little bit on Earth so we can have everything and all the eternal blessings God has in store for us?

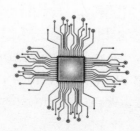

Are You Drunk?

Let's look at how the disciples lived. Do we believe God wants the same passion from us? How do people see us? I love this passage out of the book of Acts. It's Pentecost, and the Holy Spirit is coming on the disciples at Pentecost. You probably know the story. All the disciples are together in one place. Suddenly a sound like the blowing of a violent wind from heaven comes. It fills the whole house where they're sitting. They saw what seemed to be tongues on fire that separated and came to rest on each of them. Then Acts 2:4 says, "All of them were filled with the Holy Spirit and began to speak in other tongues as the spirit enabled them."

This is absolutely crazy. These guys are there, and all of a sudden the Holy Spirit of God falls upon them. I've been saved for more than twenty years. I can recount very specific times when the Holy Spirit of God has been supercharged in me, anointed me, and filled me beyond normal. Those days were not normal days. Remember you and I have already been 100 percent sealed with the Holy Spirit of God from the day we accepted Jesus as Lord.

You already have the Holy Spirit of God inside of you. But we can ask God to fill us for specific assignments and anoint us with even more of His spirit. He'll give you as much of the spirit as you request. The question is this: How much are you asking for? How much do you really want? Are we content to live our lives on the fleshly side and not willing to die to the fleshly side so we can live our lives on the spirit side? Sometimes we're scared of what God might do with our surrendered lives. I can tell you with certainty that it is much better to commit our lives fully to the Lord. I hope that's the desire of your heart.

On with the story. The disciples were now filled with the spirit of God. They were staying in Jerusalem, and when they went out into the streets, the people around them said, "Aren't all these who are speaking Galileans? Then how is it that each of us hears them in our native language?" Some of the people made fun of them and said they'd had too much wine. That was the reaction of some people. So filled were the disciples with the Holy Spirit that the people said, "This is insanity. They're drunk, speaking a different language." That would be the equivalent of me speaking Chinese or going into fluent Spanish and German. Believe me, if it happened, it would be the Holy Spirit of God doing it because I don't speak any of those languages.

So Peter addresses the crowd. He raises his voice and he says to the crowd, "Fellow Jews and all of you who live in Jerusalem, let me explain this to you; listen carefully to what I say. These people are not drunk, as you suppose. It's only nine in the morning! No, this is what was spoken by the prophet Joel: 'In the last days, God says, I will pour out my spirit on all people'" (Acts 2:14).

The disciples were drunk with the spirit of God, not with wine or alcohol, but with the Holy Spirit of God, as God had promised through the prophet Joel, "I will pour out my spirit on you in these days." I hope you see the signs of end times more in your life today, it's so obvious. I can't tell you if it's today or two thousand years from now. I don't know. Only God knows.

There is one thing I do know. We have one job. Be prepared. Live today as if this was the day God is coming so you'll be found worthy, you'll be found righteous, like the master who came back and found the slave who had done what he was put in charge to do. "That one," the master said, "who I come and find what he was doing, I will put in charge of many of my possessions, many in the kingdom of heaven."

That's what God wants from you and me. It's not like God didn't tell us exactly what's going to happen. He said, "This is exactly what's going to happen." Then He said, "This is exactly what I want you to do." What excuse might we come up with for not doing what He has told us?

That's your mission, that you'd be a drunken fool with the spirit of God for the glory of God.

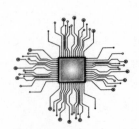

Don't Hold Back

I have a friend, a sweet Indian man who is about sixty years old. We've had several business dealings in the past. Once, I was at a renewable energy conference with him for three or four days. He has read my books. He told me, "Jack, I appreciate your books. I've given them to my children. We love God and I teach my family to always do the right thing." He's the sweetest man and he helped me tremendously in a solar project I was developing.

Then as we were sitting at the table, waiting for a meeting to begin, he looked me dead in the eye and said, "Jack, it's all about doing the right things and providing for our kids, right?"

I wanted to ignore the comment. I love the guy so much. He's only done good things for me. I wanted to let it go. The meeting was about to start. But God wouldn't let me. I said, "No, that's just a part of it. It is wonderful that you love your family and do the right thing, but for me, as a believer in Jesus Christ, it's all about knowing that I'm going to spend eternity with God in heaven. It's all about having God inside of me and the Holy Spirit inside of me as I go through life." Yeah, we should want to be faithful to our kids and to our family and do the right thing, but that's not what it's all about. It's all and only about knowing Jesus Christ and having a relationship with God in heaven.

God gave me that opportunity to share the truth with this guy at the conference. I know He's giving you similar opportunities and wants you to share your faith. If it's all about heaven, why should we bear fruit on Earth? Why should we perform the good works God created us in advance to do? Look at God's promise in James 1:12: "Blessed is the one who perseveres under trial because, having stood the test, that person will receive the crown of life that the Lord has promised to those who love him." Those who persevere under trial, having stood the test, will receive the crown of life God has promised to those who love Him. How do I persevere? You persevere by doing God's work, by responding with the will of God and the works of God to others around you.

James 2:14 says, "What good is it, my brothers and sisters, if someone claims to have faith but has no deeds?" Verse 17 says, "In the same way, faith by itself, if it is not accompanied by action, is dead." If faith is not accompanied by action, it is dead. James goes on to give us an example. He says, "Was not our father Abraham considered righteous for what he did when he offered his son Isaac on the altar? You see that his faith and his actions were working together, and his faith was made complete by what he did" (James 2:21).

I pray the same would be said of you and me. You need to respond to what God has called you to do where He's placed you. You may have a very specific personal cause that God has placed on your heart, or you may know your call is to be a light of God shining everywhere you go — in your home, in your workplace, at the supermarket.

This is critical. James 4:4 tells us, "Your adulterous people, don't you know that friendship with the world means enmity with God? Therefore, anyone who chooses to be a friend of the world becomes an enemy of God." The Lord is talking to us. What does He mean by adulterous people? God says,

"You're not cheating on your wife. You're cheating on me."

You're cheating on God because you've become a friend of the world. That makes you an enemy of God. Jesus says, "He who is not for me is against me." You can hang out in the world. You're a part of this world temporarily. You're passing through but your citizenship is in heaven. You're a part of this world, but you're to reflect God. You're to be an ambassador and a representative of God in this world, not to get sucked in by the world and be a representative of the world, of the flesh, of the devil.

You might say, "I would never do that. The last thing I would ever do is represent the world or the devil. I'm a child of God."

God says, "Then behave like it." You can say you're a child of God all you want. God says, "Behave like it," just like Jesus said to the Pharisees. He said, "You pray in the temples, and you tithe, and the outside of your cup is clean. You want to be seen by men. But I know your hearts. Inside you're filthy and rotten."

I'm looking at my own heart and examining my own life. I'm asking, "Where do I fall short of what God has planned for me?" Where have I become an adulterer to the Lord instead of staying on the Lord's side? I don't want to live like that. Yes, we're all victims of our flesh, but we can have victory over it in Christ. We're not to give in. We're to have victory over our flesh so we have victory in Jesus.

I pray our prayer would be that people would see us and know we have been with Jesus. Our lives would be such lights and reflections of Him. I pray it would be the desire of your heart for your life to be that light and reflection. When people see you, they would know you have been with Jesus. I pray we wouldn't waste this precious time we've been given, that the enemy would not fool us. I pray that the deceiver, the one who comes to steal, kill, and destroy would not rob you of your joy, joy that comes only from the Lord and your fellowship and relationship with Him. I pray you would live joyfully.

Yes, we need to do good to our kids and our family, but the ultimate decision here is whether we let Christ rule and reign in our lives.

As one Christian evangelist said, "The opportunity of a lifetime must be seized within the lifetime of the opportunity."

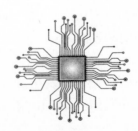

What Have You Got To Lose?

See to it, brothers, that none of you has a sinful, unbelieving heart that turns away from the living God. But encourage one another daily, as long as it is called "Today," so that none of you may be hardened by sin's deceitfulness. We have come to share in Christ if we hold firmly till the end the confidence we had at first (Hebrews 3:12-14).

That's an important verse. God is saying we need to make sure we don't have a sinful, unbelieving heart because it will turn us away from the living God. We're to encourage one another while today is today so that none of us may be hardened by sin's deceitfulness. We can be assured that sin is deceitful, and it will harden us to the things of God. Paul also reminds us we've come to share in Christ if we hold firmly until the end the confidence we had at first.

Does that mean you can lose your salvation? No. I believe your salvation is a one-time transaction between you and God. You cannot lose your salvation, assuming of course you were truly saved in the first place. God says His gift and His call are irrevocable. You can, however, miss out on the blessings that Jesus Christ has in store for you both here on Earth and in heaven forever. We've come to share in Christ if we hold firmly till the end the confidence we had at first. That means you can miss out on the blessings of Christ. God doesn't want us to miss that.

In 2014 I was worrying a lot about things I couldn't control. I'd been worried about my health. I'd been worried about my family. I'd been worried about my future. I'd been worried about my finances. I'd been worried about my father as he was suffering from dementia, so I had been concerned about a variety of things.

Then God spoke to my heart and spirit. He said: "Every single thing you're concerned about has to do with loss" — loss of time, loss of money, loss of health, loss of what the future will be. Even my kids have given me cause for concern. They were twelve and ten, and I was concerned about losing their respect as they get older. All this stuff I was focused on - health, money, finances, relationships, the future, control - had to do with the loss of things I couldn't control. God laid on my heart the reality that when my life is over on this Earth, I will have lost all of it anyway. I couldn't control any of it. I would definitely lose everything. God was asking me: What am I worried about when I have the one treasure I can't lose, which is God's love and my place in eternity? Yet all these other things I couldn't control seemed to be taking up my time.

Unlike me, Paul realized it when he said, "I've learned to be content in all situations, whether I'm abounding or have nothing. It doesn't matter because I can do all things through Christ who strengthens me" (Philippians 4:12-13). He learned to be content in all situations. Me, the opposite. I haven't learned that. Paul is a lot smarter than me.

We deal with the lies of Satan every day. Satan is the father of lies. He tells us, "It'll always be like this. You're too old. Nothing will change. Your health won't get better. Your kids won't be all right. Your finances won't be all right. Your future won't be better." That's a lie of Satan, always lying, always telling us, "No, no, no, no, no," when God has already said, "Yes, yes, yes, yes, yes," in Jesus Christ.

Yet as I was going through this period — I believe God was using these circumstances to strengthen me, mold me, shape me, and teach me something. I believe this was a teaching moment from God in my own life. At the same time, I had my own choices to make as God was testing me. I could choose to indulge in sin, and I sometimes did. Not murder and robbery or those seemingly bigger, obvious sins. Just covetousness, greed, envy, and pride. Those seem to be easy ones for me to indulge in. Yet they're just as bad as those other sins. To God, a sin is a sin.

I need to examine myself. I can't blame the world, circumstances, or Satan for everything. It might be convenient to play the blame game, but I can't. I've got to look at myself. I've got to search my own heart. It's not that I think I'm a bad person. Yet I know I don't have total victory over my thoughts and my flesh.

I've been wondering if God is looking at me like He must have looked at the Israelites when I go back and read through the Old Testament. I'm reading about how God delivered miracle after miracle. Every time, they said, "God, this is the greatest. You're the greatest. We're following you. We're all in," and they doubted Him the next day. As soon as they didn't get what they wanted (even though they got what they needed)— whether it was food, the manna, water, miracle after miracle, — their reaction was, "We're working too hard. We've got to go back to Egypt. It's not enough, God. We still don't believe."

I look at it and tell myself, "Well, if I saw those things, I'd believe." We see things that are just as amazing, and we don't always believe.

I feel that God is saying to me, "Jack, I've chosen to reveal myself to you, and yet you still sometimes don't believe me?

You still sometimes choose the world over me?" I believe He is saying the same to you today. We have to look at ourselves and answer honestly whether we choose to trust God or the things of the world.

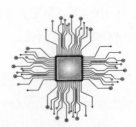

That's My Foot On Your Throat

I read the Bible almost every day. Not every day, but I try and make it most days. For two weeks, I had been picking up the Bible during my quiet time every day, but I felt like the word of God was shut off to me. I would sit there reading, but I was not receiving. God's word hadn't changed. It was me. It felt like God had closed the word to me, and it broke my heart. I said, "God, I have to have this. I have to feel connected to you."

God made me realize through that time of testing that His word is like air. It was literally like God was standing on my throat with His foot closing my air pipe and asking, "Can you breathe?" And I felt like, "No, I can't. I need your Word to stay connected. It's not enough that I have your word. I have to be connected to your word and to your spirit, Lord." That's how I have to, need to, and want to live. God reminded me of that.

Of course, God — being God — opened up the word again, and I was able to receive it and realize that the word of God is my life. That is where I get the flow of life, from God. I hope you realize that, too. Life doesn't come from the things of the world. So what do we do? I was at the crossroads with God trying to teach me something. What do I do? What do you do?

The answer is in Psalm 94:18. It says, "If I say, 'My foot slips,' your mercy, O Lord, will hold me up. In the multitude of my anxieties within me, your comforts delight my soul." If my foot slips, God says His mercy will hold us up. In the multitude of our anxieties, God's comfort delights our souls. God didn't say there wouldn't be anxieties. Quite the opposite. It's very clear in His word that we will have anxieties. God says He will comfort us through them. There is no comfort anywhere else. There is no comfort in the world. There is no comfort in your own self. The only comfort you get comes from the Lord.

We have to let God comfort us. Sometimes we don't do that. Sometimes we don't do it with people. Sometimes we get mad if somebody wants to comfort and help us. When we're not ready for it, we respond with, "Leave me alone. Get away from me. Just leave me alone." Say it enough times and they will leave you alone. Say it enough times, so will God. God will leave you alone if you don't want His comfort. I hope and pray that's not your choice.

So where is the hope? Where are the better days? If all this anxiety is happening, where is my hope? It's found in Psalm 92:10-14. "I have been anointed with fresh oil. The righteous shall flourish like a palm tree... Those who are planted in the house of the Lord shall flourish in the courts of our God. They shall still bear fruit in old age. They shall be fresh and flourishing." What a great promise from God. He's anointed us with fresh oil, and has guaranteed that the righteous will flourish like a palm tree in the courts of God. We shall still bear fruit in old age.

I want to get there. I want to do that. I say, "All right, Lord, how do I flourish in old age? How do I do that? Tell me what to do." The answer is found in a familiar verse that says, "Do not be conformed to this world, but be transformed by the renewing of your mind" (Romans 12:2). Why can't I be conformed to this world? What would be so bad?

Bad company corrupts good character. We're not supposed to pollute our bodies and minds with sin and give Satan a foothold in our lives to gain control. We're supposed to be separate from that. But why do I have to be transformed by the renewing of my mind? God's word says you must be transformed to prove what is the good, acceptable, and perfect will of God. If you're transformed by the renewing of your mind, you understand the perfect will of God, and if you do it, you can rest assured God is going to be very pleased with you.

Can you imagine going to school and the teacher not telling you what the requirements are for the test? Or going to work and the boss not telling you what your job is? Of course not. They tell you, "This is what you're supposed to do."

We are supposed to be transformed by the renewing of the mind. What does that mean? We all know what it's like to renew our driver's license, to renew a magazine subscription, or to renew a lease on an apartment or a car. What happens if you don't renew it? You lose it. No more subscription. No more car. No more apartment. No more driver's license. If you fail to renew it, you lose it.

God says we're to be renewed by the transforming of our minds because He doesn't want us to lose the connection to the Holy Spirit. The Holy Spirit is inside of us. God doesn't lose us. We get distracted by the world and move away from God. There is an action required on our part. Just like when we renew that license or lease, we have to pay or sign up or do something. We need to come to the word of God each day to renew our minds. That's the daily renewal.

Trust in Him today and every day!

Do you remember when there used to be attendants at gas stations? They would actually fill your tank at the gas station.

God's word says faith comes by hearing and hearing by the word of God. We want to increase our faith. That's how we renew and transform our minds, by connecting and getting closer to God.

Can you imagine the Holy Spirit standing there each day with a gas tank full of the spirit of God and saying, "Can I please fill you up? Can I fill you up with so much of the Holy Spirit you'll be overflowing?" and us saying, "No, God. I don't want any today"? God is there each and every day wanting to fill us with the spirit of God. Why on Earth would we ever decline that offer?

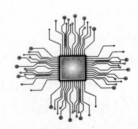

Without Care

Here's a question that is critical to our lives today. How can I renew my mind with all this garbage going on all around me? I previously told you some of my own personal worries and concerns. I'm sure you've got a few in those categories yourself. Here's a few more that were prevalent in 2015 .... what about the government running out of money? What about Ebola? What about ISIS and the Sony hackers? What about sports and politics and all this stuff that's happening and the price of oil plummeting and currencies and war and love and relationships? What about all of that? How can I renew my mind when I've got all that to worry about?

In 1 Corinthians 7:29, God is talking through the apostle Paul to the church of Corinth. He is also speaking to us today. Read God's instructions and desire for us; this will tell you how you can do it. Paul says, "But this I say, brethren, the time is short..." The first thing Paul says to the brothers, and the first thing God says to us is that the time is short. We know end times are near. I can't tell you if it's today or ten thousand years from now. Only God knows the time. Jesus told us to look for signs of earthquakes, of famine, of nation against nation, of a one-world currency, of chips that are going to soon be put beneath the skin that allow people to buy everything. Now it's in your phone. Soon it will be in your hand. It's all coming. We can see it clear as day. God says the time is short.

The scripture goes on to say, "For the form of this world is passing away." God promised the form of this world is passing away. As a matter of fact, God said we're strangers here on Earth. Our citizenship is in heaven. We should be happy we're going to die one day and get to be with Jesus. We should be delighted and excited. How lucky are we? Yet we sit there and complain about it like it's this terrible thing. It's a great thing.

Then Paul says, "But I want you to be without care... He who is unmarried cares for the things of the Lord — how he may please the Lord. But he who is married cares about the things of the world — how he may please his wife" (1 Corinthians 7:32-33). He didn't say it was a bad thing to be married. We know God provided marriage so man wouldn't be alone, and the two will be joined together as one flesh. The point is he wanted us to be without care. He didn't want us to be bogged down and worried by the things of the world. He said, "Time is short. This world is passing away. I need you to be without care so you can focus on the things of the Lord, so you can accomplish the purpose for which you are called, which is to glorify God's name and bear fruit that would last."

That's our purpose. God wants us to do it. That's why He wants us to be without care. I thought, "Oh my goodness. I'm blowing it." I've been with care. I've been with a lot of care. I've been caring about a lot of things.

Can you imagine if I gave you a remote control and I said, "The remote control will work, but one thing you've got to do is push the button. It won't work if you don't push the button. You can hold it in your hand all you want. If you don't push the button, it's not going to work," and you didn't push the button? But it's the one thing you had to do.

God says, "There is one thing I want you to do. I want you to be without care." It's so critical that you're without care.

Take a look at the perspective of people without care. Here is a practical example from the world. There was a JetBlue flight a couple of weeks ago that had severe turbulence. I hope you've never experienced that. I've experienced it. At one time I thought I was going to die on a turbulent plane flight. Not a fun thing. After this particular flight, a passenger got off the plane and said, "I'll never be mean to anybody again." He had a new perspective.

One of my friends is a pastor who rides in a patrol car with the Broward County sheriff's deputies. One night he saw two young babies die in two separate accidents. He saw the response of their mothers. He came into church the next morning, and his perspective on life was changed on what was important. Can you imagine him having to listen to somebody complaining about what song is best, or that the temperature during service was a little hot or a little cold, or anything like that when he had just seen two young lives taken away and the mothers' reactions?

What should we do? God tells us in Matthew 11:28-30: "Come to me, all you who labor and are heavy laden, and I will give you rest. Take my yoke upon you and learn from me, for I am gentle and lowly in heart, and you will find rest for your souls. For my yoke is easy and my burden is light." You hear the verse all the time, but maybe you don't know what it means. I didn't know until somebody explained it to me. A yoke attaches two animals (like cows, horses) so they stay together and go straight and forward. That's the purpose of the wooden yoke. It keeps them straight and harnessed so they go straight ahead, focused on the task at hand.

Could God be any clearer? He says, "I want to direct you. I want to guard you. Do you want a cement block on your neck or a nice, cushy foam pillow? I'm the foam pillow. I'm easy. I love you. I want to care for you and caress you and guide you and make sure you go in the right direction." That's the purpose of that verse. "I want you to take all your troubles and put them on me."

Can you imagine if I tried to walk through life carrying a refrigerator around everywhere I went, in case I wanted something to eat at any given place? Now say two strong friends approach me and say, "Put that down and let us carry that for you." And I tell them, "No, no, no. I've got to carry this around." How stupid could I be when there's someone who would carry it for me? Or when I don't have to carry it in the first place? It is better I put it down and go on to do what I'm supposed to do. Imagine not eating a pizza today because it will get moldy in a week. Or not driving a car because you know one day it will rust. Absurd, right? Yes! That's absurd! Equally absurd is not living our lives to the fullest right now.

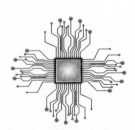

Greatest Present Ever

What's the greatest present you've ever received from anybody? I'll bet you know. I'll bet you can immediately think of the most fantastic, greatest present you received. Of course, from God, the greatest gift is our salvation through the sacrifice of His Son. But what about from another person? I remember getting a new car from my parents for my eighteenth birthday. That was an amazing present. I've tried to give my kids some amazing presents. Not new cars, but some amazing presents they'll remember.

Guess what? That's how God is thinking about you and me. Sometimes we shortchange God. But He is sitting there thinking, "How can I bless these guys?" Can you imagine God thinking about how it's going to be for us when we get to heaven? He must be laughing, thinking, "This is so amazing. You guys have no clue. I can't wait for you to get here to show you."

In Yonkers, New York, where I grew up, there is a little pizza place. It's called Capri Pizza, a tiny pizza place with only three tables. I think it has the best Sicilian pizza slices in the world. Every summer, when my family visits New York, the kids and I go back there because it's so amazing. It's the best pizza I've ever had. Because I know how amazing it is, I know you'd love it if you were to go there.

That's how God is looking at us in regard to heaven. He wants to share. He wants to show you what He knows is so great.

Isaiah 25:1 says, "Oh, Lord, you are my God. I will exalt you. I will praise your name. For you have done wonderful things." Has not God done wonderful things for you and me? How about salvation? How about heaven? How about the gift of the Holy Spirit? Isaiah 25:8 tells us, "He will swallow up death forever, and the Lord God will wipe away tears from all faces. The rebuke of His people He will take away from all the Earth." I don't know about you, but that sounds pretty wonderful to me. Swallow up death, take away all my tears, and take away the rebuke of His people. Thank you, Jesus.

So what should we do? How do we react to this abundance that's been poured out on us of love, of grace, of mercy, of the Holy Spirit? Isaiah 26:3 says, "You will keep Him in perfect peace whose mind is stayed on you because He trusts in you." If you don't have the peace of God, the peace that transcends all understanding right now in your life, perhaps you're not focused on God. God has made a promise. He will keep you in perfect peace when your eyes are focused on Him. That's how you get the peace of the Lord. You keep your eyes focused on God.

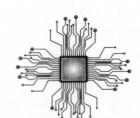

Impact Player

In Matthew 21, Jesus tells a parable. First, He asks a question. He says, "Look, what do you think?" Then He goes on to tell the story:

> *There was a man who had two sons. He went to the first and said, "Son, go and work today in the vineyard."*
>
> *"I will not," he answered, but later he changed his mind and went.*
>
> *Then the father went to the other son and said the same thing. He answered, "I will, sir," but he did not go.*
>
> *Which of the two did what his father wanted?*
>
> *"The first," they answered (Matthew 21:28-31).*

The obedient son was the one who said he wouldn't, but then did. He is the one who did what the father wanted. Let me get this right. It's not about what you say; it's about what you do. That's right it doesn't matter what you say. It matters what you do. God says we must, "Die to self" (Luke 9:23, 1 Corinthians 15:31). John says, "He must increase, and I must decrease" (John 3:30).

This is how we get where we need to be. It's not about

what you say. It's about what you do. That's how you become an impact player.

An impact player is someone who has an impact on the game. Do you think those who leave their homeland to go on mission trips have an impact on the place they go? I think so. I think they got up off their butts and decided to do something really impactful. It's also an impact every day when Christians serve the church or the community in which they live. They're choosing to be impactful players.

We look at Tom Brady's football career and say, "Oh, he's an impactful player." In 2016 LeBron James carried the Cleveland Cavaliers to a championship on his back. Oh, there's an impact player. No question, an impact player. We need to strive to be the same in our walk with Christ.

The one who is not impactful is the one who doesn't contribute to his team winning. A pastor buddy of mine said when he was a young man in college, he and his buddies had gone out for a night to celebrate a buddy getting married. He said the guys decided they wanted to go to a strip club. They lived in the Midwest and it was winter. He said it was freezing. My buddy was in the truck with four other guys who had decided to go to this club and he said, "I'm not going into the strip club." He was a Christian kid.

His buddies said, "Well, tough. We're going in. We'll see you when we come out." He waited in the car for four hours in the cold. There was no heat in the truck. He froze his butt off. The guys came out four hours later and that was the end of that, or so he thought.

Twenty years later, he got an email from a guy who was in the car that night. He wrote, "I want to tell you I became a Christian. One of the reasons was that I'll never forget the night you stood up for your faith when we all went into the strip club and you wouldn't go." What an impact! What an impact he had on somebody's life just by being faithful to the Lord.

Another friend of mine sells fences in Orlando, Florida. A customer sent a letter to the president of the company and said, "Thank you so much for sending Sean. You have no idea what a Godsend he was. I'm a veteran. I was hurting and depressed and Sean came and encouraged me and spoke the word of God into my life." In his job selling fences, he impacted the world for Christ.

You may be the only Jesus some people see. My unsaved friends often call me when they're in trouble. "Can you pray for me?" they ask.

"Of course I can pray. Of course I will. But I tell them you can do it too. You don't need me to pray. You can go directly to Jesus."

They might not think they have access to Jesus but you know what? I'm glad they call me. I'm glad that they associate me with Jesus Christ.

I think it's very important that people know what team you play for. I think there should be no question. I don't think it should be, "Well, I want to hang out with these guys and they tell dirty jokes, so I don't tell them I'm a Christian. I'm certainly a Christian on Sunday morning in church. I'm a Christian here, but not there. I am a Christian sometimes but not all the time." That's wrong! Really wrong! The world should know what team we play on at all times.

Another guy was showing me some business stuff in an industry I was not familiar with. He was teaching me some operations in the business. The guy who introduced us said, "This is Jack. He's going to be hanging around with you for a day. He's a Christian."

The guy looked at me in horror and said, "Oh. I hope you're not one of those Christians because I curse all of the time."

I answered, "Listen, you can say whatever you want. I'm here to learn. Of course I'm not going to curse, but you do whatever you want to do." But I thought, Man, how great this is they are taking note... There is no doubt I am a Christian. (I pray it was not from a prideful point that I thought it was great, but from a spiritual point.) I think the world should know the same thing about you. It should be obvious by how you live and how you present yourself that you're a Christ follower.

What does a life of impact look like? It's just reflecting Christ wherever you are. Do you have to be big and strong to have an impact? No. Mother Teresa, Nelson Mandela, Gandhi — not all of these are Christian, but it's a list of people who aren't big and strong — the Dalai Lama, and Nick Vujicic all impacted the world in some way.

Do you know who Nick is? He is a young man who was born without arms and legs. He goes around speaking and telling his testimony. What a great Christian guy. It's not about your physical strength or size. It's about the size of your heart, the amount of your passion and your trust and faith in God. That's what allows you to live out fully the wonderful life God has planned. That's what allows you to receive all of His blessings.

You have a choice. You can have the truth, but you have to choose it. You have to use it. Not everyone has to be a quarterback. But we're supposed to play our position with excellence and to the best of our ability no matter what position we play. We're not all wired the same. God created us to be all unique parts of the body. Each with a purpose and function that benefits the entire body! Each necessary, relevant and important to the body's overall success and future!

I know guys at the church where I was saved who go out knocking on doors every Tuesday night. It's called witnessing. They go knocking on strangers' doors, "Can I share the love of Christ with you?"

I am not wired to do that, but I see the value of that because I've seen the transformed lives as a result of their faithfulness to do what God has called them to do. I need to be clear on this. I've seen people who have come into the church who were suicidal, who were depressed, who were lost, who were lonely and said, "Thank God you guys knocked on my door Tuesday night. Thank God someone cared enough to come and knock on my door and share the word of God with me." I've seen the results. I've seen God working through these guys' lives who have the faith and courage to go out and knock on doors.

I'm not wired that way. I am wired to share the love of Christ with everybody who comes into my path. I am wired to make sure they know I'm a Christian and why. I want people to know my life before Jesus, and then what happened after I met Him. I had everything by the world's standards. I had money, success, and power. I did drugs, gambled, and had girlfriends. Anything you would think might satisfy, I had. It was worth nothing to me.

Now that I have Jesus, He is worth everything to me. He is why I want to make a difference. He is the reason I choose to live a life of impact.

One son said yes, but his actions said no. One son said no, but his actions said yes. Your actions speak louder than your words. What will your life show?

Be Careful What You Ask For

In the summer of 2015 I was in Cazenovia, upstate New York. I was sitting by the waterfalls, thinking that I'd had a lot going on in my life the past year. I was thinking about the future and what might happen, what the Lord might have in store for the upcoming year. I had this feeling of... I couldn't quite pinpoint it. I called it a "holy dissatisfaction." It was an overall sense that I was not satisfied with where life was.

I felt I wanted to do more for God and the kingdom and didn't see the next plan coming forward. I was sitting there at the waterfalls, watching the water crashing down on the falls. Then, in my mind's eye, I saw myself standing under the falls. I saw that the water was Jesus' blood being shed and washing me, cleansing me from all my sins. There I was, standing at it looking, and I could see myself under those falls. I could see the water crashing down. I could see the blood of Jesus being shed for me.

I remember saying to the Lord, "I need a personal story, God." I had met Erwin McManus (author and pastor) a couple of months prior to that, and he shared with me a personal story, an experience he had in college. He was witnessing to a girl, and she was pretty depressed, maybe even suicidal.

He told the girl, "God loves you so much. Trust me. It's going to snow today. That's how much God loves you." There had been no snow in the area for years and years. He told me he went back to his dorm room and sat there on the floor, thinking, "What did I do? God, this is crazy. How can I make it snow? What did I just say? I've given this girl false hope." Sure enough, it snowed that day. To this day, Erwin shares that story, an incredible story of faith and trust in God and God delivering.

I said to God, "God, I want a personal experience story too. I know you. I love you. I know you know me. I know you love me. I know you died for me on the cross, but I need that kind of experience and I need it now."

Be careful what you wish for.

My wife, who in 2015 was fifty-two years old, got pregnant. Now, most of the time, fifty-two-year-old women do not get pregnant. I was fifty-seven, and we have three kids already. Our oldest son, Ricky, was twenty-seven. Jackson was thirteen, and Talia was eleven. The last thing we were planning on was a baby.

God really shocked me with that. I think God was talking to me, as He talked to Abraham and Sarah. He asked me, "Jack, is there anything too hard for me?" He didn't ask me audibly. He asked me in my spirit. "Is there anything too hard for me?" I think He wanted me to know very clearly that God's power can accomplish anything.

Needless to say, we were shocked, nervous, excited, and panicked about the thought of bringing another baby into the world. But Beth and I accepted it immediately and said, "God, if this is your will, we're all in. We're going to do it. We'll take it, and we'll do this. Let's see what you have in store, God."

About a month later, Beth miscarried, and we didn't have the baby. The good part is that we were willing to trust God no matter what happened at any point in time.

When I was up in Cazenovia watching those waterfalls, the verse that came to me was that He washes us whiter than snow (Isaiah 1:18). Instantly, at that moment, as the water was crashing on the rocks, I looked up. The water foamed up, and it looked just like snow. I couldn't help but turn my thoughts into a prayer. "Thank you, Lord, for that graphic image of your sacrifice and death for my life. I hope and pray that I live it fully for you."

We don't have to ask God for a story. He is faithful. God gives each of us a story, a unique story that tells of His design for our lives in an incredible way. And within that story, He gives us other stories. Stories that we are meant to share with others to bless their lives. Stories that we are meant to take to heart, to better understand God's plan for us. Stories that show us God is real. Stories that enable us to glorify Him.

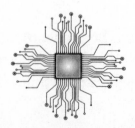

We Love You, Buddy

My son Jackson and I were at Universal Studios a while back. We were going on the Krusty the Clown ride, and Jackson didn't want to go. He hates rollercoasters. He gets violently sick on rollercoasters due to motion sickness. I said, "Buddy, I know, but it's a simulator. You can't get hurt. There is no reason to fear." He wound up going on the simulator, and he loved the ride. He wanted to go back again and again.

I thought that was just like what God does to us. God assures us we're going to heaven. He tells us our life on Earth is temporary. It's like the simulator ride. You can't get hurt here. Just enjoy it because your place is really in heaven. It is secure, paid for, and definitely designed and inspired by God. It is difficult, however, to maintain that perspective on life. Sometimes things come our way that make us feel sick, or like we can't carry on. Sometimes we face life-changing, heartbreaking tragedy.

While we were up in Cazenovia, there was a sad, local news story about a twelve-year-old boy named Joey Eisch, who was riding his bike and was hit. He didn't survive the accident. The newspaper reported that his parents' last words to him before they left the house that day, had been, "We love you, buddy." At the memorial, they spoke of how grateful they were that the last thing they told him was how much they loved him and that he knew that he was loved.

We should pray that God would help us to do the same thing. We should remember to tell the people around us that we love them and we care for them. Most importantly, we should know that God loves us each and every day.

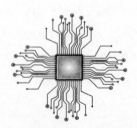

Peace Beyond Understanding

One day I encountered a storm on the turnpike going back and forth from Orlando to Boca. It was a crazy, blinding storm. I was driving along, and everything was fine. Ten seconds later, I was being pelted by rain so hard it was blinding. There was bumper-to-bumper traffic and no visibility. I thought, Man, this is what hell must be like. All of a sudden you're stuck. You thought everything was fine. You thought you could live your life apart from God. You decided not to trust God. Now you die and you find out, Oh goodness, I'm in hell. This really stinks, and I can't get out. It's this blinding rain, bumper-to-bumper, lightning, no visibility. It's terrible.

Then I drove through it, and right beyond was a blue, gorgeous, rainbow-filled sky. How was that possible so soon after being in hell, after going through this storm where it seemed that there was absolutely no way out? It seemed like it would never end, but all of a sudden I was there in heaven in this beautiful surrounding.

That's exactly what our lives will be like when we're done living, after we're done going through the storms of this Earth. When we get to heaven, after all the storms are over, there is no more pain. There are no more tears. There is no more suffering. There is an eternity of joy with God forever and ever. What a great bargain.

On another day and another drive, I had been up straight since 12:30 the prior night, without any sleep. I was driving all night to Orlando, exhausted, burned out, splitting headache, too tired to drive another mile. That moment, the spirit of the Lord came over me. I don't know how to describe it. I don't know if you've ever been in the dentist chair and gotten nitrous oxide. They call it laughing gas. I don't know if I'd describe it like that. I don't know if you ever got a morphine shot in the hospital. I had back pain and was in the hospital. With that morphine shot, in one second my whole attitude changed.

This time driving on the turnpike everything changed. It wasn't a drug. It wasn't morphine. It wasn't nitrous oxide. At my worst moment, God came over me and gave me immediate relief, peace, joy — a spiritual high unlike anything I've ever experienced in my life. I started appreciating being alive and not being sick. I was appreciating the traffic. All this even though I had a headache, I was tired, I was behind schedule, and I was frustrated. All of a sudden I was loving every moment of it as God and His Holy Spirit used that moment to transform me into His peace. It's one of the most unbelievable things, feelings and experiences I have ever had in my life. It was a great moment in time with God seeing His power at work.

One morning on another day, on yet another drive I was heading back to Orlando (as we were moving there I had to make many trips back and forth over a two-week period) to take care of signing the lease on the home we were about to rent, and I started to cry. I realized my only concern had been about my stuff, my comfort, and getting my life settled. I wasn't so concerned about lost souls. I asked God to please align my heart with His. I wanted to understand and live for things that are important. Our righteousness is but filthy rags before the Lord because here I was just thinking about myself. I was very grateful that I was clothed in God's righteousness, not my own.

Then the spirit of God spoke a special and specific verse to my heart.

Isaiah 43:18: Do not remember the former things nor consider the things of old. Behold, I will do a new thing.

That's God's promise each and every day. God says His mercies are new every morning. He promises as far as the east is from the west He'll remember your sin no more. He tells us to not remember the things of old because God is going to do a new thing.

He will meet us wherever we are — on the turnpike, in the storm, stuck in traffic — and He will show us that He is real, He is good, and His promises are true.

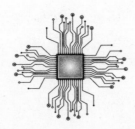

Section 4

INSTALLING VIRUS PROTECTION

Unlocking God's Treasure in Your Heart

Virus Protection is a software utility designed to protect your computer or network against computer viruses. If and when a virus is detected, the computer displays a warning asking what action should be performed.

If a virus infects a computer without virus protection, it may delete files, prevent access to files, send spam, spy on you, or perform other malicious actions. In some situations, a computer may not meet the requirements of a virus and the computer is only used to help spread the virus to other computers that may meet the requirements.

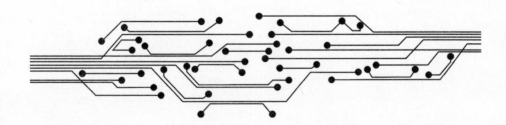

Do You Really Know What It's Worth?

We live as if Jesus is not coming back and judgement day is never coming. God says in Romans 13:11, "And do this understanding the present time. The hour has already come for you to wake up from your slumber because salvation is nearer now than when we first believed." Another version says in New King James, "Do this knowing the time. Now is high time to awake out of sleep for our salvation is nearer than when we first believed." It's high time. Listen, this is the same mentality — this herd mentality. I can't stand it. This "I just do what everybody does" mentality. It's the same mentality that gets everybody slaughtered in the stock market and destroyed in the real estate market. Why? Because if everybody's buying this, it must be good. I'll just do what they do. Oh, and if everybody's selling. I'd better get rid of this. I'm in danger. What?

Let me ask you a question. If you knew value of something, would you panic if it went up or down? For instance, if you knew the value of a certain car was $10,000. So there was no doubt in your mind it was worth $10,000, in parts alone. And I said to you, "Hey, you can have as many of these cars as you would like to buy for $25,000. How many do you want to buy at that price?"

You'd say, "Oh, Jack. Why would I buy a car for $25,000 when it's only worth $10,000."

Very good question. "How about at $35,000 or $40,000?

How many do you want that price?"

"None, I'm not going to do that. It's only worth $10,000."

What if I said to you, "You can have as many as you want for $5,000 per car"? How many would you want? What if I said it was $500 a car? How many would you want then? A lot? Oh yeah, a lot.

"Wait a minute. Why? Why do you not want it at $35,000 but you wanted it $500?"

"Well, because I know it's true value. It's worth $10,000."

Exactly, you know the value. If you know the true value of a company's stock or you know the true value of real estate, you would know if you're overpaying or underpaying regardless of what the market did at a particular time. Assuming, of course, you had the time to wait it out to see the true value ultimately reflected."

So here's the big question. What is the true value of God? What is the true value of our eternity in heaven? What is the true value of Jesus Christ to your life and my life? My answer would be, it's worth is incomparable, more than all the riches, treasures, pleasures and things of this world. Worth trading girthing I have for.

Here's how Jesus explains it in Matthew 13:44-46 "The Kingdom of heaven is like a treasure hidden in a field. When a man found it, he hid it again, and then in his joy went and sold all he had and bought that field. Again, the Kingdom of heaven is like a merchant looking for fine pearls. When he found one of great value, he went away and sold everything he had and bought it.

It's A Choice

God wants you to have the benefit of the abundant Christian life. God doesn't want you to miss it. God doesn't want you to have regret. God wants you to do it right. What should you do? I think you have to make a choice. I assume most of you are going to vote in an election, so you're going to make a choice. I assume you're going to decide what to eat for lunch today, so you're going to make a choice. I assume when you're done attending church this week, you're going to go home, so you're going to make a choice. We know how to make choices.

Here's the choice David made, and I ask if we would consider the same choice. In Psalm 101:1, he says, "I will sing of mercy and justice, to You O Lord I will sing praises." He made a choice. "Lord, I'm going to sing and glorify You." In verse 2 he says, "I will behave wisely in a perfect way." He says, "I'm going to make it a point to do the right thing. Not only am I going to praise and worship You, but I'm going to make it a point to do the right thing." Then he adds, "I'll walk within my house with a perfect heart." I'm going to make sure my heart is in line with yours, Lord. Then the one I love the most, verse 3, he says, "I will set nothing wicked before my eyes." I will set nothing wicked before my eyes. David made a choice. He said, "Listen, I'm not going to do that. Wicked, no! Pornography, no! I'm not setting anything wicked before my eyes." Yet we know David had a failure in his life and we know God restored him.

I'm very heavily involved helping people drug addiction recovery. If somebody fails to be sober, we don't tell them, "Oh, you failed. You're done. You're worthless. As a matter of fact, just go and commit suicide because you'll never get this right." No, we say, "Come back and try again, you can do it." If somebody fails their driver's license test, we don't say, "Oh, you failed. You can't drive. No, you're not driving." How about the Bar exam? "No, you can't be a lawyer." No. We say, "Listen, go study again. Go focus again and do it right because we want you to have that benefit. If we didn't want you to have that benefit, we'd say, "Well, it's one time and if you don't get it right to heck with you." No, no, no. We want you to get it. It's so important to us that you understand what's right that we don't even care how long it takes you. If you can get it right on the first time, great. Here's your license.

If you can't, keep coming back until you get it right because it's so important you get it right. God says the same thing to you and me, but He also says, "Listen, know what you're supposed to do. Know what it looks like, what you're supposed to do." When David says, "I'll set nothing wicked before my eyes, that was a choice, a conscious choice. It was a conviction, a promise, a definite plan of action, not a maybe, not a might, not a "we'll see," not if things go my way. It was a definite choice to follow God. When Joshua said, "As for me and my house, we will serve the Lord," he made a definite choice to follow God.

Remember one thing. The first time you do something wrong, you can say is a mistake. But if you continue to repeat mistakes, they're no longer mistakes. They are now decisions!

Greatest Sermon Ever Preached

I was praying one day and I said, "God, is there a way I could possibly preach a sermon that people would remember for the rest of their lives?" I don't know if there are too many sermons that you can really say, "Whoa. I remember that sermon. It was amazing and changed my life completely." Wouldn't that be cool if each time I preached I could do that? Of course, God reminded me it's not about me. It's about Him.

He spoke to my spirit and said, "Jack, if you had died during the sermon, people would definitely remember that."

I said, "How about a plan B? How about we just hit them with your word, and there's something in your word they would remember?"

I'm hoping we go with plan B.

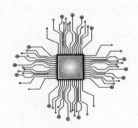

Outcasts Stick Together

In Orlando in 2016, during the time of the Pulse nightclub shooting where forty-nine innocent people died, obviously there's been a spotlight on the gay, lesbian and transgender community — and all the other letters that go with it. Here's an interesting quote that a pastor made the other day. He said, "They're accepting everybody. They're adding letters now. LBGTQI. (Q and I now standing for questioning and interested.) Anybody who is an outcast they are welcoming into their organization. They're saying, "Oh, the world doesn't understand you? You're an outcast? Come. You can be part of us." Isn't that exactly what the Church is supposed to be doing? Isn't that exactly what we're supposed to be doing? Instead of creating differences among us, we're supposed to be welcoming everybody. After all, we were the outcasts and Christ welcomed us into the kingdom. He assumed we would go and love others with the same love we have been shown. That's our job, your job, and my job.

My son Jackson is fourteen, and we went to a MegaCon conference a couple of weeks ago. That is a comic book, superhero, animae convention. Very cool. A couple of hundred thousand people come through the convention center over the course of a weekend. It struck me. I'm looking at all these people, and I'm thinking about outcasts. I'm looking at adults and children, a ton of adults were there, many of them dressed in superhero costumes. Some were there for the comics. Some were there for the superheroes. Some were there for the anime art. Some were there for movies or TV shows like Dr. Who or Harry Potter. Just a wide variety of stuff. Whether you agree with what they like, here's my point.

I'm looking at all these people and, for those three days they were there, they were in their element. They were accepted. They could wear costumes, roleplay and not be laughed at or called weird or crazy or juvenile. They were loved. They were appreciated. They were encouraged for who they are, what they're doing, and what they believe, even though when they leave, they immediately become outcasts again. As a matter of fact, there is nowhere else but there that they can come and be accepted and encouraged for what they enjoy and for what makes them happy. Can you imagine if you walked into a church, and there was a guy in a Captain Marvel costume? You'd be calling the police or the insane asylum to take the guy away.

Yet all these people are looking for something. What are they looking for? Love, acceptance, encouragement, community, family. Isn't that exactly what they're supposed to get from the Church? Aren't we supposed to be that (like Jesus) to a lost generation and world? Aren't we supposed to be that place where they can come and be loved and accepted and encouraged? Now, that doesn't mean we condone sin, but I'm reminding us there is not one righteous. Not me. Not you guys. Only Christ was righteous.

We have a world also looking for acceptance and freedom. Jesus didn't condone sin, but He loved sinners. I believe that's my purpose and your purpose in this life. Many churches have been struggling with how to deal with the gay and lesbian community. How do we welcome them in our church? How do we deal with them and make sure they feel welcome while not condoning their behavior — the same approach and issue we would have with any particular sin. We should be making sure we love the sinner. We have to be able to do that and figure that out, or we are going to fail in our purpose as a church and in our purpose as representatives of Jesus Christ.

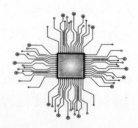

Who Is The King?

I was in a Bible study and pastor George Cope (a true man of God who has blessed me so much with his teaching and tremendous insight into the word and heart of God since I moved to Orlando) was talking about making choices. He said we need to settle in our minds once and for all the issue of the lordship of Jesus Christ. When you settle in your mind the issue of the lordship of Jesus Christ, you have settled all other issues. That issue must be settled.

I share with you today, unless Jesus is the Lord of all, He is not Lord at all. Unless Jesus is the Lord of all of your life, He is not Lord at all. We too have a decision to make, like the disciples, like the angels. Are we with God or against God? Joshua said, "As for me and my house, we will serve the Lord." I pray it will be the decision of every one of us today to serve the Lord proudly.

You're going to love this. Pastor George reminded us in the Bible study the battlefield is in our minds. The only place Satan can fight us is in our minds. Everything else has long been decided. Jesus has crushed death and the sting of death and paid the penalty of sin at the cross. That's done and decided forever. God is the same yesterday, today, and tomorrow. He is the "I am." He is everything. That's a fact. The issue is in your mind whether you believe it or not. That's where Satan is fighting you — in the battlefield of your mind. That's the only battlefield Satan has to fight us.

I want you to see it in a way I pray you'll never forget; in a way it was shown to me that I've never forgotten. Take a look. Who is the king? That's the question you have to answer today. Who is the king? We have our spirit, our soul, and our body. Those parts make up who we are.

Your spirit is the eternal part of you, the part that will live forever, for all eternity when you're here and gone. Your body, that's the five senses: sight, touch, hearing, smell, taste, feel. We know our body will die, and then we have our soul. What's our soul? Our soul is our emotions, our will, our feelings. That's our soul.

The soul is the servant. It will serve whoever is in charge. The question is: Who is the king of your life? Is the king of your life the spirit, in which case your soul, your will, mind, your emotions will serve the spirit? Or is the king of your life your body, in which case the spirit is the slave? One is king and one is slave. It can't be both. If your king is your body, then your soul, your will, mind, your emotions will be the servant of the body.

Take a look. Who's the king? That's the only question that needs to be answered. We need to make sure we live for the spirit. God said don't live for the flesh. Don't work for the flesh, the things that rust, moth, and decay. Work for the things of the spirit that last forever, where no man can break in and steal.

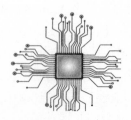

Good Stress Can Kill You

I was driving in Orlando the other day. We bought a new house. We had been renting for a year but now we just bought this new house, and we were closing on the house that day. It was a stressful day. You know, marriage, having a baby, starting a new job, and other seemingly good things can still be very stressful. Also, we were trying to start this drug and alcohol rehab center, and we had this piece of land, and the county had just shot us down on the land and told us if we wanted to do our project on that land we need to build out a road for half a million dollars because it was a business, not a residence. I'm thinking, "You've got to be kidding me."

I was driving along, extremely frustrated and aggravated. It was about three in the afternoon. I was just extremely frustrated — details, contractors, closing, and this and that. God said to me — not audibly but in my spirit (that's how the Holy Spirit speaks to me very clearly) He said, "Look over to the right."

It's a cemetery. I said, "God, I go by that cemetery three times a day every day for the last eleven months. I see the cemetery. Big deal."

He said, "Look again."

I looked over again, and God spoke to me very clearly and He said, "Those people have no problems. They're not worried about anything," reminding me that at His discretion and His timing I could be there, and I'd have nothing to worry about.

My attitude changed in a second from one of frustration and aggravation, truly in less than a second, to pure joy and gratitude. I got it immediately. I was like, "God, thank you for the things I'm thinking about. Thank you for the things that got me aggravated and frustrated. I am so happy to be alive. I get it. I see it. Thank you for showing that to me."

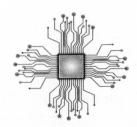

Does It Matter How You Die?

A missionary told this story. He was overseas in a foreign country where the Taliban was, and he was with a friend of his. They were going to look at some land. That was part of his job. They'd go from time to time to scout out land to put in a new camp. He was sick that morning, (and he was rarely sick) So he couldn't go. He said to his friend, "You go scout out the land. I'm sick. I'm staying here."

The other guy went to scout out the land, and he was killed by the Taliban. Shot dead. This missionary guy was sitting there going, "Wow. It clearly wasn't my time to die because I'm rarely sick. I should've been there, and I wasn't. Wow. That's amazing."

The wife of the guy who died was extremely upset and miserable, mourning the tragic death and loss of her husband. It was the most horrible thing ever. How could it be? It wasn't fair.

She said one day as she was mourning in her bedroom, her dead husband appeared to her. Was it a vision? Was it a spirit? No clue. I'm just telling you the story as I've heard it. Her husband appeared and said, "Why are you mourning? I'm in the presence of the Lord." There was not one mention of how he died a tragic death because he didn't know it. Oh, I'm sure he knew he was dead. But like the thief on the cross... Who knew right then, based on Jesus's promise that from this day on, he'd be with God in heaven forever.

You've got to understand this, okay? We should never

worry about how we're going to die. We should only worry about how we live because no matter how you die, (some deaths I can think of would be gruesome, painful ones) you're not going to know it when you get to heaven. You're not going to relive it. You're not going to suffer it. You're going to be in the presence of the Lord. That's all you're going to know. It's not going to matter how you died. It's not going to matter if you died in a car crash, got shot, died peacefully in your sleep, or died from lingering cancer.

I wouldn't wish any of the bad ones on anybody. I hope you all die peacefully in your sleep. I have actually checked that box, and we'll see if my request will be answered. At the end of the day, it doesn't matter. You'll be in the presence of the Lord. There is no more pain, no more suffering, no more tears. You're not going to know how you died. It doesn't matter.

But our human minds don't perceive that. We don't look at the way God perceives it. We don't see it, and we fear and worry. "Oh, how am I going to die? This will be terrible." Why aren't we celebrating the fact that we have life and we're alive? We're to be joyful always, pray continually, and give thanks in all circumstances. For this is God's will for us. We're going to be in the presence of the Lord.

The great news is that you and I have the presence of the Lord with us just right now. God said the Holy Spirit comes to live inside of you when you accept Him as Lord and Savior. God is living inside each and every one of us. It's the "Footprints" poem. He's with us every step of the way. Sometimes we just don't know it. My prayer for you today is that you will make the decision of who is the king in your life and the king of your life would be the spirit, and you would do things that have eternal significance with the short time we have here on Earth.

Perspective Shift

Here's a few things that changed my perspective in 2016, I believe they will change yours as well. Twenty-one-year old Andrew Esquivel, an MIT student, who died when a drunken driver plowed into him and other pedestrians in Brooklyn New York. The Newspaper reported one of his family members said, "He was this great kid with a bright future, whole world going for him. It just makes you think that everything can change in a split second." For this kid it did! He was walking along the street one minute and next instant he's dead. Oh, what's that God? Everything can change in a split second so I should be ready, sober and alert because You're coming at an hour I do not know? Absolutely.

Do you know the book and movie The Fault in Our Stars? It's about two older teenagers -a girl and a guy. They both had life-threatening cancers and were going to die soon from their diseases. Well, there was a real life "Fault In Our Stars" couple named Katie and Dalton Prager whose story and romance resembled the movie couple., There was no question they were going to die young. They found each other online, met, and actually got married. However both within the last couple of months have died. September 12 the wife, Katie Prager, died. Her husband Dalton had died a couple of months earlier. She was twenty-six. He was twenty-five.

Katie, as she prepared to leave this Earth, had messages for those who will remain. Here's what she said, "Just love each other and if somebody makes you mad just forgive them." This is a twenty-six-year-old girl who suffered all her life with cystic fibrosis that she knew would kill her, and it did. That was her message. "Just love everybody and if somebody makes you mad forgive them." She went on to say, "Do what makes you happy. I always wanted to go to Florida and I never went. I wish I had just gotten in my car and gone, it's not that far away." She added, "It's okay, I'll be seeing Florida from heaven."

Perspective! Are there things you want to do that you haven't done? Think about it. One day hopefully you'll be really old lying on your death bed, or maybe you need to think about your perspective right now...either way you don't want to make those mistakes and live with or have regret. Take that message to heart.

Max Ritvo, a twenty-five-year-old poet who died in 2016 of cancer, knowing since he was a youth his disease was terminal and he would die young, always said, "I love you to everyone." He hugged everyone. He knew he was dying, he knew he had an irrevocable disease. He said, "I just want there to be more laughter. Just hug people and love people." Man, isn't that what Jesus said we're to do? Let me get this right, I've got these non-Christian guys who are living more godly lives, whose perspective on life, living and dying is much better than many Christians, who've got it much better together than Christians? How is that possible? Make sure you get it right!

The last perspective change for today. On October 2, a South Carolina shooting victim dies. Six-year-old Jacob Hall, an innocent child, murdered by a fourteen-year-old who shot up a school. In a statement, Jacob's parents said,

"He showed his family how to love, laugh, and smile. That boy has already forgiven the shooter because that's the kind of child he was." That's perspective. I hope your perspective and my perspective is shifting as the Holy Spirit speaks to our heart.

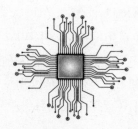

Lost Joy

In the book of Joel, the prophet Joel is talking about things to come, and he's talking about a judgment day and a land laid waste. In Joel 1:9 he says, "The grain offering and the drink offering have been cut off from the house of the Lord. The priests mourn who minister to the Lord. The field is wasted. The land mourns. For the grain is ruined, and the new wine is dried up. The oil fails." Verse 12 says, "The vine is dried up. The fig tree is withered, the pomegranate tree, the palm tree also, and the apple tree. All the trees of the field are withered. Surely joy has withered away from the sons of man."

I was reading that line, "Surely joy has withered away from the sons of man," and it dawned on me that next to salvation I would have to believe that the greatest gift God has given any of us is the joy of the Lord. If you don't have that, you have nothing. If you have that, you have everything. I believe you can go through anything in life when you're protected, when you have God as your refuge, your fortress, and your deliverer, knowing God is with you. You can handle it all.

I've done things that have grieved the Holy Spirit of God. Then, for a period of time, a day, a week, I haven't felt the joy of the Lord in my life. Usually, pretty much 100 percent of the time — it's just a question of how soon (usually rather quickly) I repent of those things that I've done, and I run back to God crying sorrowful because all I want is the joy of the Lord. I have personally tasted everything else that the world has — success, money, prestige, anything you could think of by the world's standings. I got to try all of the stuff, the drug behavior, the running around and partying, all of it (none of which I am proud of now). None of it ever brought me satisfaction, contentment, peace, or joy.

Oh, it numbed me for a day or two or satisfied me for a little while. I've had the joy of the Lord for twenty-five years, and I can tell you it keeps getting better and better and better. I can't live without it. It's like oxygen because I'm miserable and feel the life being sucked out of me the minute I don't have it.

So I want to ask you a question. How about you? Do you have the joy of the Lord? God doesn't want to take your joy away. The prophet Joel is describing a time when men have turned from God, when judgment day has come. Those who have not sought God as their refuge, those who have not made God their father is indeed separated from the Lord. He's describing all these things and, of course, losing the joy of the Lord being one of them.

Just imagine, if you will, eternity. Now imagine an eternity with God or without God, an eternity separated from God with no joy or an eternity with God full of joy. To me, it's an easy pick. If you ask any believer, anybody who knows Jesus Christ, they'll tell you that they're not guessing if there is a heaven. They're not guessing if they'll live for all eternity. They know because God has come to them, because God revealed himself to them. Remember God lives in your hearts now. God wants you to have the joy of the Lord now and forever! Remember you can and should default to that truth every minute of your life.

Whose House Are You Building?

A few years back, our dog had surgery on her back leg, a $3,600 surgery after she tore a ligament in her leg. She's been healing, and she can't run around or jump, so we keep her on a leash. She needed to be kept in a crate for two months until she healed.

One day I took the dog out of her crate this morning to take her for a walk on her leash. I came back in, opened the door, and our cat ran out.

I was frustrated. I couldn't believe the cat ran out. The dog was pulling on me, and she's not supposed to pull. I was chasing the cat as we don't want him outside and he already made it out onto the patio. I got the dog, whacked her on the nose lightly and said, "Bad dog. You stay." I got the cat. I whacked him on the nose a little bit. I said, "Bad cat. Don't do that again."

I figured I had done my duty for the day. I came back in. Jackson, my son then ten years old, and Talia, my daughter then eight, and my wife, were inside the house.

Jackson was at the computer, "Daddy..." He didn't even look up. "... Why did you hit the dog and the cat?"

I thought for a minute. "That's a legitimate question," I said. "Well, son, first of all, I didn't "hit them" hard. I didn't really "hit them" hit them. I just gave them a little slap, a little reminder, like, 'Hey, that's a bad thing. You shouldn't do that.'" Why did I do that? Because I love them. Because I don't want the dog to hurt her leg more and not have the benefit of the surgery. I don't want the cat to get outside. He's declawed. So he'd be dead quickly if he escaped. Because I love them, I wanted to remind them that this behavior is not a good idea.

I believe God sometimes wants to remind us with just a little slap, "Hey, don't do that." The word of God says in First Corinthians 4:21, "What do you prefer? Shall I come to you with a whip or in love with a gentle spirit?" I believe God wants to remind us of the type of behavior He wants us to have that benefits us most. It can be found in Haggai, in the Old Testament and I believe the spirit of God will speak to you today through it:

In the second year of King Darius, on the first day of the sixth month, the word of the Lord came through the prophet Haggai to Zerubbabel son of Shealtiel, governor of Judah, and to Joshua son of Jozadak, the high priest: This is what the Lord Almighty says: "These people say, 'The time has not yet come to rebuild the Lord's house'"
(Haggai 1:1-2).

Here is Haggai talking to the governor and the high priest, and he is saying, "These people say..." These people meaning the people of Judah "'...The time has not yet come to rebuild the Lord's house.'" The passage continues:

Then the word of the Lord came through the prophet Haggai: "Is it a time for you yourselves to be living in your paneled houses, while this house remains a ruin?"
(Haggai 1:3-4)

Whoa. What a great question. Here is Haggai challenging the people by asking them, "Is it a time for you to be living in your own comfort of your own home, in your paneled homes while the house of the Lord remains a ruin?"

I believe God is asking us the same question. "Are you focused on the house of God or on the house of Jack?"

Where are our efforts today? There is a lost generation of people out there. People are coming and going all the time in our lives. We encounter lost people in our communities and workplaces. Are we concerned more with our dinner reservations, our tickets to a game, what is comfortable to us, and what we're going to do this weekend than we are about the kingdom of God? I believe God wants us to be concerned about His kingdom.

The message from God continues into a warning found in Haggai 1:5:

> Now this is what the Lord Almighty says: "Give careful thought to your ways."

God is saying that to us today. Let's evaluate. Let's think about what we're doing. If we're doing stuff right, more power to us. Keep doing it. If we're doing it wrong, let's change it and get it right.

If we had to look at your life, as if it was a series of clips, like a silent movie — there was no audio, no words, you couldn't defend yourself with your words and your fancy talk; all we could see on the video was the actions of your life — what would that movie show? What does God see — not with your words, not with your promises, but with your life? What do the actions of your life show? That is how you will know what you're going to hear when this life is over. "Well done, good and faithful servant," or, "Depart from me. I don't know you."

I believe God wants everybody to hear, "Well done, good and faithful servant." God is giving you this chance to look at your life and, if need be, to turn around and turn back toward God. I believe God. I trust God with everything, and I'm not going to miss the blessing. I'm not going to listen to Satan. I'm not going to get distracted. I'm going to stay focused on what God has called me to do."

Many people in this world die with regrets. The biggest regret is a life half-lived. The sweetest honor is a life fully lived for Christ. As the old Christian poem states, "Only one life, will soon be past; only what's done for Christ will last."

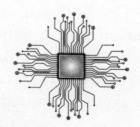

Power Over The Enemy

*They sailed to the region of the Gerasenes, which is across
the lake from Galilee. When Jesus stepped ashore, he was
met by a demon-possessed man from the town. For a long
time, this man had not worn clothes or lived in a house, but
had lived in the tombs. When he saw Jesus, he cried out and
fell at his feet, shouting at the top of his voice, "*

*What do you want with me, Jesus, Son of the Most High
God? I beg you, don't torture me!" For Jesus had commanded
the impure spirit to come out of the man.*

Jesus asked him, "What is your name?"

*"Legion," he replied, because many demons had gone into
him. And they begged Jesus repeatedly not to order them to
go into the Abyss (Luke 8:26-29a, 30-31).*

Clearly, the demons knew Jesus was the Christ, and they
knew He had the authority to cast them into the abyss. There
is no demon that does not submit to the name of Jesus Christ.
You and I have the full authority of Jesus Christ. The demons
can come, they can go, but they can't stop us.

Here's what I equate it to. I have the authority to walk on
the path God has for me. There are demons on the sidelines
trying to stop me. You know what they're shouting? My
name, that's what. "Hey, Jack!" You see I'm walking the path
of glory, in full faith of the kingdom of God. I'm walking
and they're calling, "Hey, Jack, stop! Come on over here!
Take a look here! Let's go to the racetrack. Let's have a drink.
Let's go to the strip club. Let's do anything that will get your

focus off the kingdom of God."

They do anything and everything they can do to distract me from walking on my path, but they can't stop me. That is the key point. They have no power to stop me unless I give it to them, unless I listen and say, "Yeah, I'll take a look. Yeah, I want to do that."

If I listen to them, it means they've succeeded in throwing their lies at me, a son of God, a child of Jesus Christ. It's all lies. "You're not worthy. Your father doesn't love you enough. Remember the sin you did?" What sin? The sin God says He'll cast as far as the east is from the west? The sin God says He'll remember no more? The sin about which God says His mercy is new every morning? The sin that God says if I'll confess to Him, He's faithful and just and will purify me from all unrighteousness? The sin I repented from? That sin, Satan? He has no power over us. We are children of God.

I don't even listen to Satan. That would be like a quarterback in the Super Bowl listening to the crowd. "Hey, it's third and eight yards to go. Oh, wait. Can't call the play, guys. I've got to go argue with this guy in the stands. Time out." How stupid would that be?

Focus. This is the game. Focus. This is your life. Satan can't distract you. Satan is going to yell at you. He's going to taunt you. He's going to tempt you. You have the power to go straight ahead. Only you can give Satan the power to sidetrack you. Don't give it to him.

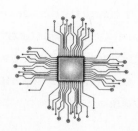

Quit Complaining

What do we do with our attitude here on Earth? God gave me an example. One day I was out on the football field with my buddy watching his son play football. Summer didn't end early this year. It was hot. People had sunscreen on and were carrying umbrellas or looking for a shady spot. I was thinking, "Man, this is extremely uncomfortable," and it was for about twenty or thirty minutes. Then my thoughts started to go to our soldiers fighting in Iraq and Iran, in the desert with hundred-pound backpacks on every day. I turned to my buddy Sean and said, "This is inconvenient, but I'm thinking about those soldiers and what they're going through."

God must look at us the same way sometimes when we complain. "You're going to heaven. You're going to be there for all eternity. This is but a minor inconvenience you are experiencing now. Plus, it's a joy. I want to accomplish wonderful things for your life." Our attitude should be that, hey, it is great to be here. Thank God we're alive, even if the weather is hot. Thank God we're alive to be used for the kingdom of God.

A buddy of mine is struggling with some business issues and some spiritual issues. He told me God spoke to him and told him, "You need to decide what really matters to you. What's really important? Is it earthly things, or is it the things of God? You must choose to live accordingly."

Here is the key to life. Get this right, and you will live the abundant Christian life. Get it wrong, and you're likely to miss it. That's how important this is. The word of God says, "Your faith should not be in the wisdom of men but in the power of God" (1 Corinthians 2:5). That's it. That's the bottom line. I was reminded of the power of God by a few great examples in my own life.

I had a friend in Orlando who was in the FBI. we knew he was dying of cancer. He told me two months before he died, "The one thing I want to do with the time I have left is pour into people the love of God. It's the one thing that I won't be able to do when I get to heaven." What unbelievable faith. That's what he wanted to do because he knew what's important — pouring into people the love of God.

Another buddy of mine is a pastor at Faith Farm, which is a drug and alcohol rehab center, a nine-month program for young men trying to overcome the struggle of addiction. My friend doesn't make a lot of money. He's got four kids. He told me that every night, when his head hits the pillow, he and his wife give thanks that God allows them to be used to impact lives for the kingdom of God. He said, "I see the transformation. I see people coming in strung out, drugged out, broken, with nothing. Then I see God move in their hearts. I see in the months that come amazing transformation as many break free from the bondage of addiction. I wouldn't trade having a part in that for anything." He so values his part in that. It's not for financial reward, but for spiritual reward.

What great examples to me of the power of God at work in lives today. They served as reminders that our faith should not be in the wisdom of men but in the power of God.

Salvation was a finished work on the cross. Our place in heaven and our salvation are assured as we trust in Christ as Savior. God has promised that all things work together for our good. He's told us to seek first the kingdom of God and His righteousness and all these things would come. He has told us to trust in Him with all our hearts, lean not on our own understanding, acknowledge Him in all our ways, and then He would direct our paths.

I pray that we would be childlike — pure, believing, trusting, loving and not polluted by the world. The Lord said He would use the foolish things of the world to confound the wise. My prayer is that we would be fools for Him and not focused on ourselves. I pray that our faith would be in the power of God and not in the wisdom of men.

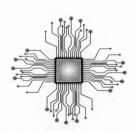

You Really Smell

We've all been there. We've all had our hands dirty. We've all had our armpits smell and our breath stink. What do you do at times like that? You wash your hands. You brush your teeth. You take a shower. Why? So you can bring an aroma of joy to the people you're around. While it may not bother you so much, it would certainly stink to the people you're around if you didn't make the effort to clean yourself up.

Therefore, having these promises, let us cleanse ourselves from all filthiness of the flesh and spirit, perfecting holiness in the fear of God (2 Corinthians 7:1).

We are supposed to be the children of God. We're supposed to bring the fragrance of the Lord to the people around us. They're supposed to smell, see, touch, and feel the fragrance of God through us. We're not God, but others are supposed to see that we've been touched by God, that we're abounding with gratitude for God's grace. That's why Paul says, "Therefore, having these promises, let us cleanse ourselves from all filthiness of the flesh and spirit, perfecting holiness in the fear of God."

What do we smell like — spiritually — to God? What do we smell like — spiritually — to the world? This is the key, and it is critical to the Christian. We tend to forget it, but listen to God's purpose. It is so exciting. "God is able to make all grace abound toward you, that you, always having all sufficiency in all things, may have an abundance for every good work" (2 Corinthians 9:8). That means you have everything you need. Of course you have everything you need. You have God. You couldn't need anything else.

You can do anything God needs you to do because you have God. You have all sufficiency in all things. Why? So that you may have an abundance for every good work. God gave it to you — this abundance — so you would do good works. He gave you the sufficiency so you would use it for good works for the kingdom of God. That's why you have it.

He goes on to say, "You will be enriched in everything for all liberality, which causes thanksgiving through us to God" (2 Corinthians 9:11). Why are we enriched in everything by God? So we can give it away. God wants us to have stuff, not so we can keep it, but so we can give it away — His love, His mercy, His grace, your money, your time, your talents, your treasures. Everything you have, God gave to you. Everything you have, God wants you to give away in the name of God.

That doesn't mean you don't pay your electric bill and plan for college. But we're to live a life that glorifies God. God gives to us so we can give, not so that we can have. It's by giving you'll receive. God Himself was our example. He gave His only son, His beloved Son that we may live. The thing He valued most, He gave in sacrifice for us. He gave Himself. What more could He give?

I know you would join me and say, "Thanks be to God for His indescribable gift," as Paul said, but there's more. Paul didn't stop there when he was writing to the Corinthians. He could've stopped there, but he then wrote, "And this also we pray, that you may be made complete" (2 Corinthians 13:9). Two verses later he writes, "Finally, brethren, farewell. Become complete." It's an instruction.

Now wait a minute, God. Just a second here. You told me that on the cross your work was finished. You died for me. You said, "It is finished." I know I didn't earn salvation. As a matter of fact, you did it. It was your work completely. How could I need to be complete? Wasn't I sealed in salvation with the Holy Spirit of God? Wasn't I indwelled with your Holy Spirit upon believing? Don't I have all of you I would ever need upon salvation?

Yes. Yes. Yes. God's work is complete. Now we're talking about our work. Your salvation is a completed work of Jesus Christ. You did nothing to earn it. Jesus died for you on the cross. He is your ticket into heaven and eternity. Thank you, Jesus.

Your sanctification — which means your rewards in heaven, what you did with your life, what you did while you're here on Earth — is a different process. Your decisions after salvation will determine your rewards in heaven. It is like God is saying, "I need you to do something. I gave you this life. I did my part. Now could you do something so I can bless you more?"

If you have kids, don't you wish they'd listen to you so you could bless them more? I do. I want my kids to listen to me so I can bless them more. When Paul says be complete, it has nothing to do with our salvation. It has everything to do with our sanctification, our reward in heaven, what we do with the gifts we've been given on Earth.

How do you become complete?

One: You know the full riches of Christ to which you were called.

Two: You know that without faith it's impossible to please God.

Three: You live a life for God. You're faithful. You run the race of your life for Jesus.

That's how you do it! Take as much time as you need, but make sure you download that!

Are You Talking Too Much Or Not Enough?

In Malachi 2:17 God's word says, "You have wearied the Lord with your words. 'How have we wearied him?' you ask. By saying, 'All who do evil are good in the eyes of the Lord, and He is pleased with them,' or, 'Where is the God of justice?'"

We need to realize how critical this is. God is saying, "You have wearied me with your words," and we're going, "Lord, how have we wearied you?" God is saying, "Because you say, 'All who do evil are good in the eyes of the Lord, and He is pleased with them.'" Do you think God is pleased with adulterers, with murderers, with thieves, with fornicators, with idolaters, with homosexuals, with sorcerers, with people who are angry, people who are filled with rage, malice, jealousy, envy, and greed? No. God is not pleased with that. Does God love those people? Of course He does. He died for each and every one of them. But He's not pleased with their sins. He hasn't changed His mind on sin. Just because NBC and CBS and HBO did doesn't mean God has. God's view on sin is the same, and He is very, very specific on it. God loves the sinner. God hates the sin.

We're the Christians. We're God's representatives. We're the ones who should be saying, "No, it's not okay." It should not come as a surprise that, as we get closer to the end times, people will accept doctrine that they want to hear preached and turn away from the word of God. It was foretold in God's word. It's no surprise that people would start to say sin is acceptable. No, it's not. It's our job to be clear on that. You don't need to go up to your neighbor's face and tell them, "You're a sinner. You're going to burn in hell." That's not what I'm talking about. However, when your opportunity to speak comes up or it's your turn to comment, you need to say the truth, regardless of who likes it or not.

In the passage from Malachi, God also says, "Or you say, 'Where is the God of justice?'" Now, that's one I hear from some Christians sometimes. "God, where are you? How could you let this happen? How could 9/11 happen? How could the Newtown shootings happen? How could Columbine happen? God, where are you?" God is on the throne, and Jesus sits at the right hand of God. You have nothing to worry about. God has promised there will be a Judgment Day, all nonbelievers will be judged for their actions (denying God) and all believers will be rewarded for their faith (accepting God). God is not lying. God didn't change His mind. God didn't forget. God said in His timing, a thousand years are like a day, and a day is like a thousand years.

He said no one knows the hour of His second coming. No one knows the day when He is returning except the Father. Your job is to be on guard, alert, vigilant, ready, and sober so that when Jesus comes again, you'll be found doing what you're supposed to be doing, so that your blessing and your reward will be great, regardless of what anybody else does.

If anybody else says, "Hey, I don't believe God's coming. I can go do whatever I want," that is their choice. If I didn't believe God was coming, maybe I'd engage in some of the sin the world has to offer, certainly any that I thought was pleasurable. But I believe God is coming, and I hope you believe God is coming. We need to remind ourselves of that great truth, and we need to base our daily decisions on that truth.

Jesus said we will be known by our fruits. Let us pray that our fruits will be recognized by Him. Let us seek His will so that our lives will bear the fruit He has ordained for us to bear as we live.

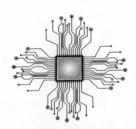

Severe Storm Warning

God is coming. Jesus is coming again. Who can stand before the refiner's fire, He asks? Do you know what that fire is? It refers to the fire over which gold or silver is placed in order to cleanse it. All that is not pure is burned away and only the pure metal remains. That is what the second coming of Christ will resemble.

Who can endure the day of His coming? Who can stand when He appears? For He will be like a refiner's fire or a launderer's soap. He will sit as a refiner and purifier of silver. He will purify the Levites and refine them like gold and silver. Then the Lord will have men who will bring offerings in righteousness, and the offerings of Judah and Jerusalem will be acceptable to the Lord, as in days gone by, as in former years (Malachi 3:2-4).

God will have men and women whose lives will be an offering in righteousness. I pray this will be our story as well.

Do you think the sinners, adulterers and idolaters are going to enter into God's heaven for all eternity on that day? No. They're going to be separated like the wheat from the tare. One is going to be thrown into the fire. One is going to be taken into the barn. One enters into the feast, and the others are outside forever as the doors are shut permanently.

That is the entire premise of the Gospel. That's exactly what's going to happen, or God is a liar. Listen to what God says in verse 5 of the same passage above:

"I will come to put you on trial. I will be quick to testify against sorcerers, adulterers and perjurers, against those who defraud laborers of their wages, who oppress the widows and the fatherless, and deprive the foreigners among you of justice, but do not fear me," says the Lord Almighty, "I the Lord do not change. So you, the descendants of Jacob, are not destroyed."

God says, "I'm going to bring justice quickly on the world, and it's going to come like a thief in the night. It's going to come so fast and so furious, like no hurricane, like no tsunami, like nothing you've ever seen." There it will be, quick and astonishing. But God also said, "You don't have to fear. You don't have to worry. I don't change. I didn't change my mind. You're a believer. You're clothed in the righteousness of Jesus Christ. You don't have to worry. You, the descendants of Jacob, are not destroyed." Think about the reverse of this. If God was not God, you would be destroyed. It's because God is God and you believe in Him that you're not destroyed. If God wasn't God and you didn't believe, you would be destroyed.

It's almost as if we're like the Pharisees trying to trip Jesus up in His words. Why don't we just believe what He says? Why do we have to question Him on every word? "Oh, God, was it this interpretation or that interpretation?" What part of "love the Lord God with all your heart" is unclear? What part of that is open for interpretation? What part of "love your neighbor as yourself" is open for interpretation? What part of "forgive seventy times seven" is open for interpretation? None of it. It's so simple and so pure and so clean.

Why Do You Look So Miserable?

Listen to what God says in Malachi,

"Your words against Me are harsh," says the Lord. Yet you ask: 'What have we spoken against You?'"

"You have said: 'It is useless to serve God. What have we gained by keeping His requirements and walking mournfully before the Lord? Now we consider the arrogant to be fortunate. Not only do those who commit wickedness prosper, they even test God and escape" (Malachi 3:13-15).

Admit you've thought that once in a while. Those thoughts go off your mind, don't they? "Why am I doing this, Lord? I know you love me. I love you. But sometimes it seems like there's no purpose. I don't understand. Sometimes it seems like the people who aren't serving you, Lord, are better off than me. How could that be if you're God?"

We might even go so far as to consider the arrogant to be prosperous. Those who don't worship God seem to escape all the consequences. Not if God is telling the truth. Not if Second Corinthians chapter five is true and we all stand before God on Judgment Day, each to be judged by his actions. Oh, it may not seem like things are fair right now, but God is in control.

It is fair. God's not lying. There's a reward, a hope to come. You're going through this life with trials and tribulations and struggles. Peter talked about this, saying that your suffering will be for a short while, but all of this is so that the glory of God will be revealed in you and God can bless you for your obedience.

You have God walking with you through this life. It's not like you get God later. You have God walking with you now. Yes, the rain falls on the righteous and the unrighteous, the sun shines on the righteous and the unrighteous. Yeah, they can make money, and they can have good families, and they may appear to have the things of the world. In the end, the things of the world are worthless.

Malachi 3:13 is scary… "You have said: 'It is useless to serve God. What have we gained by keeping His requirements and walking mournfully before the Lord?" Can you actually walk around like a mourner, not believing that the word of God is true, not believing there's a payoff for your faith, not knowing the hope through which you've been called? As the apostle Paul prays in Ephesians 1:18, "I pray that the eyes of your heart may be enlightened in order that you may know the hope to which He has called you, the riches of His glorious inheritance in His holy people and his incomparably great power for us who believe." That power is the same as the mighty power that raised Jesus from the dead.

Could you be a Christian and walk around like a mourner? I see some Christians walking around like that. I'm sure you do as well. I say, "How could that be?" That doesn't equal. It shouldn't be like that. We shouldn't see Christians acting like miserable, mourning people. We should see joyful people. Yet some people think it's futile to serve God. Their mindset is, "The reward isn't coming. The payoff isn't coming. There are other people who are not serving God. They're getting away with everything. They're ahead of me. They seem to get what they want because they take advantage of the law. They take advantage of people. Maybe I should do that. That's okay, right?"

No. It's not okay for a Christian. It's not okay to steal or cheat. It may be okay for somebody else, and they may get away with it. It's not okay for you as a child of God. If you're faithful with little, you'll be faithful with much. If you're not faithful with little, even what you have will be taken away.

God has shined a flashlight on my life in these areas. I hope He's shining that same flashlight of truth on you in your life to look at the areas that may not be glorifying or pleasing to God.

I love this final passage in the chapter. It starts in Malachi 3:16: "Then those who feared the Lord talked with each other, and the Lord listened and heard" this is a great reminder for us that God loves us, hears us, and listens to his children. Thank you, Jesus!

Here's how God sums it up in verse 17:

"On the day when I act," says the Lord Almighty, "they will be my treasured possession. I will spare them, just as a father has compassion and spares his son who serves him. And you will again see the distinction between the righteous and the wicked, between those who serve God and those who do not."

That is a promise from God's word. You will see the difference between the righteous and the wicked, between the one who serves God and the one who doesn't.

Which side are you on? There is no in-between. There is definitely a difference between the decision to trust Him and the decision to go our own way.

The disciples asked Jesus, "Lord, what are we going to get? We've left everything to follow you. What's in it for us?" It's a legitimate question. "Hey, God, we've given up everything. We've sacrificed a lot. We're following you. By the way, what's in it for us?"

Jesus responds by saying, "No man who has left his home or plow for the kingdom of God will fail to receive thirty, sixty, or a hundredfold in this time or the time to come." You can't out-give God. You can't out-give Him financially. You can't out-give Him with your time, with your love, with your heart, with your soul, with your mind. You've just got to love Him with all your heart, soul, and mind.

How's that for good advice?

God promises "On that day, when he acts. You will see the distinction". Make no mistake about it. There is a heaven and a hell. There is a life and a death. We who were born again will live forever and ever with Jesus Christ. God promises you will see the distinction on that day. You won't be asking questions then, as every tongue will confess that God is Lord. Every knee will bow.

Let us pray that when that day comes, when He returns to burn away the chaff, our lives will show the purity of a heart that followed after God.

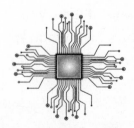

Separate But Not Equal

Apostle Paul, in Romans 5:20, says, "Where sin abounded, grace abounded much more so that as sin reigned in death, even so grace might reign through righteousness to eternal life through Christ Jesus, our Lord." He said that, where sin abounded — where Satan was there throwing his fiery darts — grace abounded more. The grace and peace and love of God comforts that divorced kid, comforts the single mom, comforts every lost person and every sick person who wants the comfort of Jesus Christ. When scripture says that sin reigned in death, reign means was in charge, was in control.

Sin was in control in death, but grace is now in control through the life and mercy of Jesus Christ. We have this marvelous, wonderful gift of grace from God. It's available to each and every one of us, available to everybody in the world. God says He died that all would be saved, not just few, not some, not most. All.

If we're going to walk in this grace-filled life, what does it look like? I believe God wants to show you what walking in His grace looks like. The first thing it looks like is that we are separate from the world. God has called us to be separate from the world, to be sold out to Jesus Christ. What does that separation look like? It looks like Romans 1:1, where Paul describes himself as "a bondservant of Jesus Christ, called to be an apostle, separated to the gospel of God."

Paul acknowledged he was separate. He was called by Christ to be an apostle. You and I are called by Christ to be a royal holy priesthood, to be children of God, to be ministers of God, to be light to a world of darkness and salt to tasteless generation. We are called, as God said in Ephesians 2:10, "To do good works, which God prepared in advance for us to do." We are called to be separate.

First Corinthians 6:19 says, "Do you not know that your body is the temple of the Holy Spirit, who is in you, whom you have from God? You are not your own, for you were bought with a price. Therefore, glorify God in your body and your spirit, which are God's." God is telling you this life doesn't belong to you. God gave you this gift of your life, but He owns it. It's His. It belongs to God. It's supposed to be separate, belonging to God.

I assume you park your car in your garage or driveway at your house, not at a neighbor's house or in the house of some stranger walking alongside you at the supermarket. It's yours. Your money, I assume, it's in your pocket and your bank account because it belongs to you. You don't go around leaving it in other people's bank accounts or pockets, why? Because it's yours!

God says, "You are mine." You belong to God and you are to be with Him, in His possession, that the world may see that you belong to God.

So if we belong to God and life is about the moments we live, may we let every moment we live reflect our love and gratitude for God.

Protect Your Valuables

On the old television show *Lost In Space* the futuristic robot would say "Warning!!!, Will Robinson, Warning!!!" whenever trouble was coming near Will Robinson, one of the shows main characters. Here is a warning from God for us. "Watch out!" Something is wrong when scripture says, "Watch out!" You can be assured you need to pay attention to that.

Watch out that you do not lose what we have worked for, but that you may be rewarded fully. Anyone who runs ahead and does not continue in the teaching of Christ does not have God; whoever continues in the teaching has both the Father and the Son (2 John 1:8-9).

Watch out that you don't lose what you've worked for. Watch out, so that you may be rewarded fully. What does that mean? It means there is a full reward God has for you. If you don't do what you're supposed to, you're not going to get it.

Now God is talking about your reward in heaven. He is saying watch out that you don't lose what you've worked for so you'll be fully rewarded. Watch out that Satan, who desires to sift you like wheat and is throwing darts at you, doesn't fool you, doesn't make you buy into a theology that says Jesus isn't the way.

First John 2:4 tells us, "Whoever says, 'I know Him,' but does not do what He commands is a liar, and the truth is not in that person." It's just that simple. Either you follow God or you don't. Either you believe this, or you don't. Either you live your life based on this, or you don't. We know a tree by its fruit. You can say anything you want. Like the guy I know who was a deacon and went to church all his life but never knew Jesus Christ. He could say he knew Jesus, but it is sad to think what Jesus would've said to him on Judgment Day. "Depart from me. I never knew you." I am so grateful this man came to know Jesus truly, in his heart.

God wants your heart. The actions follow after. God doesn't need your attendance, your money, or your stuff. All of that should come out of love and gratitude for God. God doesn't need it. Of course, He wants it. I would love my kids' respect and honor. I'd love to hear, "Yes, Daddy, anything you say, oh, most wise and wonderful father." That's not exactly what I get. But that's what I want.

A great key to happiness is found in First John 3:1: "See what great love the Father has lavished on us, that we should be called children of God! And that is what we are!" That's the bottom line. It's the key to life. We're children of God. That is what we are. That is the gift from God. John, the beloved apostle, speaks a lot of Jesus' great love because he experienced it personally. John said, "This is how God showed his love among us: He sent His one and only Son into the world that we might live through Him" (1 John 4:9). If we're not living through Jesus, we're dying through self. He came that we might live through Him.

Of course, we know it's not enough to love with words. John also speaks of our love for each other, saying, "Dear children, let us not love with words or speech but with actions and in truth. This is how we know that we belong to the truth and how we set our hearts at rest in His presence" (1 John 3:18). It's mandatory, if you want to live a life that pleases God, to live with action and truth, not just words.

We know a tree by its fruit. It's the litmus test. If we're living with actions and truth, our heart should be at rest before God. If we're not, if it's just words and there is no action and no truth, we won't have any rest with God.

How are you living? Do you have rest? Is your heart at rest with God? Do you know if you die today, not only would you be in heaven, but you would hear, "Well done, good and faithful servant"?

"Watch out that you don't lose what you work for" and you will be fully rewarded.

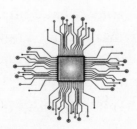

Making The Most Of Every Day

I ran into a lady a few nights ago. She is a mother with a nine-year-old daughter. We met in our neighborhood for the first time. She told me about when God came into her life. She said, "I used to have the weight of the world on my shoulders. When I found God, it all went away."

The weight of the world was on her shoulders. People who don't have God have the weight of the world on their shoulders. When we know God, truly know Him, the weights will be lifted. He will bear our burdens. Jesus said that His yoke is easy and His burden is light (Matthew 11:30).

So much of the time, the burdens we bear are the ones we allow into our own lives. They are not burdens that God puts on us. We bring them on ourselves by seeking things of the flesh rather than things of the spirit. The trouble that you and I have with our flesh in so many areas of our lives is why we must feed the spirit and starve the flesh. There will always be a war between our flesh and spirit until the day we die.

I have a buddy who is dying of leukemia. I called him and I said, "I'm coming up to New York in July. I'll see you in July."

He told me, "I don't think I'm going to be around in July." But as we spoke, I learned what a fine appreciation he has for the little time he has left. He knows he has such little time left, yet he was describing going out to Central Park and walking around praising God, and I was deeply impressed by his words. God has brought him so close to God's own heart. Whatever time God gives him, he has such a great appreciation for God and the gifts of God.

Hopefully, in our lives, it won't take a catastrophe to bring us closer to God. God willing, it won't take knowing our end date. There is the prayer that says, "Lord, make me know my days' end so that I can give value to this life I have." (Psalm 39:4) We take so much for granted.

I have another buddy. The guy was a very wealthy man. He had somewhere over five million dollars. I consider that very wealthy, but overnight he lost all his money. Literally overnight, in a business deal gone wrong, he lost everything. Things can change in a moment, but our faith in God is the one thing that should never change. I'm happy to say my buddy, even though he lost all his money, did not lose his faith. To God be the glory for that.

Our circumstances can change. God stays the same. The question is: Where is your faith? Who is it in? Is it in your body? Well, that's going to let you down at some point in time. Is it in your money? That's going to let you down. Our faith needs to be in God all the time.

My friend with leukemia knows his days are numbered, and he is choosing to glorify God with the few days he has left. We don't know how many or few days we have, but we know our days are, likewise, numbered. Only God knows the number. I pray we also choose to glorify God with the few days we have left.

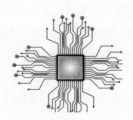

What's It Worth To You?

The value of gold, at the time of this writing (late in 2016), is roughly $1,325 per ounce. A single gold coin is worth between hundreds and thousands of dollars depending on its weight. The psalmist says, about the word of God, "I love your commands more than gold, more than pure gold" (Psalm 119:127). He goes out of his way to say, "Hey, I love your commands more than gold. Just so you're clear how much I love them, I love them even more than pure gold because that's even worth more than the other kind of gold (the kind that's not pure but still valuable). That's how much I love your words.

In Psalm 119:72, God's word says, "The law from your mouth is more precious to me than thousands of pieces of silver and gold." I asked myself that question. Is the word of the Lord more precious to me than a thousand pieces of silver and gold? At today's gold prices, that's a lot of cash in gold. Ask yourself that question. Is the word of God of more value to you than thousands of gold and silver coins? Of course, the textbook answer is yes. But what do the actions of our lives truly reflect? It was a tough moment for me, in my spiritual walk, when I asked myself that question. A good moment, but a tough moment.

Another tough moment came when I asked myself if I could say the same prayer the psalmist wrote in Psalm 51:10. It says, "Create in me a clean heart, O God, and renew a steadfast spirit within me." If God is going to create in me a clean heart, that means I've got to be ready for Him to remove all the dirt out of my old heart. It sounds good because we don't want a dirty house. We say, "Oh, come, let's vacuum that up. We don't want that."

But sometimes, in our hearts, we want it dirty. We like it dirty. We want the things we like and we want, even things that aren't of God. We have a place for God in our hearts, of course, but we have a place for all these other things as well.

God says, "Don't be lukewarm. You can't be half in, half out, or I'll spit you out" (Revelation 3:15-16). Don't have one foot in the world and one foot in the things of the spirit. It's a conscious choice we must make. You have to choose to serve God or not. It's not a halfway thing.

Can I say that? Can you? Can we say, "Create in me a clean heart, oh Lord"? I asked myself, "If I would dare to ask that of God, would I dare to pray for it and mean it?" That's a radical transformation. "Create a clean heart in me, oh, Lord. Renew a steadfast spirit within me."

Imagine if you were sitting there dying. Would you want someone to revive you? You know the paddles they use, the electric shock paddles when the guy is dying. "Revive him! Clear! Revive him! Shock him! Wake him back into life! Do something to get this guy back up because he's dying." Is that the prayer of your heart?

I hope that, as you look at your life, it is the prayer you want to make to God. "Create in me a clean heart, oh, Lord, and renew a steadfast spirit. Make my life count for something."

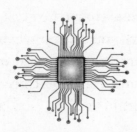

What's Better God Or Pizza?

I'm doing a Bible study with some young adults in their early twenties who play on my softball team. A couple of them are not saved. I went over to one of their apartments for the Bible study and I told them, "I'm going to do for you guys what I wish somebody had done for me when I was your age. I'm going to answer all your questions. Fire away at me. I could sit here and read you bible verses, but I know you don't understand them yet. So just ask me questions about God. I'll just tell you what I know."

One of them, a college kid, said, "I've grown up in the Catholic Church, and I've heard this stuff all my life, and I just don't get it. I don't get the Holy Spirit thing. I don't feel it."

I thought about it and said to him, "God says if you ask you'll receive. If you seek Him, you'll find Him. If you knock, the door will be opened. There's an action required on your part. You've got to ask. You've got to seek. You've got to knock."

I brought it home like this. "Let me ask you this question. If I tried to explain to you how great the taste of pizza was, how could I explain it to you? What would I say? It's great. It's amazing. You'll love it. It's the greatest thing ever. But I could not explain it to you until you experienced it yourself. I could tell you about it, but I could never explain to you exactly what it was until you experienced it yourself."

I saw the light go on in his head when he actually realized, "Okay, you can't explain this to me. I have to go experience it. I have to taste it for myself. I have to take this step forward toward the Lord, and so I'm going to open up the book of John, and I'm going to read and pray and seek God's face. I'm actually going to do what God says. I'm going to seek Him because God promises, 'If you seek me, you'll find me. If you ask, you'll receive. If you knock, the door will be opened.'" Unless God is a liar, that's going to happen. I have faith it's going to happen for that kid.

I believe the same thing applies to us in our desire for revival. It's not enough to hear it. You've got to do something. You've got to be the one who prays. You've got to be the one who seeks God. You've got to be the one who wants it. Don't seek it if you don't want it. Don't seek it so you can look good and go, "Oh, Lord, I sought it."

Here's the difference between being a disciple of God and a son of God. God loves you as a child no matter what you do. I love my children no matter what they do. There is nothing they could do to make me not love them. If you want to be a disciple of God, you need to pick up your cross. You need to follow God. You need to leave your life behind.

Are there different rewards in heaven for the disciple and the son? Absolutely. God loves you both, but He clearly laid out if you want to be a disciple, this is what you have to do. He tells us to forsake all and follow Him. He tells us to take up our cross.

You can hang out and just be a son. You can be a son and say, "Look, Dad, I don't want to work for the company. I'll just take my inheritance. I'm not going to work. I'm going to do nothing because I'm your son. I get all this, right?"

Technically, that is correct. You do get salvation and eternal life in heaven because you are a child of God. You are loved the same, but the eternal reward is different. The guy who worked for the father — the guy who was a son and worked and built the company and built the kingdom — can you imagine his reward? It's the same love. The father loves you the same. It's not about God's love. God loves you no matter what. But it is a different reward.

We have a choice before us. We can have more of God if we want it, but there's a requirement. We have to have "less of me." Man, that's a hard thing for us to do when our flesh is so greedy and covetous. He told us we're to put those things aside. He didn't say we wouldn't have them. He said we're to put them aside. He said we're to get rid of them. We're to take them off permanently like we throw out something in the garbage.

I pray that you would take the opportunity to say yes to Jesus. All you have to do is pray, "Lord, revive me, change me, and make me into a different person. Let me be a new creation in Christ. Let me live for you. Let the world see it because that will truly satisfy, and nothing else will."

That's the point you've got to get to where nothing else will satisfy you. I pray that's the desire of your heart, that nothing else can satisfy you except having more of God. God wants you to have it. You know God will answer that prayer.

God said, "I've come that you have life abundant and life eternal." God wants you to have the abundant life now. If you're a believer in Christ, I pray that you would ask God to change your heart to a heart that seeks revival so you would have the abundance of God flowing out of you in your life.

I pray that the young man I spoke to during that Bible study has discovered for himself that God is far better than pizza. I pray that, in our lives, God would be the only thing that matters, and that His loving kindness would mean more to you than life.

Get Righteous Right Now

How do we know if we're righteous or not? We want to be righteous, right? It's a very simple thing for me. Before I preach, before I pray for someone, before I begin to write, I ask of God a simple thing. I want to be able to say, "Lord, right now, at this moment in time, I know of nothing between us. I know of no sin I haven't confessed. I know of no person I haven't forgiven. At this very moment in time, I know of nothing separating me from your Holy Spirit, from Your love, from the flow of Your spirit. Fill me, Lord."

No sin. No disobedience. That's how you know if you're righteous at the moment. If you have a grudge against somebody, forgive them. If you have a sin, confess it to God. You need to turn and repent from it. That would be my definition of how I could stand before the Lord and fit that definition in the book of James: "the prayer of a righteous man is effective."

I want my prayers to be effective. God wants your prayers to be effective, but there is a requirement. It says a "righteous man's" prayers will be effective. It doesn't say an unrighteous man's prayers will be effective.

The key to it all is found in Proverbs 21:21: "Whoever pursues righteousness and love finds life, prosperity, and honor." Don't ever say God didn't tell you how to get life, property and honor. That's how God tied it all together for me and brought His point home. I recently had an experience where I spent two weeks studying the word of God and every scripture was exploding on righteousness, righteousness, righteousness.

Here's the one that finished me off. Two weeks after studying every day, I read, "God made Him who had no sin to be sin for us so that, in Him, we might become the righteousness of God" (2 Corinthians 5:21).

It's not enough that we seek the kingdom of God. That's a wonderful thing. Now, not only are we to seek His righteousness, but He want us to become it. "I want you to be it. I want you to be the righteousness of Christ to a lost world. I want them to see My righteousness in you."

I believe that's what God wants from you today. God wants us to be the righteousness of Christ.

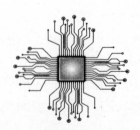

Sometimes I'm Just Stupid

I've been saved twenty-five years, and I think I'm stupid. I really do. I think a lot of people matured a lot quicker than me in their walk with Jesus Christ. It's probably because they weren't as stubborn as me; they were willing to do what God said right away.

It took me time to get to that point. God had to lead me step by step. I'm stubborn and I'm sure I paid a price for that. But I can tell you that once I got there and saw it, I was on board completely. It's like when a math tutor explains how to solve a problem you say, "Okay, now I understand the equation. I get it now."

Now I want to follow God's way because I love God and I trust Him. I believe all blessings come from God and I know the closer I get to God, the closer He comes to me. I know the more of God I get, the happier I am, and the more I can do.

In my spirit, I knew God was telling me something really important (as I shared with you in the last chapter) when He said, "Jack, you need to become my righteousness. It's not enough to just be righteous when you want to. It's not enough to just be righteous when it's convenient or you think it's a good idea."

That's not what Jesus did. Jesus was all about His Father's business all of the time, not some of the time. Jesus embodied the very being of God, His Father. He was the very righteousness of God. He represented it here on Earth when

He came down in human form. We know the purpose for all Jesus did. It is found in John 3:16: For God so loved the world, He gave his only begotten Son that whoever believes in Him shall have eternal life.

Jesus did it all for us.

Let's take this thought a step further. We are clothed in the righteousness of God when we accept Jesus into our hearts, but it's not the same as being the righteousness of God here on Earth. You have the righteousness of God when you accept Jesus Christ. God took out your old heart. He put in a new heart. He now sees you, as holy, blameless, and above reproach because you have been clothed in the righteousness of Jesus Christ. You have your ticket into heaven because of Jesus' blood. He paid the sacrifice for your sin.

That's not the same thing as reflecting the righteousness of Christ here on Earth. That's something we also need to do.

Of course, we want to be grateful that we're clothed in His righteousness. If we believe in God and accept the sacrifice of Jesus on the cross as atonement for our sin, we couldn't not get to heaven no matter what we did. Some people have a problem with that. "How can somebody call themselves a Christian and do X, Y, Z?" I don't know that I have the answer to that question. But I do know what God says a Christian is supposed to do.

It's my desire and my goal to live a life where I can become as the righteousness of God. I'm praying that God changes my heart, my mind, and my soul so that my thinking is aligned with Him all of the time. I know that my joy comes from serving God and living a sacrificial life to God, and I want to do it more because I know that's what God desires from all of us.

God's purpose for our life is found in Isaiah 43:7. God says, "Everyone who is called by my name, whom I have created for my glory, I have formed him." That's the purpose of your life. You were created for the glory of God. We shouldn't be sitting there wondering, "Why am I alive? What's my purpose? What's my meaning in life? What should I do?" All you've got to do is glorify God with your life and your actions, and God will be very, very, very pleased with you and your actions.

You know that when you die, you're going to heaven forever and ever. There's no doubt. We can be so grateful for that one thing because, if we didn't know that, we know we would be going to hell. It makes you think, "Going to heaven is the greatest thing ever!" Yes, it is. Because that is the "righteous" truth! Not only should you download that but you should share that information with everyone you know!

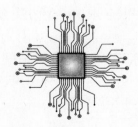

Do The Right Thing

I recently read in the news about a cab driver in Las Vegas. He was taking somebody from one hotel on the Vegas strip to the other. He found a brown bag in the back with $300,000 cash inside. It belonged to a poker player who was going from one hotel to the other. The guy was frantic when he realized he had lost his money. The poker player said, "I wanted to shoot myself in the head and kill myself." Three hundred grand is a lot of money.

The cabbie returned it all. He said, "That's what I was brought up to do. My parents taught me the difference between right and wrong." He didn't even think about keeping it, $300,000 cash. Nobody would ever have known. Nobody could have ever proved it. But he chose to be honest, to do what was right.

That should be our attitude. It should be righteousness first and always. James understood that concept. Do we understand? James said, "Dear brothers and sisters, take note of this. Everyone should be quick to listen, slow to speak and slow to become angry because human anger does not produce the righteousness that God desires. Therefore, get rid of all moral filth and evil that is so prevalent and humbly accept the word planted in you which can save you" (James 1:19).

James understood anger and bad morals don't equal God's righteousness. He said, "Get rid of your moral filth and cling to the word, which can save you."

God's guidance is so clear. His wisdom is perfect. In First Timothy, Paul is writing to Timothy about a love of money. He tells Timothy that godliness with contentment is great gain. He advises young Timothy not to be a lover of money and the things of the world.

He instructs Timothy and God's word instructs us in 1 Timothy 6:11: "But you, man of God, (you, woman of God, you, child of God), but you, child of God, flee from all of this. Run for the hills." It's not about money. It's not about things of the world. Flee from those things and pursue righteousness. The first thing Paul tells Timothy to do is pursue righteousness. He then adds, we should also pursue godliness, faith, love, endurance and gentleness. Fight the good fight of faith, take hold of the eternal life for which you were called.

Isn't that the message the Lord has for us today? Isn't that how He is calling us to live? Take hold of the eternal life to which you were called. Grab it. Hug it. Live it. Love it. Be it. There's a purpose for your life, a purpose here on Earth. Take hold of it. How do we do that? Pursue righteousness, godliness, faith, love, endurance, and gentleness. Flee from the things that the world is telling you are so important.

A buddy and I were talking about provisions for the future and related issues. He's concerned about his family and their future. I said, "I get that. I understand, but do you know what? Keep thinking about that and God just might say to you, 'Come on home. You don't have to worry about any of that. Come on up to heaven and we'll see how much of that you're worried about.'" God had been speaking to my heart about this same thing, and I was just sharing with my friend what the Lord had shown me. I said, "Keep thinking about that. Is it really so important? God is the one who gives us life and provides us with life. God has provided for every need."

You Can't Trade

A casual business acquaintance and I talked one evening after a conference. I had a chance to witness to him about Jesus Christ. He didn't want to hear any part of it. He said, "I'm a scientific guy. I hear what you're saying. It's nice, but I don't buy it."

I got a call out of the blue from the guy a year later. "Hey, can I talk to you?"

I said, "Sure. I'll meet you in Starbucks." He lived in the same city as me.

When we met, he told me, "I've done a terrible thing."

"What happened?"

He said, "I cheated on my wife, and I gave her a sexually transmitted disease. She is pregnant and our baby tested positive for hepatitis in the womb." He was beside himself. He was torn and upset. He said, "I know I've done this horrible thing." He came to me, probably because I was the only Christian he knew.

The same will be true in your life. You may be the only Christian some people know. You are God's representative; I don't mean from the pulpit. I mean from a human witnessing standpoint and by the way you live your life people should see God in you and through you.

He said, "I want to trade. I'm ready. I'm ready to accept Jesus Christ. I want to trade. I'll trade. I'll accept your Jesus if my new baby son or daughter can be well, if you can remove that hepatitis."

I had to tell him, "It doesn't work like that. That's not the deal. Here is the deal. You need Jesus Christ in your life for you, not for your unborn child. You can't make that decision for your unborn child. You need to make it for you. You've struggled. You've run all your life from God. Here is God bringing you to your knees through the thing you care about the most. Now you see the value of life, and you're willing to trade."

God wants you for you and your heart. God doesn't want you to go in as a slave. "Oh, you got me. Finally, there is something I'll trade. Okay, Lord, I'm yours." God loves you too much to take you that way. God wants you the real way.

I watched the scales come off his eyes. I watched him understand. I watched him accept Jesus on the spot. I said, "Now we can pray for your unborn child. We can pray, and I believe God will hear our prayer. Your prayer needs to be, 'God, I would like this child to not have this disease and not have to suffer the consequence of my sin but, Lord, your will be done. If the child is born with this disease, we will accept it and deal with it accordingly.'" Wouldn't you know? He accepted Jesus, we prayed and the hepatitis Ct test came back as a false positive. He is rejoicing in that, and he understands and accepts Jesus for the real and right reasons. To God be The Glory!

The word of God cuts like a two-edged sword to reveal the truth in our life and hearts. I pray that God's word will do that for you. I pray that your prayer would be that we don't stand in God's way. I pray that we would be willing to remove anything we've put in God's way and lay it down at the altar of God. I pray that our prayer would be that we obey God rather than man; that it's no longer about obeying man or pleasing man but about pleasing God.

Stay Focused

I was at a crossroads recently with so much going on in my life. God reminded me that He's tested us, and we need to pass the test for Christ's sake. For Christ's sake and our sake, we need to pass the test.

I realized that I wasn't doing what God had instructed us in Colossians 3:2. I had not been focusing my mind on things above. Quite the opposite, I was focusing my mind on the things of the world. God showed me the key, and it's the key for you, too. It's simple. We're to live in the moment.

There are some religions — Buddhism and a couple of other ones — that have many good things about them. A lot of religions have many good things about them. Yet they miss the one key blessing — Jesus Christ. There is only one way to heaven. "I am the way and the truth and the life. There is no other way to the Father but through me" (John 14:6). There is no question that our salvation comes from Jesus Christ.

What do these religions have? Buddhism in particular claims that the one who is truly enlightened has awareness, for he lives in the moment. He's not moved or changed by circumstances of the world. He lives his life on a journey, enjoying and embracing each moment, not looking at circumstances as a moment to be judged good or bad, but rather as a moment in life to be appreciated. He lives in the present moment and appreciates it for all it's worth. To him, the moment and being in it is worth everything. In their search for truth, they believe they're connected to all living things. They don't live in worry, in fear, or anxiousness, or anxiety about what will happen in the future. They're not devastated by the happenings of the past for their strategy is to simply live in the moment, believing that each and every moment is a wonderful experience and is what they were created to do.

How is it that Buddhists and other religions are better about practicing, engaging, and living their faiths than we as Christians are? I was looking at this and was thinking, were we not told the exact same thing as they were by Jesus Christ? Are we not to be anxious for anything? Are we not to, with prayer and thankfulness, present all our requests to God? If we do that, does God not promise the peace that transcends all understanding will guard our hearts? Did God not say we're to bring all our anxieties, burdens, and cares to His feet and cast them upon Him, thus taking them off ourselves and putting them on God and that He will handle it?

Were we not assured that all things work together for our good when we love God, regardless of whether we see them as good or bad? For that reason, are we not to embrace each and every circumstance, each and every moment of our lives as a gift from God? Were we not reminded to be joyful always, to pray continuously, to give thanks in all circumstances, trusting that this is God's will for us in Christ? Were we not told to leap and rejoice, for this is the day the Lord has made, and therefore we should be glad and rejoice in it?

God reminds us that we're already rich. We have all we want because we have Him, we are promised an eternal kingdom, and our salvation is assured. Jesus came that we might have life abundant and life eternal. Isn't that how we're supposed to live? Yes. That's how we're supposed to live.

I admit that I recently fell victim to Satan's trap to get my focus off God and onto the things of the world. Satan must have been laughing hysterically at me, as I would laugh at a little boy who is trying to jump up and catch a ball that I held just out of his reach. That's us when we try to control the things of the world. That's us when we try to control things that we're going to lose anyway.

I believe the answer for us is to live in the moment. I have to practice it. I'm not good at it, but I intend to practice it. We should be one hundred times happier than any Buddhist or any other religious guy, one hundred times more peaceful. Not only do we have the knowledge of how to live life, but we also have eternal life guaranteed and the Holy Spirit of God to guide us. How lucky are we? When I started living like that, my joy returned.

Psalm 89:15 promises, "Blessed are the people who know the joyful sound! They walk, O Lord, in the light of your countenance. In your name they rejoice all day long, and in your righteousness they are exalted." We need to be those people. That needs to be the description of you and me. We need to be the blessed ones who are joyful at the sound of the Lord, who are walking in the light of the Lord. God promises if we do that, He will exalt us.

A good place to start is with this prayer. "Teach us to number our days that we may gain a heart of wisdom. Oh, satisfy us early with your mercy that we may rejoice and be glad all our days" (Psalm 90:12).

God help us live and love in the moment and rejoice for our eternity is secure.

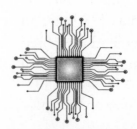

Can I Have A Do-Over?

I love my children so much, all three of them. All I want is to be with them, have a relationship with them, and know them. All I want is to be a part of their lives. The greatest joy I have is to be with my wife and my children. That is only a hint of how the Lord feels toward us. James 5:11 says, "The Lord is full of compassion and mercy." That means He has plenty to give to you.

What if you've messed up, and you've made some mistakes? What if you're not sure, and you think you've let God down? What if you haven't been good enough? Maybe you haven't lived up to the calling you've attained. Isaiah 55:6 says, "Seek the Lord while He may be found. Call upon Him while He is near." Verse 7 then gives this promise: "For He will abundantly pardon."

Joel 2:13 says, "Return to the Lord your God, for He is gracious and merciful, slow to anger, of great kindness, and He relents from doing harm." That's what you should do if you made a mistake. You should return to God immediately, ask for forgiveness, and receive and accept the abundant forgiveness, mercy, and grace that God has given you. He has ordained for you to have His grace and mercy in abundance, just as He has for each and every believer and child of God. That is the reason Jesus died on the cross.

How Else Can Scripture Be Fulfilled

How do we live a life of impact for the Lord? Let's look at the ultimate man of impact, Jesus Christ. In Matthew 26:52, Judas is about to betray Jesus. You know the story. Jesus is speaking and Judas comes. He's armed and has a whole crowd around him, guards and soldiers.

Jesus says, "What are you here for, buddy?" The NIV version says, "Do what you came for, friend."

The men step forward. They seize Jesus. One of Jesus' companions (said to be Peter) reaches for his sword. He takes out the sword and strikes the servant of the high priest, cutting off his ear. We have this confrontation. Judas has betrayed Jesus. Peter is ready to fight back and he ends up cutting off the ear of the high priest's servant.

What does Jesus say? "Put your sword back in its place." He then says, "For all who draw the sword will die by the sword. Do you think I cannot call on my father and He will at once put at my disposal more than twelve legions of angels?"

But if Jesus did that, how would the scriptures be fulfilled that say it must happen in this way? Jesus could have changed things. Instead, Jesus said, "Don't fight back. Don't you think I can call on my father? Don't you think I can bring angels down? I can do anything. I'm God. I can do anything. But then, how then would the scriptures have been fulfilled?"

(Matthew 26:54). Jesus was more concerned about fulfilling the will of God than saving Himself.

When I look at the world today, all I see is scripture being fulfilled. I'm excited. I'm not excited that people are going to hell, but I am excited God is coming back and is in control. Our job is to be that light of Jesus Christ and show people Jesus on Earth like our brothers and sisters in the faith are doing all around the world. There are Christians in countries around the world giving their lives for the testimony of Christ. They die a hero's death. As we discussed earlier in the book, when nine Christians in Charleston, South Carolina, were shot and killed in June of 2015 by a troubled and hate-filled young man, they died doing exactly what God wanted them to do — sharing His love. You can rest assured their reward in heaven is great and mighty.

Jesus said to the Pharisees, "You're mistaken because you don't know the scriptures" (Matthew 22:29). He called them out for not knowing the word of God. He also said to the people of Israel, "My people fail because of their lack of knowledge, because they don't understand." We are told not to be fearful. We are to be strong and courageous. Jesus is with us always. He'll never leave us or forsake us.

Why would we be scared when God said, "Perfect love casts out fear" (1 John 4:18)? Is Jesus' love perfect or not? It's perfect enough for me and I hope and pray that it is perfect enough for you. How awesome is it that we get to play our role for the kingdom of God? That we get to do our part by living out the life God has called us to. A life that glorifies him and fulfills Scripture.

Section 5

COPY & PASTE HIS POWER & PROMISE

Mirroring God's Word in Every Action

Copy & Paste is the act of duplicating text, data, files, or disks by producing two or more of the same file or segments of data. Selected original text is highlighted and stored on an internal clipboard. The original text is copied in its originally created form and is duplicated or pasted into its newly desired location. This makes the original text faster to reuse in the same word or sentence over and over, while still appearing as the original. The pasted file of the original copy then becomes part of the newly created data.

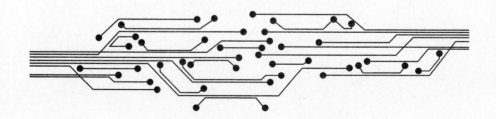

Christian Suicide

It was January and I got an invitation to attend a Christian Mastermind Conference, fifty of the top minds of the world gathered together in a room — business minds, ministry minds, some very heavy weight people. To give you an example, Erwin McManus (Pastor, Author and Futurist) was there, the great evangelist Reinhard Bonnke, Steve Strang, the president of Charisma Media, motivational speaker Peter Lowe, David Green, the president of Hobby Lobby, the fortieth wealthiest man in the world who counts his money in billions, not millions. Just fifty very high level business profile guys...it was a very intense group.

I didn't get invited because of my own net worth and success or because people thought I am a great guy. I got invited because a buddy of mine was tied into the Program and said, "Would you like to come?"

I said, "No, I'd love to come. Please let me come." I got to come and meet the guy who organized it. He was an entrepreneurial guy and he was obviously well off. This was the first time I had met him.

I met the guy who put it on and he had everything. He had a beautiful wife who I met, he had beautiful kids, and he was entrenched in the financial community and in the ministry community. He knew all of these people and brought them together to take a look forward at what we could do as Christians to change the world. I thought, "Man, I am honored to be here. What a great thing." I spoke with the guy briefly, shook his hand, and we had the Seminar. It was a two-day event. I thought, "Wow, this is amazing." I was blessed. It was truly, truly a time of great blessing.

A month later he committed suicide and I was shocked. I said, "Wow, here's this guy who by the world's standards had everything. He had a beautiful family. He was wealthy. He was tied into the most heavy weight people in ministry and business you could imagine. He seemed to have it all and yet he committed suicide." I thought, "What could he have been thinking? What could his problem have been that he thought he had no other way out."

That boggled my mind, because wait a minute. He had the most godly guys in the world there. He could have talked to, called on or asked for help or prayer from — Erwin McManus was there; James Davis, the head of World Leaders Group; Reinhard Bonnke. I mean he could have gone to three of these heavy weight Christian guys and said, "Hey, I have a problem." He could have gone to David Green or Steve Strang or Peter Lowe or these heavy weight business guys and said, "Hey, I have a problem."

He had the top guys in the world who could have helped him if he had just said, "I have a problem." Somewhere inside of him — I am speculating now — I would assume he couldn't say it. Whether it was pride, whether it was embarrassment, whether it was shame, a money problem, clearly it was something. He chose instead to take his life and that really impacted me. Remember, I'd only met him once, but I thought, "I just can't believe there was nobody for him to talk to."

I want to remind you and me today that we need to make sure we're that somebody who people can talk to. When you say to somebody, "Hey, how are you doing?" and they're going, "Okay" or "Just hanging in there." That probably means, "I'm drowning." Unless you hear, "Everything is great. I couldn't be better unless I was having breakfast with Jesus," you need to look a little further or at least make sure they know you are available for them if they have an issue or just need to talk This issue cuts across every social class, every demographic, geographic and psychographic profile and other categories the world uses to classify and judge people. This is about life and saving it!

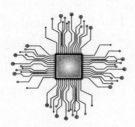

Who Am I To Judge

The last story about Christian suicide doesn't end there. I know another guy named Walter who I've known for many years. He was a very, very successful guy when I met him down in south Florida. He had a company that was worth tens of millions of dollars. He got offers to sell and didn't sell. Unfortunately at the height of the NASDAQ bubble, the market crashed and he lost everything.

Smart guy, wife and kids, but over the years he was never able to rebound from that devastating loss. He would try to start some new business ventures. He borrowed $100,000 from another guy I knew and it was gone in two months. He blew through it and was off raising funds for his next deal. That really upset me. I thought, "You know, he took advantage of my guy there."

He'd only call you when he wanted something. That's the best way I can describe it. He was a taker. If the phone rang it was because he wanted something. At one point he called me years down the line, again he'd been spiraling downward. He said, "Listen, I know I haven't been a really good friend and I know I only call when I want something, but I'm going to change. I'm going to really become a good friend. I'm going to change and I just need to borrow $3,000 for this next business/project I am trying to get off the ground."

I very lovingly said to him, "Listen, I'm not going to give you that money, but I really hope you do change because I would like to see that.

I was just really ready to write this guy off. I just thought, "It's just not worth my time." He's just a guy who takes, takes, takes.

God spoke to me after the Christian Mastermind organizer committed suicide. He said, "You need to go talk to Walter."

I said, "I don't want to talk to Walter. I am done with Walter."

He said, "No, you need to go talk to Walter because what if he's thinking about suicide."

I said, "Okay, God." I called him up and arranged to meet him for lunch. I sat down with him and I said, "Listen, I'm worried about you. I'm worried that you might commit suicide. I'm worried. I see you've been knocked down, been hit, and taken hits. I'm worried."

We talked deeply and intensely. I don't believe he's committing suicide, but I think it was a good thing I went to see him.

The reason I share this with you is God changed my perspective. It's not that I thought, "Oh, the guy's not a taker." No, I thought that way. It was the same exact situation, but God changed my perspective and my heart of how I looked at the guy. Instead of looking at him in the flesh, instead of judging him, I looked at him through the eyes of God and I hope and pray that I had compassion and did the right thing.

I want to remind you of that. Often we're right in our thinking. "This guy is wrong. This guy deserved that, doesn't deserve this, etc." But you know what? God wants to use us as agents. What if somebody had reached out to the Christian Mastermind guy? Would he still be here? We want to be the guys who make a difference.

Are You Still Hungry?

Do you find yourself not satisfied at times? Look at God's word and let's use it as a flashlight to examine what's really inside of us.

You have planted much, but harvested little. You eat, but never have enough. You drink, but never have your fill. You put on clothes, but are not warm. You earn wages, only to put them in a purse with holes in it (Haggai 1:6).

What a frightening thought. Planting, but not harvesting. Eating and drinking, but not being filled. Clothing ourselves, but remaining cold.

Does this reflect our lives with Jesus?

The above passage, from the book of Haggai, portrays the life that the people of Judah were living. They were putting their own pleasure and satisfaction before God, and He could not bless it. In the next verses, God clearly states His will.

This is what the Lord Almighty says: "Give careful thought to your ways. ... You expected much, but see, it turned out to be little. What you brought home, I blew away. Why?" Declares the Lord Almighty. "Because of my house, which remains a ruin, while each of you is busy with your own house" (Haggai 1: 7, 9).

I can't stress enough this aspect of our lives with Christ. God is trying to tell us, "I need you to live a life that glorifies me. I need you to be focused on the things of the kingdom, not on the things of the world. I've told you to build up for yourself treasures in heaven where rust and decay cannot come in and steal. I've told you what to do because I love you."

Are we so busy pursuing the things of the world, pursuing the goals of our mind and the desires of our flesh, that we are ignoring completely or putting on the back burner the things of God? Or worse yet, we are ignoring completely or putting on the back burner God himself? Or perhaps we are paying attention to God or serving God out of fear or obligation. But not out of the true desire to know the God who loves us and who we love.

Can you imagine taking your teenage son out for his birthday to his favorite restaurant. Yet instead of talking to him you're constantly on the phone answering emails and taking calls from work or other things you deem a priority. Even though you're present with your son, he can tell your focus is not on him. Even on the special day when he deserves your complete focus, your attention is elsewhere. How do you think he's going to feel? He knows by your actions and attitude you're there out of obligation not because you want to be. He may very well think, "You don't love me. You're here because you have to be, not because you love me." How sad and tragic that would be.

When you love somebody, you want to be with them. You want to spend time with them. You want to hang out with them. You want to know everything about them and be a part of their life. You don't want to be apart from them.

That's what love is, and that's what God wants with you and me — an individual relationship. Yes, you should tithe. Yes, you should attend church. Yes, you should sing in the choir, if you have the voice for it. Yes, you should serve. Yes, you should do everything you can to glorify God out of love for God, not out of obligation.

Listen To Daddy

There are parents of a wayward girl, and they made this chilling remark. They are Christian parents, and they said, "We brought our kids up in the church, but we didn't bring them up in Christ." How scary is that?

In Haggai 1:12 God's word states, "Zerubbabel, the high priest, and the whole remnant of the people obeyed the voice of the Lord their God and the message of the prophet Haggai because the Lord their God had sent him. And the people feared the Lord."

"And the people feared the Lord." They had heard from God. They had heard from the prophet Haggai earlier (as we just read in the last chapter). That's a pretty chilling warning that God had given them. "Hey, listen. You're going to want stuff. You're not going to get what you want because you're not paying attention to the things of God. You're paying attention to the things you want. You're not paying attention to the spirit. You're paying attention to the flesh."

Do we obey the one the Lord has sent us? Do we listen to the words of Jesus? God has sent us Jesus, His Son, the Most High to us. Do we obey Him? The people were fearful, and they obeyed. Why should I be fearful and obey? Should I fear the punishment of God? No, I should fear missing the blessings of God.

I made a decision three years after I came to know Jesus as My Lord and Savior. It took me that long after I had been saved to come to the realization that either all of God's word is true, or none of it is true. It's not a case where the parts I like are true and the parts I don't like aren't true. It's not that the verses I like or suit me well are "Gospel truth," and the ones I don't like or wish God hadn't said, in those cases God didn't know what He was talking about. It's either all true, or it's all a lie. That was my "aha" moment.

I believe it's all true. For me, there is not even a question that God is God. You should have that same belief. Not because you're reading it here but because of the Holy Spirit inside you. God said the Holy Spirit will come upon each believer upon salvation, and He will teach you all things. He's your compass. He's your reminder, your counselor, your guide to what is right and what is true. Yet sometimes we let the roar of the world drown out the whisper of the spirit. God speaks in a whisper. We need to shut up so we can hear God.

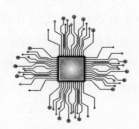

Keep Swinging For The Fences

How can God's power work through us? His word tells us, "Therefore, whether you eat or drink, or whatever you do, do all to the glory of God" (1 Corinthians 10:31). That's the purpose of our lives. Whatever we do, we need to do for the glory of God. Earlier in the chapter, Paul writes, "Let no one seek his own but each one the other's well-being." We know we are to love others as we love ourselves. Do unto others as we want them to do to us. We all know it. The problem is we don't do it.

We need to strive to live a sacrificial life. We need to teach ourselves and train ourselves to live a sacrificial life, to put these things in practice because they actually matter. We train our minds when we want to learn something. We train our bodies when we want to accomplish an earthy feat. We need to put forth the same effort to focus and train on spiritual things because they actually matter.

We know it. Why don't we do it? God was speaking to my heart. As I was reading through the books of Corinthians and came to the powerful message in First Corinthians 13, it comes down to love. I think the reason we don't do so many of the things is that it comes down to a lack of love. "Love does not seek its own" (1 Corinthians 13:7). Love isn't selfish. It's about others. We love ourselves really well. We don't do as good a job of loving others. We do it when it's convenient.

We do it when it's profitable, when it will benefit us. How about when it's not?

Here is a great reminder from the word of God:

The sting of death is sin, and the strength of sin is the law. But thanks be to God, who gives us the victory through our Lord Jesus Christ. Therefore, my beloved brethren, be steadfast, immovable, always abounding in the work of the Lord, knowing that your labor is not in vain in the Lord (1 Corinthians 15:56-58).

Those are God's instructions to us. Because of this great gift we've received, because our salvation is assured, because Jesus is with us and walking with us in the spirit every step of the way, we're to be steadfast. We're to be immovable. If I was coming after your family to hurt them, you'd be immovable. I couldn't push you out of the way in order to hurt your family. They are important to you. "Always abounding in the work of the Lord." Always. Not sometimes. Not once in a while. Not when it's convenient. That's our purpose, to abound. Abound means to be plentiful. Abound in the work of the Lord, knowing that your labor is not in vain.

I know my labor is not in vain. I know your labor is not in vain. How do I know that? Because God is real. Because that's what God has promised us. We need to stand upon the promises of God. We can know it and believe His promises, but our actions need to speak it. It's not enough to know it and believe it. You have to act it out and live on it.

1 Corinthians 16:14 says, "Let all that you do be done with love." Is all that we do done with love? Perhaps we need to train and practice to learn that? Let's say you try to make that your New Year's resolution. "All that I do I will do with love." I know a resolution like that won't last one day. I know I can't make it until tonight acting in love in all that I do.

Does that mean I shouldn't try? Of course not.

It's like our walk with God. We're not perfect. Only Jesus was perfect. Does that mean I shouldn't try? No. Jesus said, "Be imitators of me." We're to try to attain perfection. God knows we can't do it perfectly. He still calls us to try and do the best that we can.

The teacher teaches the best lesson they possibly can, yet not every student learns. Does the teacher get discouraged and say if I can't save everyone why should I bother to save anyone? Of course not. They do the best they can by using the gifts and talents God has given them to change and impact who they can. The baseball player knows he can't get a hit every time up, but that doesn't prevent him from trying his best each and every at-bat.

We're supposed to do the same thing. Think about a minister who wants to save the world, but he only saved a few million people. Or a hundred. Or maybe he only saved one person. Was he a failure? No.

It's not about us or what we accomplish. It's about what God accomplishes through us. Our job is to be obedient to God and let God use us. We strive for perfection, but we achieve greatness in the midst of our failure because by trying we succeed.

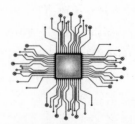

Reflecting His Greatness

God says, "'My name will be great among the nations, from where the sun rises to where it sets. In every place incense and pure offerings will be brought to me, because my name will be great among the nations,' says the Lord" (Malachi 1:11). God is looking for pure offerings. Any offering made in the name of Jesus Christ is pure. It's washed. It's clean.

When you and I live a life that glorifies Jesus Christ, our offering to God is pure. That's when we don't have to worry about whether we made a left turn or a right turn, whether we work at this job or that job. When we've sought God's face for everything we have done, we have the peace of God living in us. The Holy Spirit is guiding us every step of the way. We can be certain that we are walking according to the will of God when we seek His face.

God says in Malachi 1:12, "But you profane my name by saying, 'The Lord's table is defiled,' and, 'Its food is contemptible.' And you say, 'What a burden!' and you sniff at it contemptuously, says the Lord."

God is upset with us when we say, "What a burden to be a believer in Jesus Christ. What a burden to have this chore and obligation to serve as a believer of Jesus Christ."

No wonder God is not happy with that attitude. "Wait a minute. Excuse me? You think this is a chore, an obligation, and a burden? You don't think this is a privilege and a joy and a pleasure?" That's really what it should be. It's not a burden, a chore, or an obligation to serve the Lord. That's not the kind of service God wants from you. God doesn't want robotic, prisoner-like service or obligation. God is not interested in that. That's Pharisee-like thinking. God wants Christian believers, joy-filled, spirit-led people serving in gratitude and thanks for the gifts we've been given.

If we are not serving that way, we're not grateful enough for the gifts Jesus Christ has given us.

By the way, "service" doesn't mean you have to volunteer at church. It would be a wonderful thing if you did that, and I hope you do. God wants us to glorify and edify the Church and the body of believers and to reach the lost with the love of Christ. He wants us to use our talents for the kingdom, but it's not just about church on Sunday morning. It's about the way you live your life all the time with your neighbors, your friends, your employees, your bosses, the school, and the people around you. What do they see?

You've got to be available, and you've got to be good at what you do. If you're a bad baseball player, you won't be a baseball player very long. If you're a bad teacher ... well, you could probably stay a teacher, unfortunately, but you know what I mean. The point is you need to be good at what you do.

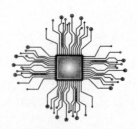

Why Do We Do What We Do?

I was praying a couple of weeks ago for God to bless our business so we can make some money. It's not a bad thing. God asked me this question — not audibly, but in my spirit God speaks to me very specifically and very distinctly. He asked me, "Jack, for whose glory are you asking this blessing?"

It was not quite the question I wanted to hear. I answered God honestly. I said, "For mine, Lord." I was asking God, claiming His promise, saying, "God, if I ask anything according to your will, it will be given to me."

I felt the spirit of the Lord say, "Well, whose glory are you asking for?" It dawned on me that I was asking for mine. Yes, I love God. But I could not honestly say, at the end of the day, that the only reason I was asking for this blessing was for Him. It was for me. Of course, if I get my blessing, I'll do stuff for the Lord. I'll be grateful. I'll serve Him.

But God asked me this question, "What would it look like if your life was totally sold out to me?"

I believe He's asking you the same question. What would it look like if my life was totally sold out to Jesus? It would be more about sacrifice. My attention would be more focused on others. My life would definitely show more sacrifice. I'd be all about Kingdom-of-God business — not just on Sundays, or some of the time or when it was convenient. I'd be all about Kingdom business all the time. I'd have less concern and worry about myself. I'd trust God with all things. I'd stand on Proverbs 3:5 and 6. We say it a lot. "Trust in the Lord with all your heart, lean not on your own understanding. In all your ways acknowledge Him and He will direct your paths." We say it. We just don't live it. My focus would be more on spreading the Gospel.

My prayer was, "Lord, please speak to my heart and let me willingly come closer to you." If I look at my evil, selfish, judgmental, and jealous heart, all I can say is this, "Lord, thank you that you paid the price for my sin, that you were the mediator, that you reconciled my sin. I'm not guilty of my sin. I still did it. I'm just not guilty of it. You paid the price for it so I don't have to be burdened by guilt and by the weight of sin. Lord, thank you that the apostles, these mighty men of God, went through the same things I did. None of them was perfect, but you used them mightily based on their faith and love for you. And finally, Lord, thank you that Jesus also took on the form of a man just like me and knew everything I felt and experienced, so that I can never say, 'God you don't understand.' You do understand, Lord!"

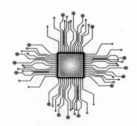

Startling Realization

In 2014 I was in Pensacola. At that time, it was a ten-hour drive from where I lived in south Florida. I was up there to speak at an Iron Sharpens Iron conference, which I love to do. I was very excited to get up there. I got up early, and I got to talk to the pastor of the host church. I'd never met him before. He had been a pastor of Myrtle Grove Baptist Church in Pensacola for seventeen years. He has a great church, a very successful church. This wonderful man with a great heart for God was talking to me after I introduced myself.

I said, "Pastor, how's it going? I'd like to just ask what God is doing in your life because I'm really interested in hearing."

He said, "I just got back from a trip to Africa, and God spoke to my heart. God showed me that I am a failure." He looked at me with humble, sincere eyes and said, "I've failed because in Africa and in Korea, I've seen what true worship looks like. I've seen people who are truly worshipping God. I realize I've failed my people. Oh, yeah, we've come to church, and we've done church for seventeen years, and I know the people love God, but in those countries, I saw true worship. I saw people coming with mats laid out on the floor praying to God, crying out to God for hours at a time..." and on and on he went.

I thought, Wow, this is amazing. This is mind boggling. Here is this pastor who, by the world's standards, even by the church's standards, by our standards, would clearly have lived a successful life, a life sold out for God. He is a great man of God. Yet the Holy Spirit spoke to this pastor's heart and said, "You have more to do. Now that I've shown you more, I want you to do it. It's okay what you did before, but now you know a better way. You need to do it this way."

I asked him, "How are you going to translate what you've seen to the people from the pulpit? How are you going to tell these people to whom you've been preaching for seventeen years that, 'Hey, there is more'? There's a true heart for God and a heart that cries out for God. There is a spirit of dedication to God that isn't being in church for an hour and leaving at noon. How will you get that across to them?"

He said, "Jack, I'm going to do it through Bible studies in the homes, through the missional community because that's how I see it happening in Africa and in Korea where I've been."

I was blown away. I was impressed. I was thinking, Wow, I need to look at my own life, and I need to see where I have failed. I could say that, by the world's standards, maybe I'm doing some good stuff. But what's the truth? What is God really saying to my heart?

Then the question came to me. "What would happen if today were the day I went to meet Jesus?" What would Jesus be saying to me?

What would the account of my life look like? There are some things I could throw up to God in my defense. "Hey, Lord, look, I've done this, and I've done that. It was in your name and for you." But I know I would think of all the things I haven't done for God.

To this day, those things exist in my life. Time that I spend on me, my pleasures, my flesh, my life, and the things I want instead of the things God wants me to do. I hope the prayer of your heart would be to reprioritize your life for God. I know that is my prayer, desire and aim.

Writing Your Own Eulogy

What if, at this very moment, it was your time to meet God in heaven?

That's the question on my heart and mind. Imagine it's your funeral. What are people saying about you? What are they talking about at your funeral? Are they saying what a great golfer you were, what a great investor in the stock market you were, what a great parent you were, what a great businessman, what a great athlete, what a great fireman you were? Is that what they're talking about? If they are, you've done something very wrong.

I'm looking at my life and I'm wondering, "What are people going to say at my funeral? What are they going to talk about?" Are they going to talk about some of the things I think I've done by earthly standards? I sincerely hope not. I hope they're only talking about one thing, and I pray the same for you. They're talking about what a good Christian I was, how I lived my life sold out for Jesus Christ, how I believed God and what He said.

I believed there's a heaven. I believed there's a reward. I believed I was supposed to live a sacrificial life for Christ. I believed I was supposed to be an imitator of Jesus Christ and follow Him and not the world. I believed in feeding my spirit and not my flesh. I knew God was supposed to be strong and I was supposed to be weak, so I lived relying on His strength for my life.

That's what I want to happen. That is what I want people to remember. Really, think about this today. Don't just give it a passing thought. Truly consider it. Who is coming to your funeral? What are they going to say? If they're not talking about the amazing Christian you were, what a light that you were for God, and how you were salt to a tasteless generation, we've got a problem.

Galatians 6:9 tells us, "Let us not become weary in doing good, for at the proper time we'll reap a harvest if we do not give up. Therefore, as we have opportunity, let us do good to all people, especially to those who belong to the family of believers." Does that describe us? Is that what people are going to be saying at my funeral, at your funeral?

"Oh, man, that guy did good to everybody. He was kind, compassionate, caring, loving, and sharing. He gave of himself. He was selfless." I have friends who have the characteristics of a Christian, they are wonderful people, yet they don't know and believe in Jesus. But for those who know Christ, we should definitely be living a Christian life. We should be the ones glorifying God.

Whether we live in Africa or Korea, California or New York, let us show the fruits of a soul that knows God, a heart that is fixed on Him, and a life that glorifies His Son, Jesus.

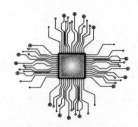

Mistaken Identity

In 2014 my dad had a stroke. He's got some dementia setting in now. We're living with that. It is caused us to take a look at our planning and future. I have an estate-planning lawyer I've known for probably for twenty years. "Estate planning" is a fancy term that just means you have a will and a health care proxy, etc. He's the guy who draws up our will and helps us with the details.

About eight or nine years ago, he and I went out to lunch. He's a Jewish guy, great guy, a highly esteemed lawyer, active in his temple, and a very charitable guy. He's one of those guys who would give you the shirt off his back. Eight years ago, he invited me out to lunch, and he wanted to talk about God a little bit.

As we were talking and I was sharing some of my experiences with him about Jesus, he leaned over the lunch table and said, "You mean to tell me you talk to God?"

I said, "Yeah, all the time. I listen to the Holy Spirit. Not audibly like you and I are talking, but I talk to God all the time, and I know He answers back."

He said, "Okay." We finished our lunch, and that was it. Every once in a while, I'll get a holiday letter from him, or I'll call him if I have a question. Well, I needed to see him again because we've needed to get some of my dad's stuff sorted out and put in order while he was still capable.

So we were at his office, talking. My parents and my

brother from New York were there. We were signing the
paper to make a trust and everything else that was necessary.

He then said to me, "Jack, we need to have lunch again."
It has been eight years since that last lunch. Okay. That'd be
great. He then said, "There are two specific questions we're
going to talk about."

I said, "Okay, what's that?"

He said, "One: what does God require and really want
from us? Two: why do bad things happen to good people?"

Okay. Wow. So I went home, and I spent some time
preparing for that lunch meeting. We set the lunch date for
three weeks later. I spent time diving into the Bible. I knew
I could only come to him with Old Testament references
because he doesn't believe in Jesus. He knows I believe in
Jesus, but I wanted to respect his beliefs. So I did research,
and I was looking at the Torah, the first five books of the
Bible, and I also started looking through the twenty-four
other Old Testament books in the Hebrew language. I
wanted to make sure I had my ducks in a row. I had studied
Deuteronomy 8, where it says don't forget God who gave
you all these things. I chose Isaiah and the prophecies, and
I was ready to show him everything. I had it all figured out.

I met him for lunch, and I was ready. We were talking back
and forth. Finally, he said to me, "I get very nervous when I
hear people say they've heard from God."

I asked, "Why is that? Wouldn't it be a good thing to talk
to God and know what God wants?"

He looked me dead in the eye, without missing a beat, and
said, "Do you know how many people have been killed in
the name of Christianity?" I felt like a deer in headlights.
First of all, the answer is, no, I don't know. Maybe I'm naïve.
Maybe I'm stupid. I don't know. I got saved at thirty-three.
I spend my time looking into the word and heart of God,

and it gets better and better each day for the last twenty-five years. So I never went back historically and looked up how many people were killed in the name of Christianity. The bottom line is I really didn't know.

He started to tell me about all these atrocities committed in the name of God, people who thought they were doing God's will. The tragedy of 9/11 is one we can relate to. We know what happened on 9/11. That was people who thought they heard from their god. How about these guys who shoot up the kids in school? "Oh, the Lord told me to do it. I heard the voice."

This is why he told me, "I get very nervous when I hear people saying they hear voices, that God speaks to them."

I was kind of hit between the eyes with that one. I finished the lunch and I told him, "Wait a minute. I'm a born-again Christian. A born-again Christian could never act as you're talking about. It's impossible. We're born again of the spirit of God, a new creation in Christ. This is not how a born-again Christian would act." I realized that I didn't have the power to sway him. This is a lawyer. He's got his facts right. He's looking for evidence, evidence, evidence. It'd be like talking to a Yankee fan and trying to make him a Red Sox fan. You can say anything you want. You can talk yourself blue. It's not happening. I tried to do the best I could for the rest of the lunch, and we parted ways.

I went home fired up. I wanted to see what he was talking about. I began to Google the statistics of people who have been murdered in the name of God, people who have been murdered in the name of Christianity. I came up with eight pages of victims of Christian faith atrocities. Eight pages! Missions, crusades, heretics and atheists, witches, religious wars, Jews. On it goes. All of these people who have been murdered in the name of Christianity. There have been plenty of twentieth-century church atrocities as well.

So I read them because I was interested, asking myself, "How am I going to come back at this guy?" As I read, I saw that while most of them were through a church or pope or some other person off the beaten path, they were all using the name of Christianity. Medicine is good. Doctors are good when they're not illegally prescribing painkillers to people who are dying. If one doctor began giving out pills that killed people, it wouldn't mean you should discredit science and medicine altogether. Police are good when they're not corrupt. One crooked cop does not discredit all honest policemen. Churches are good when they're not polluting or corrupting the word of God for their own selfish gain.

There have been plenty of organizations and people who have done terrible things in the name of God, but a true Christian couldn't behave like that. Now that I had done my research, I wanted to go back to this guy and tell him why he was wrong. This is a case of mistaken identity. That's what it is. I've figured it out. It's a mistaken identity. I wanted to say, "You thought, mistakenly, that we born-again Christians were like all these other guys. No, no, no. We're not the same. We're born-again Christians. We're the ones who do things the way God said to do them. We love. We care. We're kind. We never murder. We never hurt. We'd never do anything like that."

Then it dawned on me that most people have mistaken people's identities for a long time. It's nothing new. There are many different sects of Judaism, and they operate and think differently? Many people don't know that. They think, "Well, he's a Jew." It's a stereotype.

Is every person who went to college smart? Well, they went to college. Shouldn't they be smart? No. Not every person who went to college is smart. There are these major stereotypes we make. And we can be completely wrong.

I was ready to go back to this guy and plead my/our case in this matter of mistaken identity. I wanted to fight against that mindset to make him understand. But God put on my heart, "No. He is not the person you need to talk to."

"Excuse me? You heard what he said, Lord."

I felt the Lord say, "No. It's not about him. It's not about changing his mind. You need to talk to the born-again Christians."

Why? Because we need to do a better job. It should be that every single person who knows you or me has this response, "I hear the bad things they're saying about Christians, but it has to be wrong because it is impossible that the Christians I know behave like this. I know Christians, and it is impossible they would ever engage in this type of behavior. It's impossible that they're hypocrites, liars, cheaters, thieves, adulterers, angry, resentful, jealous, and envious. It is impossible they are murderers. All they do is love people... Even their enemies! I've seen it in their actions and by the way they live their lives."

God told us in the third chapter of Colossians to take all of that stuff off. He says we're a new creation in Christ. We are meant to throw away the old ways of the carnal man and to reflect God. What does the world see when they see you and me? Do we need to behave differently so we are certain they see God reflected in our lives.

First Peter 2:12 tells us, "Live such good lives among the Pagans that though they accuse you of doing wrong they may see your good deeds and glorify God on the day He visits us." That's God's direction to you and me. Live such good lives that even though they might accuse you of doing wrong, your good works glorify God.

People might say, "Oh, but there are eight Google pages of Christians killing people in the name of God." There may be eight pages, but I can tell you this: for those who are born again in the spirit of God, it is not even a possibility they would engage in this type of behavior. There are many people saying, "I'm a Christian," who are clearly not Christians by their works. God knows. God says, "If you're not a Christian, if your heart is far from me, when you get to Judgment Day, you'll hear, 'Depart from me. I did not know you.'" That's what you'll hear instead of, "Well done, good and faithful servant."

Could you believe that anyone who lives like Jesus commanded is capable of murdering people? His word says, "If any man is in Christ, he is a new creature. Old things are passed away. Behold, all things are new" (2 Corinthians 5:17). Ultimately, God will settle the accounts of those who have blasphemed His name. That's between God and them. Our job is to make sure that when the world sees us, they see something different.

"Therefore, as God's chosen people, holy and dearly loved, clothe yourselves with compassion, kindness, humility, gentleness, and patience. Bear with each other. Forgive one another. If any of you has a grievance against someone, forgive as the Lord forgave you. Of all these virtues put on love, which binds them together in perfect unity" (Colossians 3:8). Does that list of virtues sound like a murderer to you?

Galatians 5:13 says, "You, my brothers and sisters, were called to be free, but do not use your freedom to indulge the flesh, rather serve one another humbly in love. For the entire law is fulfilled in keeping this one command: Love your neighbor as yourself." John 13:34 says the same thing. "A new command I give you. Love your neighbor as yourself."

If we are faithful to follow His commands, to put others first, to love others as we love ourselves, we do not have to fear mistaken identity. We will be known as His and will be as lights shining in this world. We will enable others to see and know that true, born-again Christians are capable of one thing only — living lives that honor God and bringing glory to His name.

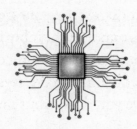

The Key To Happiness

God says better is a little with righteousness than much with wickedness. Yet sometimes we act like we don't believe God. We say, "No, Lord. It would be better if I had all the stuff I wanted and your righteousness."

Now let's look at the attitude of our lives and the attitude I believe we need. This is what God showed me as He broke my heart with this verse. In fact, He has kept it broken for quite some time now, broken in a good way. Psalm 63:3 says, "Your loving kindness is better than life. My lips shall praise you."

I thought to myself, Wow! First of all, it's true. Second of all, if I simply had that attitude about my life, if I just looked at God truly from my heart and believed that His loving kindness is better than life, if I desired the loving kindness of God more than this life, I would never have a problem. I'd be the most on fire, focused Christian you ever knew.

If we valued the loving kindness of God more than life, we would be content. We would be happy. We would be peaceful. We would be joyful. The things of the world and the ways of the world wouldn't drown us. The pressure of the world wouldn't crush us. We have everything because we are blessed with the loving kindness of God.

That's what we need to remember. Because it's true. God's loving kindness is better than this life. And we have God's loving kindness. We already have it. We have everything.

Only we can choose to live each day in a way that gives glory and honor to God. I pray that we would download that and never forget it!

As lights shining in this world. We will enable others to see and know that true, born-again Christians are capable of one thing only - living lives that honor God and bringing glory to His name.

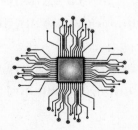

Born Into Royalty

I had just finished reading the Bible chronologically. It was a great experience. It really touched my heart. I said, "God, I want you to examine me and look at my heart and show me everything about me." When we go to the grocery store, in order to purchase an item, they scan it, and it tells them everything about the item. It tells them the price. It updates the inventory so they know to replace it. It's all computerized. I said, "God, I want you to scan the barcode of my heart. I want you to see everything about me because I want to know what can be different and what can be better."

I don't want to kid myself. I want to be honest. God said He desires truth in the innermost parts of us (Psalm 51:6). As I want my kids to be truthful with me so that I can bless them and help them, I want to be truthful with God for that very same reason.

Consider what God said to the prophet Jeremiah in the days of old. I believe He has the same message for us today. "The word of the Lord came to me," said Jeremiah, "saying, 'Before I formed you in the womb I knew you. Before you were born I sanctified you'" (Jeremiah 1:4-5). That's the same promise God gives to us. Before we were formed in our mother's womb, God knew us, and we were sanctified by God.

It's like being a trust-fund baby. In the old days, it would've been the Vanderbilt, Morgan, and Rockefeller families.

If you were born into that lineage, in that family, you had nothing to worry about. You were taken care of. Today it would be Buffett, Gates, Trump, or the family of any sports star or athlete because they all have what seems to be endless supplies of money. You'd have nothing to worry about. You'd be taken care of. You'd be set.

Upon hearing that, Jeremiah responds to the Lord. His response is, "Ah, Lord God! Behold, I cannot speak, for I am a youth" (Jeremiah 1:6). Just like Noah, like Moses, like Abraham, like Jonah, and like us, Jeremiah heard God's call and he's looking for the first way out. Jeremiah's excuse... "God, you don't mean me because I'm too young."

"Oh, God, you don't mean me," said Moses, "because I'm old." Sarah said, "You don't mean me because I'm ninety years old. I can't have a baby."

God says, "That's exactly who I mean." God says to you and me, "I do mean you. I want to talk to you. I'm God, and I want to talk to you."

God goes on to tell Jeremiah, "Do not say, 'I am a youth,' for you shall go to all to whom I send you. And whatever I command you, you shall speak. Do not be afraid of their faces, for I am with you to deliver you" (Jeremiah 1:7-8). What a great promise from God. Do not be afraid because I am with you to deliver you.

God gave Jacob the same message — be strong and be courageous — and He gives that message to us today. Do not be afraid. I am with you to deliver you.

No matter what happens, our lives are in God's hands. Our families are in God's hands. We are in God's hands. And He does all things well.

Yes, You Can You Have It All

Paul writes to the Corinthians, "We speak wisdom among those who are mature, yet not the wisdom of this age, nor of the rulers of this age, who are coming to nothing" (1 Corinthians 2:6). The rulers of this age, the wisdom of this age, will all come to nothing. You don't have to worry about that.

Paul continues, "But we speak the wisdom of God in a mystery, the hidden wisdom which God ordained before the ages for our glory. ...It is written: 'Eye has not seen, nor ear heard, nor have entered into the heart of man the things which God has prepared for those who love Him'" (1 Corinthians 2:7, 9).

It's for your glory that God has revealed Himself through Christ Jesus. But we can't even imagine the glory that is in store. My kids can't even imagine what Beth and I are doing for their futures. They can't even imagine it, but we know because we're the ones doing it. You can't imagine what God is doing.

At the same time, Paul says, "God has revealed them to us through His spirit. For the spirit searches all things" (1 Corinthians 2:10-11). God has revealed them to you through the spirit. The next passage states, "Now we have received, not the spirit of the world, but the spirit who is from God, that we might know the things that have been freely given to us by God" (1 Corinthians 2:12). Only when the spirit of God is showing you the things of God can you understand and know God.

You must know the Holy Spirit to know God. If you don't know the Holy Spirit, the part of Himself that He deposited inside of you, you don't know God. If that is the case, you can change it today. Simply pray, "Okay, God, I'm accepting you into my heart. I'm inviting you into my heart. I want to know your Holy Spirit. I want to see these things you've revealed."

Who has known the mind of the Lord that He may instruct Him? But we have the mind of Christ (1 Corinthians 2:16).

Do you understand how powerful that line is? We have the mind of Christ. We have the mind of Christ because God has put His heart and His mind inside of us with the Holy Spirit so that we would understand these things, so that we would be certain, so that we wouldn't foolishly waste our lives living for our flesh and the things of the world that are worth nothing.

I was at a Christian concert with my wife around Christmas time. One of the band guys came out, and he said, "Imagine how cool it would be to get to heaven and see Moses there. The first thing I'd want to say to Moses is, 'Moses! Tell me how it felt to part the Red Sea. Tell me how it felt when you stood there and the Spirit of God came upon you and the sea parted at the command of God through you. How amazing was that? Could you just please tell me about that? That has to be the most amazing thing in history.'"

The guy said that, before you could finish speaking, Moses would say, "Oh, no. Forget that. You tell me what it feels like to have the spirit of God living in you twenty-four hours a day all the time." In Moses' day, that hadn't happened yet. Jesus hadn't been resurrected yet. The spirit of God would come on them from time to time, but it wasn't dwelling within them.

We have everything. Moses would be envious of us. He's going, "You have God 24/7. This is amazing. You must be the happiest guys in the world. You must be dancing in the street like in a New Orleans Mardi Gras parade every day, 'Whoa, we can't believe it. This is amazing. We've got the greatest lives ever.'" How could anything bother us?

I understand. I'm just like you. I'm in the flesh. Things bother me. But they don't have to bother us for long because we can test everything against the word of God. There are things I don't like. There are things I wish I could change. But I'm not God. I trust God. I love God. Football players get hit in the football games, but they know they're going to get hit. They're prepared for the hit. They practice for the hit. They're running for the goal, for a super bowl trophy.

We run for a prize that will never get taken away. We know we're going to get hit. We have an enemy who wants to kill and us and destroy us, who is throwing his fiery darts at us, who is trying to hit us. God said put on the full armor of God in Ephesians 6:11. There is a spiritual warfare going on down here. Your uniform should say, "I play for Christ. I'm out there to win for Christ." That's my job. God has promised you're going to get the reward both now and in heaven. The reward now is the joy and peace and love and glory and hope and mercy and kindness and goodness and righteousness that comes in your life. Everybody should see it in you and through you.

God wants to take our joy to the next level. Eye hasn't seen it, ear hasn't heard it, but the Holy Spirit reveals it to our heart, and we know true joy.

Don't Leave Home Without It

If you travel out of the country — whether it's to the Bahamas or Jamaica, Canada, Mexico, anywhere you may go — you would never leave America without your passport because you can't get back without it.

When you travel, you always guard your passport. It's important if you want to travel without any problems.

The Holy Spirit is our passport to the abundant Christian life. We should have the Holy Spirit as close to our hearts and always a part of our lives, just as we keep those passports on us when we travel, fearful that if we lose them, we're in trouble. You can't lose the Holy Spirit of God once you have it. When you accept Jesus, He takes out your old heart, He puts in a new heart, and you're a new creation in Christ, indwelled with the Holy Spirit of God. You can't lose it, but you can certainly push it aside. You can drown it out. You can push it to the back of your life where it won't be effective. That's exactly what Satan wants. It is not what God wants.

In the book of Acts, John and Peter were on their way to the temple to pray when a crippled man asked them for money. Peter then says the famous line; you probably know it: "Silver and gold I have none, but what I have I give you. In the name of Jesus Christ of Nazareth, arise and walk" (Acts 3:6). This lame beggar was healed. He gets up. He's walking. It's a miracle.

Later in the chapter (Acts 3:16), Peter says, "By faith in the name of Jesus, this man whom you see and know was made strong. It is Jesus' name and the faith that comes through him that has completely healed him, as you can all see." In Acts 3:19, he says, "Repent, then, and turn to God, so that your sins may be wiped out, that times of refreshing may come from the Lord."

When you repent of your sin and turn to God, times of refreshing will come from the Lord. Your passport, the Holy Spirit of God, is your key to the full joy, the full peace, the full life God intended for you to have where the Holy Spirit reigns in your heart. I pray that you may experience times of refreshing from the Lord right now, at this time in your life. Claim that passport as your right of entry into the presence of God.

In Matthew 16, the Pharisees and Sadducees had come to Jesus, and they were testing Him by asking Him to show them a sign from heaven. They didn't believe what He had said. They wanted to see proof. They wanted a sign. Jesus replies in Matthew 16:2, "When evening comes, you say, 'It will be fair weather, for the sky is red,' and in the morning, 'Today it will be stormy, for the sky is red and overcast.' You know how to interpret the appearance of the sky, but you cannot interpret the signs of the times."

Jesus was saying, "You guys use your brains to figure stuff out here on earth, and make assumptions and conclusions based on obvious things and signs you observe. Why is it you cannot or will not do the same regarding heavenly things?. Why not? Why don't you understand? Why don't you get it?"

Let us trust the words of Jesus. We do that by allowing His Holy Spirit to reside in our hearts and speak to us. Your spiritual passport is vital to your spiritual life and growth. Never leave home without it!

It All Depends On How You Look At It

My buddy Andrew has stage four cancer (I mentioned him in a previous chapter). He knows his days are numbered, and he's satisfied with his days. He's going out walking in Central Park, spreading the joy of the Lord, and he's happy. The other things don't matter to him anymore. He is satisfied.

I have another buddy, forty-five-year-old guy with four kids. He is a hardworking guy. He got a prostate cancer diagnosis a couple of weeks ago. He said, "The first day I was mad. The second day, I came home, and I didn't go to my night job." It was a pest control company he's trying to start. He said, "I'll spray them another day. I just wanted to be with my family. I just wanted to be with my kids. I just wanted to laugh with them. All the rules and regulations I had put in place didn't matter anymore." He had a new perspective on life in light of his diagnosis.

This same buddy was thinking about his wife and family and how he's going to provide for them. He said he was sitting on the porch and thinking about his wife and how, when they got married, she trusted him to provide for the family. That was twenty-something years ago. She could have married a lawyer or a doctor and been certain of her provision, but she wanted to be with him. She loved him so much that she said, "I trust you. I'd rather be with you because I love you so much and trust your provision. I want to be with you. I couldn't imagine not being with you. I'm going to trust you for our provision."

My friend had the thought that this is exactly how it is with him and God. He said, "Of course, God, I want to be with you so much. I love you so much. I'm going to trust you for the provision of my life. I'm not going to trust anybody else. I'm going to trust you. You've always provided."

How tragic would it be if his wife had turned on him somewhere down the line and thought, "You know what? I know you've provided for our life all these years, but maybe you can't do it now. Maybe you're too old. Maybe you don't have what it takes. Maybe you've lost it"?

Do we do that sometimes with God when we don't get what we want? "God, maybe you've forgotten me. Yeah, I know you've done all these miracles, but maybe you won't in the future. Maybe you can't. Maybe you're not able." We should not do that with God.

I got an email from a buddy of mine — I'll call him Dave — who is struggling with severe financial problems and health problems. He wrote, "I'm pretty sure my luck could get no worse. If I were a weaker man, I would walk out into traffic. I'm at my wits' end. I'm so tired of struggling and struggling and struggling. There is no way to express how I feel right now. I'll just keep trucking along until a plane decides to land on my head. I wouldn't be surprised if that happens. It seems if it weren't for bad luck I'd have no luck at all."

Then in a letter from my friend Andrew, who is in stage four of cancer. He wrote me, "What I need to tell you is that with my cancer there are good days and bad. On the bad days, you just don't feel like living. I now face the possibility of having lymphoma in addition to my leukemia, but God has blessed me with all of this so I can continue on. If you don't have or have not ever had cancer, it's difficult to explain. I seek no sympathy. I am here because it's God's will. Many times over I should've passed this life. The trials I have faced throughout my life I would not wish on anyone, but I never quit. I keep going until I finally ask God to guide my life. Even though I still face trials, as we all do, I always thank God for my trials. God promises us that prayer works, and it does. I'm a testament to that. Today I faithfully and joyfully walk His walk for my life. Today and each day I pray for each of my family and friends, and I pray that God gives me the strength, courage, and wisdom to do His will and to spread His love and salvation to all people that I can touch and witness to."

Wow. Let me put it together for you. I phoned my friend, Dave, the guy who is struggling financially and said, "I know you're going through a lot of tough times. I get it. I'm praying for you, buddy. But I just want to share this with you. Let me share with you my buddy Andrew's situation. If he were in your spot, Dave, he would believe he was the luckiest man in the world. If he could just have your problems, those that you think are the worst, he would be so grateful. To you, they are crushing. I'm not diminishing the significance of that." But it was all about perspective. What perspective are you going to take? Are we going to take God's perspective or the world's perspective?

I sometimes look at my children as extremely spoiled. They have everything. They have everything they could ever want. Yet they complain all the time the minute they don't get what they want, whether it's what restaurant they're going to, what flavor ice cream they get, what television show we watch or what game we play. The minute they don't get what they want, all they do is complain. My wife and I say to them, "But you have everything. You have everything not only by the world's standards but by God's standards. There are kids with nothing. You throw away bags of toys every six months. All these things you're getting for Christmas; we're going to be donating in six months or a year because you'll be bored with them. You have everything, yet you're fighting about what food you eat when there are kids who don't have food. You're fighting about how much time you can spend on a computer not even grateful that you have the privilege of watching the computer and watching television." Many children have nothing. No food, no toys, no free time, and no education. Some don't have loving parents and some have no parents at all.

I'm hammering them on how spoiled they are and thinking how spoiled they are, and God put upon my spirit this question: "You mean, Jack, just like you are with me? You look at the things you don't have that you want, instead of being grateful for the things that you do have." I learned from that parable in my own life.

I learned from my friend Andrew who is likely in the final stages of his life, but is reveling in each new day God has given him. God, help us to number our days, and glorify You with every breath we have.

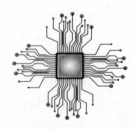

Lunatic Fans

Sometimes we complain. I remember complaining in New York when it was too cold and complaining in Florida when it was too hot. It seems we're never quite satisfied unless our eyes are focused on the Lord, and then we're always satisfied. It is vital to our spiritual growth that our eyes be focused on the Lord and on all that He's done for us, all that He's given us — this wonderful, abundant life, this wonderful planet to be a part of to spread His ministry and His word, and then the ultimate promise that we're with Him forever for all eternity in heaven. Our place in heaven is assured. If nothing else, that is reason for unending praise and worship. He has shown us the way to eternity with Him through His Son, Jesus.

One year I remember Brazil lost the World Cup match to Germany. The fans of the Brazilian team had a variety of reactions, but a few of these reactions, after their team had just lost the World Cup Soccer match, were quite telling. It was quite an upset to the Brazilians, and a couple of quotes from the newspaper article stated, "In San Paulo, Brazil's biggest city, thousands gathered in the bohemian neighborhood of Vila Madalena, the streets carpeted with yellow, green, and blue, the colors of the Brazilian flag. Fan Samir Kelvin clung to a street pole and loudly cried, 'I have nothing left! I'm Brazilian and humiliated! I want to kill myself!' Nearby, a woman cried out, 'What shame! What Shame!' As another man was banging his head against a table."

As I read that newspaper excerpt, I thought, "Wow, these guys are committed." They were genuinely upset. This was not, "Oh, our guys lost. Let's go bowling or to a movie have some fun and forget this." No. This was life affecting. These fans were truly bummed out, and this was a soccer match. I wondered why sometimes we, as Christians, don't have that same passion for our God that these soccer fans have for their soccer team. They take it very, very seriously.

Here are these Brazilian soccer fans so intense over their team that they're moaning. They're banging their heads on the table because their team lost. It was as if they were living or dying based on the success of their team. I pray that your passion for Jesus would be similar and that it would increase based on the blessings that are flowing in your life and the abundance that God has provided for you. Let us focus on the Savior. Then our souls will be satisfied by the abundance of His love. We will stand in awe of all that He is and all that He has done for us.

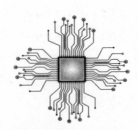

Walk This Way

In the world today, there are so many celebrities and so many leaders who are admired (some living and some dead). There are so many opinions and so many styles. So who do we imitate? Who is our role model? Is it Snoop Dogg? Is it President Obama? Or is it Donald Trump? Maybe it's Justin Bieber, Michael Bublé, Sinatra, Capone, John Gotti, Mickey Mantle, LeBron James, Woody Allen, Brad Pitt, Madonna, or Lady Gaga?

Who do we imitate? Who do we want to be like?

For a Christian, there is only one answer. Our role model is Jesus. We are to be followers of Jesus Christ. We are ordained to imitate Him with our lives. Our decisions each and every day — big and small — should be based on the life and person of Jesus Christ. When we seek to please Him, to follow Him, we will know the way we should walk.

Paul says, in First Thessalonians 4:1, "That you should abound more and more, just as you received from us how you ought to walk and please God." The apostle is saying, "Look, brethren, we urge and exhort you in the Lord. We're not just telling you, by the way. We're urging you. We're exhorting you. We're making sure you know this is an important thing you should do. You should abound more and more, just as you received from us how you ought to walk and please God." This isn't a thought or a suggestion for us as Christians. It's our responsibility. It's our calling. It's our purpose to walk in a way that pleases God.

But not out of obligation. Not out of, "Oh, crap. I better walk in this way that pleases God, or He is going to be mad at me forever and ever, and this is going to be a bad thing." No. It's supposed to be, "Oh, God, I love you so much for what you've done. You've given me this life. I'm so grateful.

Luke 6:45 tells us, "A good man out of the good treasure of his heart brings forth good. An evil man out of the evil treasure brings forth evil. For out of the abundance of the heart his mouth speaks." What's in your heart? What's in my heart? If I have an abundance of anger, jealousy, rage, and malice, that's what's going to come out of my mouth. If I have an abundance of the fruit of the spirit, of love, peace, mercy, joy, grace, loving kindness, that's what's going to come out of my mouth. Out of the abundance of our hearts, out of what we have a lot of, that's what's going to come out.

Second Corinthians 1:5 says, "For as the sufferings of Christ abound in us, so our consolation also abounds through Christ." God's comfort abounds in us. So our comfort to others should abound. Others should see the comfort and love of God from us that we receive from God. That's how we're supposed to look, like Jesus was. We are supposed to share this comfort and love with others, and we're supposed to share it abundantly.

Look how Jonah describes God. In Jonah 4:2, he says, "For I know you are a gracious and merciful God, slow to anger and abundant in loving kindness, one who relents from doing harm." Jonah says, "I know this." He doesn't say, "I think it," or, "I hope it." I know it. And I know it, and you know it too. This is how God is. He is gracious and merciful, slow to anger and abundant in loving kindness toward you and me. How lucky we are!

Whose Fault Is It?

When we see some bad people, real rotten apples in the world, when we see a mass murderer or a shooting take place at school, we want to place the blame somewhere. Who is to blame? I have Christian friends who are the most wonderful people and parents in the world, and they have raised some crappy, rotten kids. They have kids who are drug addicts, kids who are thieves, a kid who is a murderer, or a rapist. Is that their fault?

The parents did everything they could. Those "rotten apple kids" have godly, Christian parents. Is it their fault the kid turned out wrong?

I also know some crappy parents who have raised some amazing, good kids. Amazing. Do they get all of the credit? No.

Wait a minute, that's a little confusing. You mean it's not about the result? That's right. We don't control the result. It's about your effort and obedience; that's how we're judged. We don't judge the parents based on the kid. Rather, we can say, "Oh, I know these parents. They are wonderful. I can't believe this kid chose to make these bad decisions."

It is the same when we look around at the world today. We see bad things happen and many people automatically ask, "Why did God let this happen? Where was God when this was happening?" Is it God's fault when people choose to do the wrong thing and sin and go far from the Kingdom? No, it's not God's fault. God gave you everything you need to make the right choice.

It's not those parents' fault. That kid made an individual decision. So did the kid who made an individual decision to live a good life. When God looks at you and me, He's looking at our effort.

It's like the Parable of the Talents. What did you do with the life God gave you? He's not holding you responsible for the outcome of who got saved, who didn't, how your kids became, what they did or what they didn't do. Obviously you want them to be wonderful, and you want to do the best you can to raise them in the way of the Lord. But you can't control every outcome.

I'd like my kids to choose to serve the Lord with their lives, but I know my job is to be the best parent I can be. If I've done that, I've done my job regardless of the outcome.

It's the same in your Christian life. It's not necessarily about seeing thousands of people come to the Lord or this and that. It's were you faithful with what you have?

We see the Christian evangelist and actor Kirk Cameron and the impact he has on the world, both with his personal testimony and starring in God-inspired movies such as Fireproof and Left Behind. Well, what about a lady working at the counter at Dunkin Donuts? All day long, when people come into Dunkin Donuts, she loves on them with the love of Jesus Christ. She shares her smile and shares the love of Christ. People can see Jesus bursting out of her every single day. People come in there and they want what she has. I don't mean the donuts. They see and want the peace and joy of the Lord.

Do you know what? She may never see the impact she had on people, but she glorified God with the life she lived. I believe when she gets to heaven, her reward will be the same as Kirk Cameron's because they both did the same thing.

They both said yes to God. That needs to be our answer to the Lord. Yes.

There is a spiritual warfare going on. We know that, in our Christian walk — whether we're pastors, ministers, daughters, sons, ambassadors, or warriors — we are representatives of the Lord. Our job is to glorify God. The outcome is up to God. We simply need to keep praying and keep trusting.

Proverbs 19:8 says, "He who gets wisdom loves his own soul." You're supposed to love yourself. You're not supposed to hate yourself. You're not supposed to beat yourself up. You're supposed to love yourself. God loves you. Satan wants you to beat yourself up. He wants you to condemn yourself and say, "I'm not good enough."

That's right. You're not good enough. Thanks be to God that Jesus was good enough. God's goodness and sacrifice got us into heaven. We're supposed to love our own soul. We're supposed to love this life we have, this gift from God. Stop letting Satan beat you up and condemn you.

God says in Romans 8:1, "There is no condemnation for those in Christ Jesus." Is any part of that unclear? There is no condemnation for those in Christ Jesus. God did say our own hearts would condemn us, yes because they're a part of our flesh. I get that, but then I stand focused and fixed on Jesus, the author and finisher of my faith, and I see what He said. He said when God sees me, He sees me clothed in the righteousness of Christ. I am holy, blameless, and above reproach.

That's the way God wants you to live. That's freedom. When God says, "Whom the son sets free is free indeed" (John 8:36), that's freedom to live a life that glorifies God with no fear and no concern for the outcome.

Someone Wants To Shut You Up

The first pastor I ever met, Truman Herring, a wonderful man of God and a great teacher of the word, wrote a book asking whether God was judging America. I wonder in 2016 if God is crying today for America? Oh, man, I don't know about you. I think God is crying today for America. I'm not surprised at what I see. I'm not surprised that I see the world going to hell in a hand basket because it's fulfillment of Old Testament and New Testament prophesy, of God's word talking about the end times coming. It said we'd see these signs. People would be lovers of themselves. They put teachers who say what they want to say and not the true Word of God and nation would fight against nation. It's all there.

In pastor Truman's book, he brought up some very interesting dates. Of course September 11, a day we'll always remember, when the terrorist planes crashed into and brought down the World Trade Center. Most of us were alive to remember that day, where we were, what happened. Some of you remember December 7, 1941. Instantly, you go, "Pearl Harbor," the day the Japanese attacked. Those two days changed America forever. Our freedom that we'd taken for granted was all of a sudden under attack. What did America do? We responded accordingly. We got tough. We fought back. We did well.

Without getting political, I want to mention these next two things to you because there are a couple of other dates that are very historical in America that maybe you're not as familiar with. One is January 22, 1973. That's the day the Supreme Court decided in Roe v. Wade that abortion was now legal in America. Another day was June 26, 2015. That's the day the Supreme Court ruled against God's standard of marriage as being between a man and a woman and basically ordered fifty states to recognize same-sex marriages.

It's very important, before we talk about this, that you understand we have no hate or issues with people who have already had abortions. As a matter of fact, you may have had an abortion. When I say no issue, I mean I would not stand in judgment of the action you took at a certain time in your life. (You can rest assured, if you have had an abortion, your baby is in heaven with God because God covers all little kids and babies who were not old enough to decide for themselves to accept or reject Jesus's as Lord). This is not a condemnation or judgment of anyone who has had an abortion, nor is it a condemnation of anyone who engages in a homosexual lifestyle.

We're supposed to love everybody. We're supposed to love all sinners. Jesus did. We're sinners. God loves sinners. I'm not going to judge their individual sin. I may not agree with it, but that's not the issue from my point right now. The issue here is America has   taken the absolute word of God and the morality of God, (what God has said is an absolute, not open for negotiation) and changed it. God has said marriage is between a man and a woman. God has said homosexuality is a sin. He said many other things are sins, not just those, but those are the two that seem to have been legislated. And He said taking a life (killing) is a sin.

Instead of the absolute morals God has instilled, we now have America making up its mind based on how it feels in a present time or place. "God, that wasn't such a good idea. So here's what we're going to do. We're going to take the morals we think are accurate, and we're going to make those the new morals." We call that socialist morals, when society is determining what the morals should be, based on how they feel at that particular moment in time.

The scary part of that, to me and other people I've heard speak on it, is the lesson we're teaching our children. The lesson we're teaching them is that God's word isn't absolute. As a matter of fact, God's word is wrong. When we don't like it, we just change it. We're not bound by it. If it doesn't apply or it doesn't appeal, we'll just change it. That's a bad lesson. Either God's word is true, or it's not, but it's not half true. It's not, "The parts I like are true, and the parts I don't like aren't true." If it's not true, why follow any of it? If it is true, why wouldn't you follow all of it wholeheartedly? I know we as believers believe that.

We have the country changing things, and here is the problem. It's getting worse. America today, the society that is changing the legislation, is calling you and me and all Christian believers religious hate mongers. That's what we are to them.

"How dare you say homosexuality is a sin? How dare you say I don't have the right to choose if I want an abortion? As a matter of fact, if you continue to say that, we're going to put you in jail for a hate crime. That's a hate crime. You must hate us to say that."

No, I don't hate you. As a matter of fact, I love you very much. I love my family very much, and at times I say things they don't like because I love them. I'm telling them what the truth is.

We have a society saying, "Wait a minute. If you don't believe like we believe, you need to go to jail, and your haters."

Wait a minute. All I've ever said — when I say I, I mean

we — all I've heard Christians ever say is, "Hey, listen. This is the word of God. We believe it 100 percent. We're not telling you that you have to do or think as we do. We're just telling you what we believe and what and how we choose to live. We never said we should put you in jail or cast you out of society or you shouldn't have a right to live here in America because you do those things. Quite the opposite. All we've said is this is what God's word says, and we believe God. So let me get this right. You're going to take away my right to believe what I want, my free speech, my right to believe what I want because you don't agree." That's right. That's exactly what's happening.

If you and I, as Christians, don't stand up and recognize this, we will be legislated into not even being allowed to speak our minds. Now, that is insane when you think about it. Who is the hate monger now? Don't be influenced or swayed by the newspaper, politics, athletes, governors, college students, and presidents who are celebrating this as a victory for individual freedom. "Oh, this is great, same-sex marriage, abortion. Everybody has got their rights. This is how it should be." Not according to God.

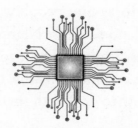

Struggling with Sexuality

I want to share this with you very intimately. I got saved at thirty-three years old. At that time, I had a raging drug problem. It took me three years to really deal with my drug problem and give it over to God. God was always willing to take it from me, but I wasn't willing to give it to Him.

Let me explain something to you very clearly because I need you to understand. I was extremely saved, radically saved at thirty-three years old. God started to work on different areas in my life, one by one, changing me and my behavior to his way of thinking in many areas over the course of three years. Finally there was one big area left... My drug use.

For the three years before we got to that one, I was very happy to indulge in my drug addiction. I knew it was wrong. But I was happy to indulge in it. I loved God. Had I died during that three years, I certainly would've gone to heaven because I can tell you I was definitely saved. Fortunately, I believe I have victory over that today, but I still struggle with other issues and areas in my life. (I think all humans do... even Christians...SMILE!)

Recently at a meeting of a group of pastors, (who got together right after forty-nine people were shot and murdered at a shooting in Orlando at Pulse Nightclub, a gay and lesbian bar) we were brainstorming on how to specifically deal with the gay and lesbian community. How to welcome them into their churches. How to deal with them and make sure they feel welcome while not condoning their particular sin.

We met a guy there who was a pastor who had struggled with being gay. His insight was both fascinating and heartbreaking. Obviously there are questions regarding abnormal sexual behavior we need to look at. Some of them are very legitimate questions, one of the main ones being, "Hey, am I born that way or do I choose this?" I don't know the answer. I'm sure there are some kids who are absolutely predisposed to same sex attraction and some who have those feelings that they're not in the right body, but they're actually born in the wrong gender. I totally get it. I don't deny people feel that way.

This pastor guy, in particular, made a very interesting comment. He said, "Jack, I knew I was gay since I was eleven years old. As a matter of fact, it's always about love. It's never about the sex. My father had not shown me much love. There was an older man who came around and started showing me some affection." This is the chilling part. He said, "All I had to do was have sex with him to get love," like it wasn't even a big deal. Then he said these words that broke my heart. He said, "I prayed every day that God would take this from me, take this feeling. I don't want to have this feeling of being gay. I don't want to be attracted to other men. I prayed every day for twenty-five years that God would take this from me, all through my childhood and continuing through adulthood when I married a woman hoping and praying that would make the feelings go away so I could live a normal life by society standards. I prayed and prayed God, take this from me."

God didn't take it from him. Here is a guy who loves God. Now, there are other people who may not be praying that God takes it away who may be exactly like I was in the height of my drug addiction when I got saved and said, "Hey, God,

I'm fine with this. I love you, but I'm fine with this." (By the way, try and tell me there is not an area of your life that you're struggling with. I'd like to meet that man or woman.)

No. We're all struggling. Yet we point at the other guy's struggle. "Well, if you're struggling with homosexuality, we don't want you around here. If you're struggling with drug addiction, stay away. If you're struggling with mental illness, no way. If you're struggling with un-forgiveness, if you're struggling with lust, with theft, no way."

No. We're all sinners. Christ died for each and every single one of us. Your job and my job is to love people whether they are struggling with sin or indulging in it. We are to show them the love, grace and mercy of Christ, not forgetting that is what God gave and showed to us when he dealt with our sin, which in God's eyes as you know is equal to theirs in every single way. I hope that is both startling, humbling and heartbreaking

Your job and my job is to show people the love of Jesus Christ, everybody, every sinner. We're to go to those people with the love of Jesus hoping we can attract them to Jesus, that they see something in us that we have that they want so that they come to Christ. Christ will deal with their individual sin as He does with each one of us. That's Jesus' job to point out the sin in people's life and the Holy Spirit to convict people, not mine and yours. My job and your job is to show people the love of Jesus Christ, all of them, regardless of what they've done, regardless of our own judgments.

Through it all, I've come to the point where I'm saying, "Lord, please make me slow to condemn. Please help me be slow to condemn. Help me be quick to seek understanding, complete understanding of what people are going through." That doesn't mean I have to agree with what they're doing, but I should at least understand it. When I heard that guy talk about his homosexuality and desire for God to take it away, I was like, "Whoa. I didn't know that." That's intense and deep and complex.

I can't leave the subject without one more point because I think it's important, as you walk through the world, for you to know it. There are those who will point to scripture out of context and say horrible things about homosexuals and other types of sinners. Let me quote one of the verses they use. It's 1 Corinthians 6:9-12. It says, "Do you not know that the unrighteous will not inherit the kingdom of God? Do not be deceived. Neither fornicators, nor idolaters, nor adulterers, nor homosexuals, nor sodomites, nor thieves, nor covetous, nor drunkards, nor revilers, nor extortioners will inherit the kingdom of God."

In context, be aware that Paul was writing this letter to the church at Corinthians. As a matter of fact, he starts off in the letter by saying, "To the church of God, which is in Corinth, to those who are sanctified in Christ Jesus, called to be saints." That's believers. He's talking to believers and he's saying, "Don't you know that." He goes on to list many sins and types of sinners, idolatry, adultery, homosexuality, sodomy, thieves, covetousness, drunkards, revilers, extortioners. He says, "Don't you know they won't inherit the kingdom of God?"

Most people stop right there and some say, "Those homosexuals deserve what they got in Orlando." I've heard pastors on the air say it (but no pastor or Christian with a proper understanding of God's word would ever make such a horrible and untrue statement). However, those who did make such a statement and those who thought that way, whether pastors or believers...they don't want to read the next verse. The next verse says, "And such were some of you," you too were all of these things. "Such were some of you.

But you were washed, but you were sanctified, but you were justified in the name of the Lord Jesus and by the Spirit of our God."

The day I accepted Jesus Christ as Lord and Savior, my sins were forgiven — past, present, and future. That's not an excuse for me to sin. Of course, I want to get closer to God and do things that glorify God and have God touch my heart and impact my life. But don't let people misquote to you and take Scripture out of context.

We were all sinners and Jesus paid the price for all of our sins. That applies to homosexuality and any other sin. A homosexual — like a drug addict, like a pornographer, like a tax cheat — can certainly accept Jesus. In some God may remove your desire to sin immediately and some may struggle with that sin the rest of their lives in their human flesh. It doesn't mean they're not saved! That is for God to judge but not you.

Your job and my job is to love everybody, believers and sinners alike that is what Jesus did and we are to imitate Him. I'm sure you still struggle with sin, your fleshly desires, and nature in certain areas of your life. I know I do. I'll bet you're glad God doesn't judge you daily for your sin but instead forgives you and loves you. We are to do the same to others.

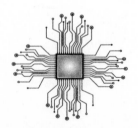

Section 6

REMOTE ACCESS TO THE KINGDOM
The Holy Spirit Is Your Conduit

Remote Access is the ability to access your computer from a remote location. However, remote access is more than just being able to connect one machine to another machine in a different location. It is the ability to mirror the original machine to another once the connection has been made. A remote access program can basically transform your local computer into a duplicate of the computer you connect to. More accurately, remote access is connecting one device to another for the ability of accessing and sharing resources.

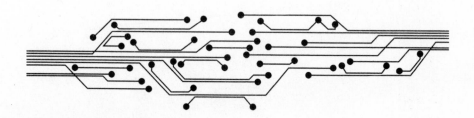

Remote Access To The Kingdom

Shake It Up

I love how the word of God is alive and relevant today, even though it's two thousand years old. Look at the promises God made to some of the Old Testament Bible heroes, and he makes the same promises to us today.

In this instance God's warning and God's promise are one and the same.

This is what the Lord Almighty says: "In a little while I will once more shake the heavens and the earth, the sea and the dry land. I will shake all nations, and what is desired by all nations will come, and I will fill this house with glory," says the Lord Almighty (Haggai 2:6).

I love God's timing. "In a little while I'll shake the heavens and the earth." In a little while. God says in his timing a day is like a thousand years and a thousand years like a day. God says, "You don't know my timing. I'll come like a thief in the night, like labor pains upon a pregnant woman." Be prepared. Be ready.

Who will be the faithful servant that the Lord finds doing His will when He comes back? Will it be you? Will it be me? Will we be prepared? Will we be doing what we're supposed to do, living that life that glorifies God by sharing what God has done with us with other people? Will God see us being diligent, righteous, faithful, longsuffering, staying the course, and pressing on to the task at hand? Will that be what God sees?

I pray we will not say, like some said in the Bible (Luke 16:10-12), "Oh, our master delays in coming. I don't have to do these things. When He comes back, I'll do them. In the meantime, I can do whatever I want. I'm going to help myself to the party stuff. I'm going to beat the slaves. I'm going to do whatever I want." God made very clear statements about the one who is not doing what he's supposed to when the master comes home. The master will take him and throw him into prison. But the one who is faithful, who is found doing what he's supposed to, much will be given to him.

God is looking at our lives and He is saying, "This is what I've given you. Will you be faithful or not?" There is no other test. It doesn't come later. This is it.

It's like finally making it to play in the Super Bowl and then saying the Super Bowl isn't really the Super Bowl. No, it's the Super Bowl. It'd be a good time to play your best game. This is it, these three hours are the Super Bowl game. This is it, these sixty, seventy, or eighty years you live that God says is a like a mist. Here for a moment and then you're gone. That was your life. Your reward in heaven for all eternity, forever and ever will be based on your obedience to God on Earth, not your accomplishments.

Your job is just to be obedient to God, wherever God has placed you. Your task is to say, "Yes, Lord. I'm going to step out of my comfort zone. I'm going to open my mouth for Jesus Christ. My coworker might not like it, my friend, my cousin, my family, but I'm going to do it. I have a mission here on Earth. You've called me to do something."

God tells us His will for us so clearly in His word. Waiting for Judgment Day is going to be too late. It's going to be too late to go back and change things, to decide that, yes, we do want to live a life that glorifies God. It's going to be too late.

God, through the prophet Haggai, speaks of the temple

He is asking His people to build for Him. "'The glory of this present house will be greater than the glory of the former house,' says the Lord Almighty. 'And in this place I will grant peace'" (Haggai 2:9).

Has not God made the same promise to you and me? The glory that is to come will be greater than the glory that is now. Has not God made us that promise? Is God a liar? That's the question we have to ask. Of course not. May it never be said that God is a liar. God says, "In this place, I will grant peace." Of course you're going to have peace in heaven. It is a place with no more pain, no more suffering, and no more crying. We will be living for eternity with God, face to face with Jesus, the most amazing thing I could ever imagine.

But you can have it now too. Jesus says, "I am your peace" (John 14:27, paraphrased). The peace that transcends all understanding is God Himself. You have God Himself inside of you. The Father and the Son have come to make their home inside of you through the Holy Spirit, their deposit inside of you.

God has put a piece of Himself in your heart so you would be sure of the eternity that is to come, so you would know how great this hope is of yours, how great this love of God is for you and me. Don't miss your peace!

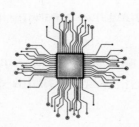

Fat Chance

Read God's word below. Does not God say the same thing to you and me? My prayer is that there are no Christians, especially you, my valued and cherished reader, who don't believe they were chosen by God to live for God. Here's proof.

The word of the Lord came to Haggai a second time on the twenty-fourth day of the month: "Tell Zerubbabel governor of Judah that I am going to shake the heavens and the earth. I will overturn royal thrones and shatter the power of the foreign kingdoms. I will overthrow chariots and their drivers; horses and their riders will fall, each by the sword of his brother. On that day," declares the Lord Almighty, "I will take you, my servant Zerubbabel son of Shealtiel," declares the Lord, "and I will make you like my signet ring, for I have chosen you," declares the Lord Almighty (Haggai 2:20-23).

God says, "I'll take you, and I'll make you like my signet ring." What does that mean? It means that on that day, you will reflect God. A signet ring was like a signature of the king. It's what he used to stamp documents. How did you know, back in that day, if a document was real? How did you know it wasn't a forgery? It needed to have the king's signet ring stamp. If something had his stamp, his signature, it had his authority.

That's the exact authority Jesus Christ has given you and me here on Earth. We're to be his signet ring. We're to represent Jesus here on Earth. People are supposed to see us and say, "Of course they're from God. Of course they have Jesus Christ within their hearts. We can tell. Just look at these guys. Look at their lives. Everything about them is about Jesus Christ."

Here's a tough question. I asked myself this question recently, and it's a good one. So I'm asking you. What if the only payoff you ever got from God is in heaven? You get nothing here on Earth. Nothing. "Just do what I said. Be faithful. Be obedient. Everything will come to you in heaven." Are you still going to do it?

Look at Hebrews Chapter 11, all those characters who died "in faith" — Abraham, Noah, Joseph, Moses and many others. They died before they saw the fulfillment of God's promises. They lived their life, and they died. They didn't see the rewards during their earthly lives.

God will record what impact we had on history. We don't have to worry about that. We just have to do our jobs. We simply have to say, "Yes, Lord."

The bottom line is; do we believe Jesus or not? In Luke Chapter 8, Jesus was performing miracles. He was on His way to the home of a synagogue leader named Jairus, whose daughter was very ill. He felt power going out of Him when He was touched, and that touch of faith healed a woman who had been bleeding for twelve years. Jesus told her, "Daughter, your faith has healed you."

We pick up the story from there.

While Jesus was still speaking, someone came from the house of Jairus, the synagogue leader. "Your daughter is dead," he said. "Don't bother the teacher anymore."

Hearing this, Jesus said to Jairus, "Don't be afraid; just believe, and she will be healed" (Luke 8:49-50).

The guy's daughter just died. He's going to Jesus, asking for a miracle. Everybody was saying, "Don't bother Jesus. Your daughter is dead. We need to focus on the people Jesus can help. Your daughter is dead already. So no sense you getting in line. Let's talk about the people Jesus can help."

Jesus says to Jairus, "Don't be afraid. Just believe, and she will be healed." The story continues.

When he arrived at the house of Jairus, he did not let anyone go in with him except Peter, John, James, and the child's father and mother. Meanwhile, all the people were wailing and mourning for her. "Stop wailing," Jesus said. "She is not dead but asleep."

They laughed at him, knowing that she was dead (Luke 8:51-53).

They laughed at Him. Can you just see this in the Bible? They're like, "Yeah, right, Jesus. You're going to bring in James, John, the mother, and the father. You're going to do something with the dead girl like bring her back to life. Yeah, right."

Do we do that sometimes in our lives to Jesus? We sarcastically say, "Yeah right, Jesus, you can't do that, or that will never happen. Jesus... you're dreaming I tell you! Do we do that in our lives? Do we do that to other people sometimes? Somebody has a dream. "I'm going to be president of the USA. I'm going to be an astronaut. I'm going to be an athlete, a movie star, a playwright, a scientist. I'm going to invent the next Internet. I'm going to start a new business. I'm going to live my dream. I'm going to get out of this place."

We say, "Yeah, right. Fat chance. No way. You're stuck in this life just like us. We're going to tear you down every moment just like we feel torn down." We refuse to believe in our God-given potential and our strength. This mindset forces us to live a mediocre life based on expectations of the world and flesh, void of the power of God and the hope of God. I call it that "Yeah, right" moment. It's a "Yeah, right" attitude.

God says all things are possible with God. God asks, "Is there anything too hard for me?" If God could save a wretch like me, there is nothing impossible for God. I believe it. I get it because I've seen it myself.

There are other "Yeah, right" moments in the Bible. How about when David went to face Goliath? Everybody was like, "Yeah, right, David. Fat chance. That'll work really well." How about when Noah was building the ark? "Ha, ha, ha, Noah. That's a good one, Noah. Yeah, right." How about Job believing in spite of his circumstances? Nobody believed, not even his wife. His own wife said, "Yeah, right, Job." His friends said, "Sure, Job. You didn't sin. Yeah, right."

How about when Jesus walked on water and nobody believed? They thought, "It's a ghost!" No, it was Jesus walking on water. "Yeah, right. It's a ghost!" Peter believed for a little while, until he took his eyes off Jesus and sank.

How about Moses parting the Red Sea? How about the walls of Jericho falling down? Can you imagine Joshua walking around a wall and the guards up there going, "Ha, ha. You're going to make the wall fall down? You guys are going to walk around this wall we built of cement," (or whatever it was made of) "and it's going to fall down? Yeah, right."

How about Abraham being one hundred and Sarah ninety when she gave birth? Abraham was cracking up when God told him. Abraham said, "God, that's a good one. Who says God doesn't have a sense of humor? God, a baby for Sarah? That's good, God." Sarah laughed as well. Abraham was like, "Yeah, right." Who had the last laugh there?

How about Mary giving birth to Jesus, claiming it's a virgin birth? "Okay, Joseph. Let's get this right. Your wife is not a whore. Here's what happened. The God from on high came down and impregnated her. Okay. We believe that one." All these "yeah, right" moments are recorded in the Bible.

The greatest "yeah, right" moment of all time was Jesus' resurrection after His death on the cross. To this day, a lot of people in the world are going, "Yeah, right. Let me get this right. Your God dies, and He's resurrected after three days, and then He's taken up to heaven. That's who you believe in? That's your God? Yeah, right."

Yeah right! That's exactly who we believe in. That's our God. We've seen the miracles. We know they're true because each and every one of us has in our heart the Holy Spirit of God confirming it. I don't believe anybody else. I don't need to. I believe God. I believe the Holy Spirit. I know He's real. You know He's real.

Well, if we believe and know He is real, we need to live like it. We need to bet our lives on Jesus Christ. Not half and half. Not lukewarm. God says, "If you're lukewarm, I'll spit you out." Not one foot in the world, one foot in the kingdom. No. Both feet in the kingdom of God. We are strangers here on Earth. We're passing through. Our citizenship is in heaven.

That concept is not something to scoff at, to sarcastically say, "Yeah, right." It is right. It is true, and if we live like we believe it, we will be confident on the day of His coming. Because we will be going home with Him. Now download that, and you will have it made.

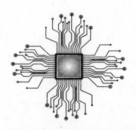

The Parable Of The Soda

Check out this amazing life promise from God: "Blessed be God who has not turned away my prayer nor His mercy from me" (Psalm 66:20). God has not turned away your prayer, nor has He turned away His mercy. He says in Isaiah 26:3 that He will keep in perfect peace those whose mind is stayed on Him because they trust in Him. If you're not feeling the perfect peace of God, there can only be one of two reasons. Either you've taken your eyes off God, or you don't trust Him.

Is it possible that we've taken our eyes off God? Is it possible that we don't trust God? We know all of God's promises are true. We know that from God. One pastor said it this way. What you worry about is what you don't trust God with. If you trusted God, you wouldn't worry.

Let me tell you the Parable of Jackson and the Soda. When my son, Jackson, was thirteen, he loved soda. He also loved coffee. I didn't like him drinking soda, and I really didn't like him drinking coffee. I issued him a challenge. I said, "Son, if you don't drink soda for six months and coffee for a year, there will be a financial payoff for you." I promised him $150. It was a big number, but I told myself I was buying a year of his health and it was well worth it.

He accepted the challenge. I didn't think he would make it a week. I told myself, "He wants the soda. He wants the coffee. This is not going to cost me a nickel, and maybe I'll get a day or two free of him not drinking soda or coffee out of it."

He just hit the six-month mark on the soda. So he won the soda part of the bet. I learned something from Jackson the day he met that challenge. There was something he wanted, something that was very important to him, and he was willing to sacrifice to get it. He wanted to drink soda, and he wanted to drink coffee, but all of a sudden there was something more important. (For Jackson in this case it was the financial reward.) So he didn't do it.

How important is God to us? What are we willing to do and sacrifice for God? Is God worth it or not? Are we going to choose the world and the flesh, or the spirit and kingdom and the things of God? That's the choice every believer has to make. I believe it's not too late for anyone who is still alive to turn around and do the right thing with God.

I was inspired by Jackson's dedication to getting what he wanted. It inspired me to remember that we should do whatever we need to do to accomplish and get what's important to us. Our lives will reflect our actions and decisions, and we see the signature of our souls reflected in the actions of our lives. It's easy to tell. That's why God says a good tree will bear good fruit and a bad tree will bear bad fruit; we know a tree by its fruit.

You hear so many opinions from so many places on what's right or wrong. Every politician, every sports guy, every self-help guru, every religion... Everybody will tell you, "Here is what you need to do." But here's the real key. Look into your heart. See if God Himself — the same God who raised Jesus from the dead — is calling out to you today.

I knew when He was calling me. There was no doubt in my mind. All you have to do is respond. God is walking with you every step of the way. That doesn't exempt you from the circumstances of life, but it does ensure God walks with you through them.

He loves us not merely in words but in actions. The greatest action of all time was the sacrifice of His Son on the cross, that we might gain eternal life in the presence of a loving creator. That is true love. That is reason enough to rejoice in all things.

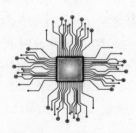

Your Honor Please

Proverbs 14:12 says, "There is a way that seems right to a man, but in the end it is the way of death." John 15:5, one of my favorite verses, tells us these words of Christ: "I am the vine. You are the branches. If you remain in me and me in you, you will bear much fruit. Apart from me, you can do nothing." Our plans are futile apart from the Lord.

In Malachi 1:4, God is upset. He says, "This is what the Lord Almighty says: 'They may build, but I will demolish.'" Why would God say that? Because they weren't being obedient. Through Malachi, God is speaking to Israel, telling them what they're doing wrong.

Is it possible that God is also speaking to us? It is possible that God would like us to examine our own lives, examine ourselves and see if there is something we need to change, if there's a place in our lives we're not giving honor and glory to God, if there's somewhere we can do better so God can bless us even more, as is the desire of every parent for their child?

God goes on to ask the million-dollar question. It's in Malachi 1:6. "A son honors his father, and a slave his master. 'If I am a father, where is the honor due me?'" Then he asks another million-dollar question in that same verse. "If I am a master, where is the respect due me?' says the Lord Almighty." How scary is that? What's your answer to God on this question?

I pray that we may be found faithful in what may seem like a very little thing because it really is a huge thing. God is saying, "You call me Father. You say I'm king of the universe and master. I see you bow down to me and I hear you praying to me, but you do it out of routine, fear and obligation. But where is the honor that's due me as a father and a master?" Where is the love you would have for a father who loves you and sacrifices all for you? The New King James Version says, "Where is my reverence?"

I pray that when God looks at my life and your life, He is satisfied with us, He sees how much we love Him, how much we honor Him, and He never needs to ask that question of us (where is the honor that's due to me as a father and as a master!) for it is so evident to God and to everyone how much we love and honor our father and master!

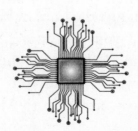

Still Time To Turn Back

If we look around at the world today, things can seem pretty scary. We're starting to see politicians today looking to oppress the word of God. To keep it out of schools, out of shopping centers, movie theaters, government, even our homes and churches if they can. We can't let that happen. God's word is alive in our hearts. He's written it in our hearts and we're to live it out with our lives.

In the Old Testament, punishment was usually pretty swift and just. We know from the New Testament that we're saved in Jesus Christ. Our sins are forgiven and we're going to be with God forever in heaven, yet we can still miss blessings that God has for us if we're not obedient to God's word.

I want to share some Old Testament stuff, as some things really stood out to me from there.

In the eighth month, in the second year of Darius, the word of the Lord came to the prophet Zechariah son of Berechiah, son of Iddo:

"The Lord was extremely angry with your ancestors. So tell the people: This is what the Lord of Hosts says: 'Return to Me'"—this is the declaration of the Lord of Hosts—'and I will return to you,' says the Lord of Hosts.

Do not be like your ancestors; the earlier prophets proclaimed to them: This is what the Lord of Hosts says: 'Turn from your evil ways and your evil deeds.' But they did not listen or pay attention to Me—this is the Lord's declaration. Where are your ancestors now?" (Zechariah 1:1-5)

God, almost mockingly, says through Zechariah, "I told them to turn from their evil deeds. Oh, but they didn't listen. They didn't think it was important to listen to God, and by the way, how did that work out for them? Where are they now?" They're dead and separated from God. The answer is the same thing for any unbeliever. If you don't believe in Jesus Christ, unfortunately, you will be separated from God for all eternity and you'll spend eternity in hell.

If you are a believer in Jesus Christ, Jesus' desire is still that you would turn from your sin, repent, and get the full abundance of His blessings. In this particular passage, the verse goes on to say, "...and the people repented" (verse 6). What we've seen through Old Testament history is Israel constantly doing the wrong thing, constantly repenting, and then constantly doing the wrong thing again. The cycle begins again. Repenting, doing the wrong thing, repenting, and wondering why they never go anywhere.

When you repent, it needs to be with Godly sorrow, that you're truly sorry for what you've done. You have to realize that this sin is separating you from God. You're grieving the Holy Spirit of God with this sin in your life, whether it's an addiction, a habit, bad behavior, anger, malice, rage, jealousy, envy, anything. God tells us we're to get rid of. It can be very individual for all of us what specific thing or things it is, but God wants to remove that from your life. God wants to take it away.

If we switch to the New Testament and look at the words of Jesus, we can get some perspective on this. Jesus said, "How foolish you are, and how slow to believe all the prophets have spoken!" (Luke 24:25) Would God say that to you and me today? How foolish you are and slow not to believe all that

Jesus has spoken? We have Jesus. We have the word of God living in our hearts. How could we not believe all that God has spoken? How could we believe some, but not all; a little, but not most? It's ridiculous, and then we expect the benefits of this full blessing and abundant life from God.

Back to Zechariah, now they're in the fourth year of King Darius. It's two years later and we read:

The word of the Lord came to Zechariah on the fourth day of the ninth month. Now the people of Bethel had sent Sharezer, Regem-melech, and their men to plead for the Lord's favor by asking the priests who were at the house of the Lord of Hosts as well as the prophets, "Should we mourn and fast in the fifth month as we have done these many years?" (Zechariah 7:1-3)

The people of Bethel sent their prophets to "plead for the Lord's favor," and they had a question. "How can we get your favor, Lord? Maybe we should mourn and fast in the fifth month as we have done these many years. Is that good, Lord? Would that please you, Lord?"

Zechariah then says this:

Then the word of the Lord of Hosts came to me, "Ask all the people of the land and the priests: When you fasted and lamented in the fifth and in the seventh months for these seventy years, did you really fast for Me? When you eat and drink, don't you eat and drink simply for yourselves?"

Get this right; they did it for seventy years. They fasted and mourned. But their motives were not pure.

I believe God is asking us that same question today. What you do, who are you doing it for? Really, who are you living this life for? God said we're a new creation in Christ. We're created anew to live a life that would glorify God. So God asks, "Who are you doing all this stuff for?"

When we look at our own lives, do we see a life reflecting fruit, reflecting good works that God prepared in advance for us to do, being lighthouses to a lost generation? Are we serving God with our lives? God called these guys out on it, very specifically. He's calling us out also. As Christ laid His life down for us, we are to lay our lives down for others as a sacrifice. We are to lay our lives down for Him.

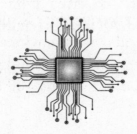

Lost Treasure

I was inspired as I was reading the book of Daniel. God touched my heart and made me want to be like Daniel — in a lot of ways, but one very specific way I want to touch on.

Three times in the book of Daniel, God says to Daniel, "You are treasured by God." In Daniel 9:23, Gabriel is speaking to Daniel. The angel Gabriel appears to Daniel regarding translating a dream and he says, "At the beginning of your petitions an answer went out, and I have come to give it, for you are treasured by God."

In Daniel 10:11, we read, "He said to me, 'Daniel, you are a man treasured by God. Understand the words that I'm saying to you.'" Then, in Daniel 10:19, the angel Gabriel said to him, "Don't be afraid, you who are treasured by God. Peace to you; be very strong!"

Treasured by God. I want that in my life. I wish and pray and hope that God would look down on me and say, "I treasure you." I know God loves me. I know He loves all of us. He died on the cross for all of us, but Daniel was treasured for his faithfulness, for his obedience, for his complete trust in God. That's what will make God treasure you. God loves you no matter what. God gave His life for you. But I want to be treasured by God. All it takes is faith and obedience and a sold out life for God.

Tough Love

The first verses of Hebrews chapter 12 give us such a great vision for our lives.

Therefore, since we are surrounded by such a great cloud of witnesses, let us throw off everything that hinders and the sin that so easily entangles. And let us run with perseverance the race marked out for us, fixing our eyes on Jesus, the pioneer and perfecter of faith. For the joy set before Him He endured the cross, scorning its shame, and sat down at the right hand of the throne. Consider Him who endured such opposition from sinners, so that you will not grow weary and lose heart (Hebrews 12:1-3).

Consider Him the word of God says. Consider Jesus so you will not grow weary and lose heart. When you're going through this life, you have a trial or tribulation or struggle, consider Jesus. Remember that. Throw off this sin that so easily entangles you. Resist the devil, and he'll flee from you. Resist. There is an action required on our part.

The next verses go on to state this:

In your struggle against sin, you have not yet resisted to the point of shedding your blood. And have you completely forgotten this word of encouragement that addresses you as a father addresses his son? It says, "My son, do not make light of the Lord's discipline, and do not lose heart when He rebukes you because the Lord disciplines the one He loves, and He chastens everyone He accepts as His son." Endure hardship as discipline; God is treating you as His children. For what children are not disciplined by their father? If you are not disciplined — and everyone undergoes discipline — then you are not legitimate, not true sons and daughters at all (Hebrews 12:4-8).

If you're not being disciplined by God, you're not God's son or daughter. I can't discipline your kid, but I can sure discipline mine. You know why I'm not disciplining your kids? Because they're not my kids. They're your kids. You discipline them.

We are God's kids. God is going to correct us and rebuke us because He loves us, because He's not going to let us waste the precious life He has given us.

God wants you to have the best of everything. When the Holy Spirit knocks on your heart and says, "Don't do this," or when you face a consequence for sin — you drive drunk and you get a ticket, or you wind up in jail because you hit somebody — you see that there's a consequence to sin. God wants to use your life. God will discipline you and correct you and rebuke you so that He can continue to greatly bless you.

The next verse goes on to say, "We have all had human fathers who disciplined us and we respected them for it. How much more should we submit to the father of spirits and live! Our earthly fathers disciplined us for a little while as they thought best; but God disciplines us for our good, in order that we may share in His holiness" (Hebrews 12:9-10). Remember God disciplines us for our good in order that we may share in His holiness.

It is God's desire that you share in His holiness as you walk this Earth and, of course, forever in eternity where you will be like God, holy and blameless forever. On this Earth, it is God's desire we share in His holiness. He disciplines us because He doesn't want us to miss it.

Today is the day. Today is your opportunity not to miss it. "No discipline seems pleasant at the time, but painful. Later on, however, it produces a harvest of righteousness and peace for those who have been trained by it" (Hebrews 12:11). Whether it's our military, our children, or a football team, discipline and the training enable them to perform at the level of greatness we so need.

Later in the chapter, we are given this commandment:

See to it that you do not refuse Him who speaks. If they did not escape when they refused Him who warned them on Earth, how much less will we, if we turn away from Him who warns us from heaven? At that time His voice shook the earth, but now He has promised, "Once more I will shake not only the earth but also the heavens." The words "once more" indicate the removing of what can be shaken — that is, created things — so that what cannot be shaken may remain (Hebrews 12:25-27).

What things cannot be shaken? Heavenly and eternal things. Verse 28 says, "Therefore, since we are receiving a kingdom that cannot be shaken, let us be thankful, and so worship God acceptably with reverence and awe, for our God is a consuming fire."

Our heavenly Father has told us we've received a kingdom that can't be shaken. He has said we're to be thankful and we're to worship Him with acceptable worship, with reverence and awe for all He has done for us. God is a consuming fire. What does that mean? For us, as believers, it's a wonderful thing. That fire refines us and purifies us like gold and precious metal that's refined in the fire, purified so its metal can shine, so all can see the glory and the beauty of the metal. Its true value can be appreciated, seen, and revealed.

The Lord's desire is that our true value as sons and

daughters of God can be appreciated, seen, and revealed here on Earth, so that we would fulfill the mission He has for us.

That same fire is the fire God, with His hand, used to separate the wheat from the chaff, the fruit from the tares, and the good from the bad for eternity. It's a refining fire. The hand that loves is the same hand that disciplines — it depends on what we need.

It's God's desire to hug us and pat us on the back and say, "Great! You guys are doing excellent! Let me give you this blessing and reward. I love you so much." If we're not on the right path, however, that same hand, that same voice will speak and rebuke us and correct us.

I pray that is the desire of our hearts, to hear His sweet, still voice. I pray we would quiet our lives for as long as it takes, to hear what the Lord has to say to our hearts individually. Where do we need to turn and repent? What do we need to bring back to the altar, to God's feet, and then walk away from? What temptation, what sin do we need to put at His feet? Who do we need to forgive? Where do we need to show mercy?

I pray that we would take the opportunity to judge ourselves. God said if we judge ourselves, we won't be judged. We can look at our own lives and truly come before the Lord with a heart of repentance so we don't face judgment. That way, we know in advance we're going to hear, "Well, done, good and faithful servant," because we've done what He has asked us to do.

I love my children so much. While it breaks my heart to discipline them, I do it willingly. My wife and I do it willingly. We do it because we love them so much we couldn't bear the thought of them going astray and not getting the full benefit of the lives they have. As much discipline as it takes, that's how much they'll get.

That's God's approach for us. As much as it takes. It shouldn't take any. It should just take a proper response to the loving word of God. That's should be gratitude from our hearts for what our loving father has done for us here on Earth and for all eternity, and trust in his guidance and directions and love for us.

If His word has spoken to your heart, don't let it go. Take the time to commit and repent and turn back to the God who loves you so much, like the prodigal son who had squandered it all. When he turned back to the father, he couldn't even make it home. The father ran to him, embraced him, put the ring on his finger, had the fattened calf killed, and called for a celebration. He said, "My son was dead, and now he's alive."

If you've been dead to God, it's time for you to live for God. God wants you to live. God can do more in five minutes with your surrendered life than you can manage to do on your own in fifty years. Won't you give it to Him today? I pray you will tell Him, "I can't bear to miss what you would do with my surrendered life." I pray your heart would surrender fully to God today and especially in all the places where you specifically need to give it over to Him.

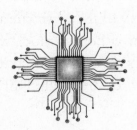

I Have Doubts About You

When God says whom the son sets free is free, indeed he's not kidding! Let's look at and absorb God's word below.

When the fullness of the time had come, God sent forth His Son, born of a woman, born under the law, to redeem those who were under the law, that we might receive the adoption as sons. And because you are sons, God has sent forth the spirit of His Son into your hearts, crying out, "Abba, Father!" Therefore, you are no longer a slave but a son, and if a son, then an heir of God through Christ (Galatians 4:4-7).

You probably know that verse. It's a pretty popular verse. You're no longer a slave. You're a son of God. You're an heir to the throne of heaven with Jesus Christ. You're Jesus' brother and heir to God's throne in heaven. The passage goes on to say:

But then, indeed, when you did not know God, you served those which by nature are not gods. But now after you have known God, or rather are known by God, how is it that you turn again to the weak and beggarly elements, to which you desire again to be in bondage? You observe days and months and seasons and years. I am afraid for you, lest I have labored for you in vain (Galatians 4:8-11).

Get this right. The apostle Paul is saying to the church, "Hey, don't you get this? I'm wondering. I'm worried that maybe all this teaching I've done, everything I've poured into your life as I've shared the love of God with you and made sure you understood it, maybe I did it in vain. You don't seem to get it." Is it possible Paul's efforts, his love, his teaching, his sacrifice could be wasted on those he taught it to? Let's bring it closer to home.

Is it possible that Jesus' love, teaching, and sacrifice will be wasted on us? That's a scary thought. The apostle Paul goes on to say in verse 20 of that same chapter, "For I have doubts about you." Think of stuff that you have doubts about and compare it to things you have no doubts about. Your spouse loves you. Doubt or no doubt? You love your kids. Doubt or no doubt? Your car will start. Doubt or no doubt? Your favorite food tastes good. Doubt or no doubt? The stock market will go up. Doubt or no doubt? The stock market will go down. Doubt or no doubt? A Republican will be president. Doubt or no doubt? A Democrat will be president? Doubt or no doubt. There are things you know for sure and have no doubt about. There are other things you have doubts about.

The apostle Paul is saying, "I have doubts about you." I'm wondering if God is looking at us and saying, "I have doubts about you."

I want to look at my life and I want to make sure that, when God looks at me, He doesn't have any reason to doubt. I hope you want the same. We know we shouldn't doubt God, but if we don't doubt God, we should act accordingly and our lives should reflect that. Then He won't have any reason to doubt us. Jesus hammered people for their lack of faith. It wasn't about perfection. It had nothing to do with that. It was about faith. God says He will bless us based on our faith. How many times did Jesus heal and say, "Your faith has made you well"?

God knows what will happen. I think I know what will happen with my kids. It doesn't mean I'm not concerned.

When my oldest son was a young man having a major drug problem, in the throes of his drug addiction and I was watching him throw his life away, I knew what would happen based on his behavior, based on his lack of obedience. We certainly had doubts about him at that point. We knew things weren't going to go well, and we had doubts about his desire to live the right life.

The good news is, now we don't have those doubts. He rebounded. Today he's a father and a husband. I'm a grandpa with a granddaughter, and I'm very excited about that. Here is the good news. Doubts can change in an instant. Our state of mind can change instantly based on our kids' actions and obedience. Thank God it can change.

I don't want God to have doubts about me.

Here is this great promise from God. This should not be a funeral verse. It's read at every funeral, but it's a life verse. It's a promise for all God's children.

The Lord is my shepherd. I shall not want. He makes me to lie down in green pastures. He leads me beside the still waters. He restores my soul. He leads me in the paths of righteousness for His name's sake. He anoints my head with oil. My cup runs over. Surely goodness and mercy shall follow me all the days of my life, and I will dwell in the house of the Lord forever (Psalm 23).

How great is that? Here is God restoring my soul, leading me in the paths of righteousness for His sake. God is anointing my head with oil. My cup is running over with good things. It's full. Goodness and mercy follow me all the days of my life.

That's a promise for your life here on Earth and your life in heaven with God. All the days of your life, goodness and mercy shall follow you. You're going to tell me that you're not jumping up and down, singing hallelujah? You're not the happiest person in the world?

I like the fact that goodness and mercy are following me. It beats the heck out of evil and judgment. We should be happy and joyful.

Psalm 36:7 gives us another key to life:

How precious is your loving kindness, O God! Therefore, the children of men put their trust under the shadow of your wings. They are abundantly satisfied with the fullness of your house.

If you're not satisfied with God, you'll never be satisfied with anything. Those who are being blessed are trusting in the shadow of God's wings. They're abundantly satisfied with God's fullness. That is the gift of God.

God Himself is this great gift of God. Yes, we get eternal life. Yes, we get abundant life. But the greatest thing of all is knowing God, having that joy, walking through this life knowing God is with us, holding our hand, and with us every step of the way. Above and beyond all that, He's prepared a place for us for all eternity. How lucky could we be? It doesn't get any better than that.

Psalm 36 goes on to say in verse 8, "And you give them drink from the river of your pleasures. For with you is the fountain of life." That's the key. It doesn't get any clearer than that. For with God is the fountain of life. If you want the fountain of life, you need to get God.

We are no longer slaves to fear. We are no longer servants to our own dark passions that seek to run wild. We are children of God. He has called us to life. He has breathed new life into us through the Holy Spirit. The moment Jesus breathed His last breath on the cross, new life, forever life, was available for all who would believe in Him.

We should never doubt. He is the fountain of life.

In The Field Of Opportunity
It's Plowing Time Again

It is amazing to me how the world searches for joy, peace, and happiness in their lives. It is amazing to me that Christians, who have everything, are not joyful, happy, and peaceful in their life. Joel 2:12 says, "Turn to me with all your heart, with fasting, with weeping, and with mourning." Turn to God with all your heart. God says rend your heart, not your garments. Return to the Lord, for He is gracious and merciful, slow to anger, of great kindness, and He relents from doing harm."

God wants us all in.

Perhaps it seems like a lot to ask us, like a lot for us to give up. So you mean I've got to give up the things of this world for the things of God? That's right. You've got to give up the things of this world for the things of God.

Does that mean I can't have anything in this world? No, it doesn't mean that. You can have a business. You can have a house. You can have a car. You just do whatever God told you to do. It's what you do with the blessings that matter, not what you have.

God says in Hosea 4:6, "My people are destroyed for lack of knowledge. Because you have rejected knowledge, I also will reject you from being priest for me." This is God's warning for every believer. If you reject the knowledge of God, He will reject you from being a priest for Him. Peter said that God has called us to be a royal priesthood. We're temples of God, living stones that He is building up. The spirit of God lives in us; our bodies are temples. We don't want to miss that. We don't want to be rejected from being a priest for Him.

He's not talking about being a pastor. He's talking about shining as a light in the midst of an ever-darkening world. We are all called to be priests for the kingdom of God. Hosea 6:6 says, "I desire mercy and not sacrifice and the knowledge of God more than burnt offerings."

Here's a verse I feel deeply matters to get this point across: "Sow for yourselves righteousness. Reap in mercy. Break up your fallow ground. For it is time to seek the Lord till He comes and rains righteousness on you" (Hosea 10:12).

"What's that, Lord? I have to sow for myself righteousness? I have to reap in mercy? I have to break up the fallow ground?" It's a farming term. It means you go in and you till the ground to make it fertile so you can plant in it. You can't just throw seeds on the dirt and expect a great crop. The farmer has to work the soil. He's got to plough the field so it's fertile, so the seeds will grow. That's what God is telling us to do. He's telling us that it's time to work the field. It's time to sow righteousness, reap mercy, and break up the fallow ground.

We need to look at our own lives and say, "I need to break up this earthly ground, and I need to plant some spiritual seeds in my life."

That's what we need to do so that when we're sitting up there in heaven with the apostles, with the faithful disciples and other saints and believers of Jesus down through the ages, we can say, "Lord, I lived a life that glorified you to the best of my ability. I know of no sin between us. I took off every weight."

Oh, there were weights and, oh, there was sin that entangled us from time to time. I get that. We're in the flesh. But we have a responsibility to recognize them and remove them as they arise in our lives.

I believe God. When God says these treasures are waiting for me, I believe Him. I have received the joy and peace and happiness of the Lord. I've had it for twenty-five years, from the day I accepted His grace into my life. I wouldn't want to live any other way.

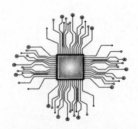

Admit It, You're Jealous!

God has had me buried in the book of Psalms for the last month and a half. God won't let me out. I don't know if you've ever been there, but it's a good thing. Lately I've been in Psalm 73, written by Asaph. Many of the Psalms are written by King David, but this one was penned by Asaph.

You might want to see how it applies to your life because it was exactly what was happening to me. The first three verses state this:

Surely God is good to Israel, to those who are pure in heart. But as for me, my feet had almost slipped. I had nearly lost my foothold. For I envied the arrogant when I saw the prosperity of the wicked.

Do we do that? Do we envy the arrogant when we see the prosperity of the wicked? "Oh, I wish I had that. If I just had that guy's money... If I just had that guy's wife... If I had that guy's job... If I had that guy's health... If I had that guy's looks... If I just had what somebody else had, I could do what you want, Lord. Then I could serve you. Then I could live for you. If I just had those things..."

Not only do we do that with the wicked or arrogant, but sometimes we do that with other Christians. This is what the Psalm goes on to say:

This is what the wicked are like, always free of care. They go on amassing wealth. Surely in vain I have kept my heart pure and have washed my hands in innocence (Psalm 73:12-13).

He's lamenting the fact that it seems like the bad guys have nothing to worry about. It seems they just keep getting more and more. "I'm a good guy, and I get nothing, and all the bad guys are getting everything. This stinks. I don't know what to do." To paraphrase it, the psalmist says it this way, "Surely, I've kept my heart pure and my hands clean in vain. Surely, it's a waste of time. It's ridiculous to follow you, Lord, and live a life that glorifies you and care about you, Lord, because I'm getting nothing. Look at all these guys who aren't following you. They've got everything." He's lamenting and complaining about it. He wonders about the value of his being righteous.

In the chapter, the psalmist goes on to say, "All day long I have been afflicted, and every morning brings new punishments" (Psalm 73:14). He's complaining, "I'm suffering for being righteous."

Hey, Job suffered. Joseph suffered. John and the disciples suffered. Jesus suffered. That great cloud of witnesses spoken of in Hebrews Chapter 12. They all suffered. You and I will suffer for the glory of God. Jesus suffered. We're to suffer, yet still live a life that glorifies God.

Of course, it doesn't mean you have to suffer. I know a lot of Christians who aren't suffering by worldly standards and I know others who are. What's the difference which assignment God has given you? He's promised He's going to reward you based on your faith, not based on your life's calling. He will bless your obedience, not your popularity. If God wants to use you, and through your suffering show others the light and love of Jesus Christ, how are you going to respond? "No, Lord, I don't want to do that. I don't want to suffer, and I don't want you to use me in that way. Can't

I be the rich guy on the beach? Can't I show them how it's good to have money, and I'll spread it around and show your love that way?"

God says, "No, I'm not going to use you that way. I'm going to use the rich guy that way. Here's how I want to use you." Sometimes we argue with God, forgetting He is the Giver of all good things, and that He is the potter. We're supposed to be the clay, yet we argue with God about how life goes and how he chooses to use our lives for his glory.

Listen to what the psalmist, Asaph, says next. "If I had spoken out like that [In other words, if I complained about it], I would have betrayed your children. When I tried to understand all this, it troubled me deeply" (Psalm 73:15-16). Here he's saying, "Look, this is crazy. I'm righteous. I'm suffering. The wicked are getting everything. But if I had spoken out about it, I would've betrayed you. I couldn't say anything, yet, it troubled me deeply. God, it bothered me, man. I was upset. I was aggravated. This isn't right."

Have you ever experienced that in your own Christian walk? You're arguing with God. You're like, "God, I know you're doing it, but this can't be right."

God says, "Remember my ways are higher than your ways."

Now here is the great truth and amazing reality of this psalm. It's found in verse 16. Asaph goes on to say, "It troubled me deeply until I entered the sanctuary of God." What's that? You were bothered, you were troubled, you were upset until what happened? Until you entered the sanctuary of God, until you came close to God?

Isn't that the same in our lives? God says, "Come closer to me. I'll come closer to you." Is there something troubling you? Come close to God. God promises He will give you understanding, knowledge, and wisdom. As much as you can handle. God shows us truth when we seek Him. When we walk with God, we get understanding.

Observe how Asaph concludes this issue.

It troubled me deeply till I entered the sanctuary of God. Then I understood their final destiny. Surely you place them on slippery ground. You cast them down to ruin. How suddenly are they destroyed, completely swept away by terror.

He is basically saying, "Now I understand. Now you've shown me. Thank God I'm not them. Thank God I'm me. I thought I wanted to be like them. I thought they had everything until you showed me their end, and I saw they were going to be separated from you.

It's like the story of the wheat and the tares. I'm going to spend eternity with you, comforted by you, loved by you, reigning with you, walking with you, laughing, and they're going to be crying, weeping in the fire of hell. I don't want to be like them. Let them keep everything they've got."

I pray my prayer and your prayer would be, "Thank you, Lord, that I am not like them. Now I see I don't want anything they have. I am blessed to have you, oh Lord. Forgive me for wanting the things of the world."

Achieving Immortality

God's righteousness is described in the Bible in a variety of ways: "His righteousness endures forever" (2 Corinthians 9:9). Jesus calls God "righteous Father" (John 17:25). Isaiah calls him "righteous Savior." Job puts it this way: "He restores to man His righteousness" (Job 33:26). God has restored His righteousness to us.

Look how God describes the attributes and benefits of those who are righteous and live righteously. Proverbs 11:30 is so great: "The fruit of the righteous is the tree of life." Isn't that what the world desires? "I want the fountain of youth. I want the tree of life." Where is it? Where do I search? Inca treasures? Is it found in Botox? God says, "The fruit of the righteous is the tree of life." If you are righteous, if you're living righteously through Jesus, your fruit will be a tree of life, both for you and those who eat of it.

Proverbs 10:2 says, "Ill-gotten treasures have no lasting value, but righteousness delivers from death." Righteousness delivers from death. God confirms it in Proverbs 12:12. He says, "The root of the righteous endures." In the way of righteousness, there is life. Along that path is immortality. What a great deal — immortality. I think we take that word for granted sometimes. "Hey, we're going to heaven and we're going to be with God forever." You're immortal. For a moment, if you can, let go of every science fiction movie you've ever watched. "How can I clone myself to live forever?

What can I do to not die?" You have it. God has gifted you with immortality. How awesome is this?

Proverbs 13:5 tells us, "Righteousness guards the person of integrity, but wickedness overthrows the sinner." You are protected because of your righteousness. It goes on to say, "The light of the righteous shines brightly, but the lamp of the wicked is snuffed out." Do you want to be a bright light for God in the world? Do you want to know what you can do to live a life that pleases God? God says be righteous. The light of the righteous shines brightly.

People are watching how you respond to sickness, to injury, to financial crisis, to health, to life, to death, and they're saying, "Well, you are the Christians. You're supposed to be the light of the world." If you don't respond with the joy, happiness, peace, and love of Jesus Christ, why would they possibly want what you have? Why would they possibly believe you have it? Why would they believe you have anything different than them? We're supposed to be different. We're supposed to respond in that light.

Listen to God's word. "The righteous eat to their heart's content, but the stomach of the wicked goes hungry." Imagine that. "Hey, have as much as you want. Eat to your heart's content." Jesus is a stumbling block to those who are perishing, but to us who believe He is the way to life. There's more. Proverbs 15:6 states, "The house of the righteous contains great treasure, but the income of the wicked brings ruin." Great treasure or ruin, which would you pick? If there was a test and you had to pick one, of course you'd pick great treasure.

"The Lord detests the way of the wicked, but He loves those who pursue righteousness" (Proverbs 15:9). God already loves you. Jesus died for everyone, the saved and the unsaved. "For God so loved the world He gave His only begotten Son" (John 3:16). Absolutely, there's a love that God has for us no matter what. Can you get more reward? I think so. If you are a parent, you're going to be more likely to bless those children who are obedient. Those children who are not, you're still going to love them, but it's going to be hard to bless them, as it's hard to bless their disobedience.

Proverbs 15:29 gives an amazing promise: "The Lord is far from the wicked, but He hears the prayers of the righteous." I am so grateful that Jesus hears our prayers. James understood this concept. I hope we understand this also. James said, "The prayer of a righteous man is effective" (James 5:16). Such simple truths. Yet living them carries such great importance. Oh that we would be those who are righteous!

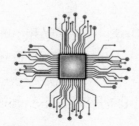

Get The Point

God is with you.

His word promises, "The Lord will rescue me from every evil attack and will bring me safely to His heavenly kingdom" (2 Timothy 4:18). If the Lord has promised to rescue me from every evil attack and bring me safely to heaven, what do I have to worry about?

You might ask, "How do I know God is going to rescue me from every evil attack?" For one, when you get to heaven, you've been rescued permanently. But here on Earth, God didn't say you wouldn't be under evil attack. Quite the opposite. You will be under evil attack. What God did say is He will rescue you from it. We often have Satan throwing his darts at us, trying to hammer us and put us on the sidelines rendering us ineffective for God and the kingdom, trying to knock us out and make us feel guilty, shamed, unworthy, and unloved. God says, "I can rescue you from that."

An amazing Christian isn't defined by accomplishment like we define a musician who earned gold records or a ballplayer who had a certain number of hits or touchdowns. An amazing Christian is defined by obedience to God wherever He placed you in life.

I was teaching a class Thursday night at a church, a "Free Indeed" class. A man called me after he attended the first class and said, "Hey, what you said in the class was great, but you need to tell people there is a rest in God they can find, and they should find this rest in God that's mentioned in Hebrews." It's absolutely true what he was saying. He continued, "I don't like that pastors have to give all these ten-point sermons or six-point sermons or four-point messages. That's crazy. All they should do is tell people about the rest of God."

By this time, I was scratching my head a bit. I knew this guy. I knew he jumped around a little bit from church to church. He is a good Christian guy, but basically there is no pastor who could satisfy him.

I said to him, "Listen, here's what it's like." I happen to know a lot of pastors. I told him, "This is what I believe is the heart of every single pastor I know. They just wish you would open up the word of God and do what it says." Just do what God says. We'll never have to say another thing. However, as I learned many years ago when I was training and managing salespeople, I would speak to salespeople and say, "Here's what you need to do," and they wouldn't do it. I'd ask, "Why won't you do that? That's your job. That's what we pay you for." But they wouldn't do it. I had to tell them different things and I had to motivate them in different ways. With some, I had to be very kind and loving. Some I had to hammer and be very tough with. Some I had to explain it one way. Some another. That was my job as a sales manager.

The pastor's job is to explain God's word to you any way that will make you get it. Any way — ten points, six points, three points, no points, etc. We shouldn't need all that explanation. We should just be obedient. We should simply be doing what God says, and none of us would need that, but we do need it. Sometimes we need to hear it different ways.

But the bottom line is, God is with us, the kingdom is promised to us, and Christ makes us free indeed.

Never Lack Again

What are the things you're envious of? Think about your own life. What are they? Maybe there are none for you, but maybe there are things you're envious of. Maybe it's the rich guy. Maybe it's the family that wins the lottery. Maybe it's a guy who hit it in the stock market or real estate market. Maybe it's the trust fund kid or somebody who just inherited a lot of money. It's clear that many of those people did nothing to earn what they got. Somebody passed away or they picked the right number, and all of a sudden they're loaded. Or maybe it's a successful businessperson, a movie star, or an athlete. Maybe it's even your neighbor. It doesn't take us much to be envious of someone else. We easily tend to be envious because they seem to have something we don't have. Something we want.

Let's take this thought a little further. How much do you have? If I said to you, "How many white blood cells or how many red blood cells do you have?" you'd know whether or not you had enough if you went to the doctor. Clearly, when you don't have enough, there's a problem.

We don't often think about it this way, but it can be a problem if you have too much. If you and I were talking about strength, knowledge, good looks, money, health, friends, and love and I asked, "How much do you have?" I'm sure, as you went through those categories, in some, you might say enough. In some you might say not nearly enough. Perhaps you'd say you have too much in other categories. The question is how much do you want?

If you knew you had enough, would you worry? I'll bet that, if you knew you had enough, you wouldn't worry. Have you ever had too much food left over? Perhaps you hosted a party. People came, but there was still so much food left over. In that case, you'd likely say, "I not only have enough. I have more than enough. It will spoil. I better give it away."

That is exactly what we're supposed to do in our Christian life. We're supposed to have so much of God, so much more than we'll ever need, that all we want to do is give it away to everybody because we certainly have enough for ourselves. We have more than enough. We have an abundance.

If you don't have enough, where do you go to get more? Well, you want to go to the source. For us, that source is God. If we want more of God, we go to the source. How do you get more? Well, you can ask for it, you can take it, or it can be given to you. Proverbs 10:22 tells us, "The blessings of the Lord make one rich, and he adds no sorrow to it." The blessings of the Lord are what make us rich. I suggest we ask God and we take what God gives. God has given us blessings to make us rich, abundantly rich beyond our belief. I am of course talking about spiritual richness.

Let's look further at how much we have and what God has given us. Romans 5:5 says, "God's love has been poured out into our hearts through the Holy Spirit who has been given to us." God's love has been poured out into our hearts. It's pouring. I lived in south Florida for over 30 years. It pours in the summer. It was pouring the other day. As a matter of fact, it was raining so hard that if you went out in it, you'd be drenched in it. That's exactly what and how your supposed to feel in the downpour of God's love. You're supposed to be drenched in God's love.

In Titus 3:5, we hear, "According to His mercy, He saved us through the washing of regeneration and renewing of the Holy Spirit, whom He poured out on us abundantly through Jesus Christ our Savior." What's that, Lord? You poured out your love on us? You poured out your Holy Spirit on us abundantly? Yes. Yes. Yes! It's overflowing — the Holy Spirit of God, for you, me and every one of us.

In First Timothy 1:14, we read, "And the grace of our Lord was exceedingly abundant with faith and love, which are in Christ Jesus." We have His love. We have His Holy Spirit. We have His grace exceedingly abundant. Do you feel that you have not received the abundant grace of the Lord? If so, it could only be for one possible reason.

You haven't asked.

God said He will give to all who ask. He who asks will receive. He who knocks, the door shall be opened. He who seeks will find. It is God's desire to bless you abundantly and exceedingly more than you can ask or imagine.

So what if someone has a better car than you. Or more money. Or a bigger house. So what if they are famous or won the lottery. We have the greatest treasure imaginable, and so much of it we cannot fathom the sheer abundance of it. Grace rains down upon us and saturates our every waking moment. The weather outside your window might be hot and sunny or freezing cold. But the abundant grace and mercy and love of God is enough to transform any weather, any circumstance, into gratefulness and satisfaction.

When I worked on Madison Avenue, I did a campaign for the US Army. It was called "Be All You Can Be." The army is telling everybody to live up to their full potential. "Be all you can be." Not only that, but, "Come on in and we'll train you and show you how." It worked for the army. God makes the same promise.

Can You Believe It?

Jesus came and declared His purpose. One of the purposes of God, very specifically stated, was to destroy the work of the devil. That's why Jesus came to Earth, to destroy the work of the devil. But He gave another reason in John 10:10. He said, "The thief does not come except to steal, kill, and destroy. I have come that they may have life and they may have it more abundantly." That's the purpose. It came from Jesus' own mouth, "I have come that they may have life and have it more abundantly." That's for you and me to have this abundant life, to grab all of it, to eat it, to take every piece of it and live every moment of it.

So here's the million-dollar question God asks you and me. It's found in John 3:12: "If I've told you earthly things and you do not believe, how will you believe if I tell you heavenly things?"

God says, "I'm telling you everything. If you don't believe me here on this, you'll miss this abundant life." You don't think you've got enough, you're not happy, you're not satisfied, what part of 'godliness with contentment is great gain' is unclear?

God says, "Hey, I have abundance for you. If you don't believe me, how are you going to believe me about heavenly things?" The abundant life is a life filled with the spirit, overflowing with joy, enveloped with peace, love, mercy, and grace, a life you have so much of you can't help but give it away.

The abundant life Jesus gives might not be the trending topic on Google News or Twitter. It might not be going viral on Facebook or YouTube. A thousand other celebrities and fame-seekers might have taken the limelight. They might even seem like good role models or great examples to follow. But we who are called the children of God have only one role model to follow, and His way is the only way that will lead to a life abundant and free.

His name is Jesus and He is the way, the truth, and the life.

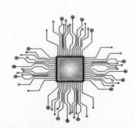

More Than Enough

While in upstate New York recently, I was at Chittenango Falls, and I was watching the falls, thinking, this is amazing. Everything comes flowing through the falls. They keep pouring down, yet their source is never expired. They always have enough water. It just keeps coming.

The waterfalls never run out. The tap doesn't run dry or turn off. They have enough to keep and keep pouring, and keep pouring. That is what our life should look like. We have a source that never runs out. We have the abundance of God. It should be flowing through us. We should be the waterfall of Jesus in everybody's life. That's what we should look like - a waterfall of Jesus.

This scripture is great news for every believer. Second Peter 1:11 states, "For so an entrance will be supplied to you abundantly into the everlasting kingdom of our Lord and Savior Jesus Christ." That's a "Hallelujah, thank you, Jesus" moment for every believer. We even get an abundance for our entry into heaven. Other versions say it's a rich welcome. There will be a rich welcome for you, an abundance for your entrance into heaven. Jesus will be there. Moses. The disciples. Daniel. They'll be there clapping when you come in.

Don't Miss It

I met a guy recently, a pastor who ministers at a church of many drug addicts. He said to me, "When I found out Jesus was real, nothing else mattered."

Talk about someone who responded to the Lord's call, "Come and follow Me and I'll make you fishers of men" (Matthew 4:19). He used to be a business guy. He said, "When I found out Jesus was real, nothing else mattered."

A couple of weeks later, I was having lunch with him. He's married and has kids. They're living in a very small parsonage. They have no space. They have no money. I don't know what they make ... I'm guessing maybe $40,000 a year because the ministry has no money. A family of four making $40,000 a year. Not room for any luxuries and probably not nearly enough for basic necessities.

In conversation, he wasn't asking me for anything. We were just talking. I asked him, "How are you doing?"

He said, "We're doing well. God is good. I'm loving the ministry. I get to see people coming off the street hurting and see God pour into and transform their lives." He then said, "My wife and I have $1.38 in our checking account until I get paid Friday." No IRA. No pension. No relatives to send them money. Less than two dollars in his checking account. As I sat there looking across the table from him, I thought, Here is the richest man in the world because God is using him so mightily. He is fulfilling his calling. He is doing what he loves. He is being blessed spiritually beyond what you can imagine and he knows it.

Oh, I'm sure he'd like to have more than $1.38 in the bank, but talk about a guy living a life of impact.

If our lives are canvases for God's work to be displayed, then I believe my pastor friend's life is a true masterpiece. You have the tools to do what you need to do. Do you want to use them? Won't you also be God's masterpiece?

How do we respond to the world's fallen condition? How do we respond to 9/11? How do we respond to ISIS, to Columbine, to Newton, to the Boston bombing and to the everyday life and tragedy of sinful behavior of a lost and fallen world made up of lost and fallen men and women? We respond with our eyes focused on the Father, reflecting Him, like the young child who imitates all of the actions of his father.

That's how we glorify God. That's how we live a life of impact. That's how we change the world. We don't let the world corrupt us. We shine and reflect the light of Jesus on the world so they realize what they're missing. So their hearts are pierced with what they're missing here on Earth and in heaven.

We respond by sharing the love of Christ to one sinner at a time. We respond by sharpening each other as iron sharpens iron, one brother and one sister at a time.

God promises in John 14:27, "My peace I give you, not as the world gives you. Let not your heart be troubled, nor let it be afraid." He goes on to say, "In the world you will have tribulation, but be of good cheer, I have overcome the world" (John 16:33). We do not need to fear. Our Lord has already overcome.

I'm choosing to believe God. I believe the Holy Spirit because He confirmed the word of God thousands of times in my life and He does it every day. Our faith is being certain of what we hoped for, sure of what we can't see. My eyes are fixed on Jesus, the author and perfecter of my faith. He is my reason for living, my reason for life. God said we are a new creation in Him.

When we know Christ is real, nothing else matters but living our lives to bring others to know that same truth. To know the glory of the Father through the sacrifice of the Son.

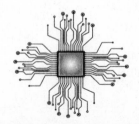

Does God Really Speak To People?

About a year and a half ago, God started to press on my heart that I was supposed to move to the Orlando area to help my buddy, Sean, start a church.

My initial thoughts were, "Lord, I don't want to go to Orlando. I like south Florida just fine." I've lived in south Florida for thirty years. I moved there in '85 from New York. I like it, and everything is just fine. But I couldn't shake the feeling that the Lord was leading me in that direction, so I got in touch with Sean in Orlando.

He wasn't ready at that point to start his church. He had kids, a couple of whom were nearing college age. He needed to take a job in the secular world to offset the cost of college. That was really the end of that.

Time went by. As we came into summertime, again, God started pressing on my heart that I was supposed to move to Orlando and help Sean start a church. I called Sean up and said, "Listen, brother. You've got this great job. You're making all this money now. How are you doing, by the way?"

He said, "Jack, I've never been more miserable because I really feel God wants me to do ministry stuff."

I said, "Well, it's funny you should mention that because God has been placing on my heart more and more that I'm supposed to come help you. I'm going to continue to pray about it."

A couple of weeks went by. A month went by. I kept on praying to make sure this was really God's will. It kept burning in my heart, refusing to let go. Everywhere I went, I would see "Orlando" this, and "Orlando" that. Every waitress was from Orlando. Every sign said Orlando.

Finally, one day I told myself, "I have to tell my wife, Beth, what's going on. Too many months have passed and I don't want to be out of God's will. I know we are supposed to follow God's call and go to Orlando." The last thing I wanted to do was try and play a prevent defense and get into this mentality of trying to hold on to what we had and what we thought was important to us.

In the Bible is a story (Luke 12:20) of the man who tried that. It's the story of a rich man who tried to build a storehouse to put away all his possessions and goods and figured, "I can eat, drink, and be merry. Now everything is accounted for and safe."

It didn't work out too well as. God said to him, "You fool. This very night your life will be required of you."

God was reminding me of that. Also, God says that a man's life does not consist in the abundance of his possessions. I was reminded not to try and hold on to what we had, not to get into this prevent defense because you know what happens in sports. It seems every time you try and play a prevent defense you lose your lead. You wind up losing the game.

It works that way in life too. Instead of taking the risks and being aggressive and using the offense that got you the lead in the first place, you calm down and start to hold on. All of a sudden, the lead dissipates and everything you've worked for is gone. Personally, I was scared of missing the blessing of God.

I know God is real. I knew I needed to trust Him completely and totally. I knew where He was trying to take me all my life and I had been refusing to go was coming to fruition right at that moment. And that was the place of trusting him completely. I knew God had so much more in store.

I've seen so much of God's miracles and blessings in my life, but God was telling me, "There's more. But you've got to step out in faith and take that leap of faith." I think what God wanted me to realize was I needed to be dependent on Him. I needed to go deeper and get to that next level of being dependent on Him.

So I took that step. I was driving with my wife, and I started to tell Beth what had been going on in my heart. I said, "Honey, it's been on my heart for three months, and I think God is telling us to move to Orlando and help Sean start a church."

She looked at me and said, "There is absolutely no way I'm going to Orlando. Out of the question. God would have to move my heart in the biggest of ways." She had been in south Florida for fifteen years. All her friends were there. Our young kids' lives were rooted in the south Florida area.

I said, "I completely understand. Would you just pray about it?"

Of course, she said yes. As the words were coming out of my mouth, as I finished telling her what was going on, I looked over to my right, and there was a huge, green highway sign that said "Orlando" on it. I thought, Okay, God. That's pretty good, considering I've lived down here fifteen years, and that sign has never been there before.

At that time, we were trying to get a drug and alcohol rehab center going in south Florida. I told myself, "This is a good idea. We'll get this center going. It will help my family financially in the future. It will help people." I had a drug problem myself in the past and enjoyed helping people attain victory over addiction, so this was a natural extension for me. I've been helping people with drug problems for over twenty years. I thought this would be a good thing. I had some investors ready to go, yet it never came together. This thing would happen. That thing would happen. We'd be looking at apartment buildings to buy, we'd be looking at people to hire, but for one reason or another, it didn't get started.

I began to pray, "God, what's going on here? I'm ready to go. Come on. Why isn't this happening?" Finally, I came to the point where I was frustrated. I didn't know why things were taking so long. I said, "You know what, God? I have got nothing. I have no plan left. All my plans haven't worked. I have no play left to call. I'm fifty-seven years old. I think I've done well, but right now I'm at a stalemate. I just don't know what to do. God, I am in your hands. You are the coach. You call the play. I am in your hands."

We'd been trying to sell our house for two and a half years. The first year, it was overpriced, but the last year and a half it was certainly priced right. Yet nobody came to buy it. We had a few people look, but there was not even one offer, not even a lowball offer to turn down. Absolutely nothing.

A few months passed by. I reminded Beth about Orlando again. She said, "I've been praying about it. If God is telling us to go, I'm in." To this day, she says she still can't believe those words came out of her mouth because it's not what she was thinking. When she opened her mouth, however, the words that came out were, "I'm going. I'm in."

I was very excited because I knew if this was meant to be, God would knit our hearts together. I knew there wouldn't be friction, and He wouldn't allow us to be torn apart by this decision. It would be a decision we would make together. I saw that God had brought her into alignment with His wishes and what I believe He was pressing on my heart.

I said, "Honey, this is great. Here's what we're going to do. We're going to go home, and we're going to start to empty out the house. We're going to take this step of faith leisurely and maybe in December we'll move up there." That was our decision. We were going to go home and start to leisurely pack up, let the kids remain at school through the end of the year.

We got home the next day. Before I could call the broker to take the house off the market, he called to say he had someone who wanted to look at it. Sure enough, the guy came and made an offer. He gave us two and a half weeks to move out of the house because he needed to move in on the fourth of September.

The minute we took our restrictions off God, the minute we said to God, "God, we're going. We're following you in faith no matter what, no matter what it costs, no matter what's at stake," God brought a buyer and took care of the house. We were blown away by God's timing.

We need to trust God and step out in faith. Now, I often feel like Elijah — and not in a good way — because one day I'm praising God and saying, "God, you're the greatest. I see your miracles everywhere," and the next day I'm fearful, and I'm scared. That's not how I want to be. I want to rest in God's peace. I want to honor God with my life. I want my heart and my life aligned with God.

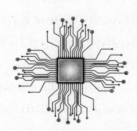

Moving Day

We had a big house, and we had lived there for thirteen years. Two and a half weeks to get out was quite the impossible task. As we were moving, as we were cleaning up and throwing things out, I saw how my values, my perception, and my appreciation for things had changed over time. All these things I once valued, things I was once trying to protect, were now worthless. Their value hadn't changed over the years, but my perception of their worth had changed. They didn't mean anything to me anymore. One thing we can know for sure is that our appreciation, our value, and our affection for God should only grow and grow and grow.

As we were preparing to move, I was looking at my kids' faces, thinking, What am I doing to them? I'm ripping them out of their lives. Jackson was born in that house. He's thirteen. Talia is eleven. This is the only home and friends they've known. I'm ripping my wife out of everything she has known and built for fifteen years — her Bible study, her best friends, and her support system.

Yet all I could think of was Noah. All I could think of was God speaking to Noah and Noah listening to God. Noah's family must have been freaking out. They must have thought he was crazy, but he didn't care. He kept going for one reason. He kept building that boat day after day, no matter what anybody said. He kept going. He kept doing it for one reason — he knew he had heard from God. He knew he had heard the voice of God.

I felt the same exact way about the Orlando move. I felt the presence of God. I know Beth was upset, and I know the kids were upset, and it broke my heart. It broke my heart, but I knew I had heard from God. I felt like a general in a war. What does the general do when everything around him is blowing up? There are casualties everywhere. The troops are freaking out. It's chaos. We're being unexpectedly attacked.

Of course, Satan wants us off the path of God and he will try to attack us and distract us at all costs. What must a general do? He must dismiss the emotion. He must dismiss the fear. He must dismiss the panic of his troops. He can't even stop to mourn the death and casualties. His job is to make on-the-spot decisions and change strategy on the spot, depending upon the minute-by-minute, second-by-second happenings. If he loses his cool or he takes his eye off the ball or he's distracted by the pain, the suffering, or the uncertainty all around him, all is lost.

At the height of my uncertainty, when I was questioning the move, I was questioning my friend Sean, I was making one of my many turnpike drives back and forth between Orlando and south Florida. At the very moment of fear, I looked up and saw a sign on the turnpike that read, "Jesus is still the answer." I saw that sign three or four more times at the most important times of my drive, of my life, in the midst of the storm.

I don't know if the move to Orlando has been a matter of God just testing my faith. Maybe He wanted to see if I'd be obedient, like Abraham offering up Isaac, or maybe it was specifically to help Sean start this church. Perhaps there was some other ministry purpose, perhaps the drug rehab center. All I know is my family and I have been blessed because of our obedience more then we could ever imagine.

God knows. All I know is that our job is to be faithful to God where He calls us. I want to be found faithful to God on all matters. I want to be found trusting of Him in all things. We've got to walk in faith each day.

I told a buddy of mine about the Orlando move and I said, "I don't know how this is going to turn out."

He said, "Well, make it good. Don't leave it to fate. Don't leave it to chance. You make it good." I believe we have that ability. I believe that's what we should do with our lives. We should make them good. I'm going to do it... what about you?

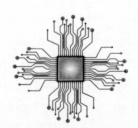

Swimming In The Deep End

Look at these great promises of God.

Isaiah 44:7: I have appointed the things that have come and will come.

God has a plan and a purpose for our life, and He will show us the way to go as we walk in the path He lays out for us one day at a time.

Isaiah 44:2: Says the Lord who made you and formed you in the womb, "I will help you. Fear not."

What problem could we possibly have? What could we possibly be worried about or upset about when God Himself has said, "Fear not. I will help you. I have created you. I will help you"? That was a tremendous comfort and blessing to me.

So we moved to Orlando. God's amazing. God's not done. God has more to do. It is now a couple of months later, and it's going by so fast. So many things are happening. God has given me witness opportunities, helping some people with addictions. I'm meeting people and plugging in. I can see God's hand all over it. I don't know where it's going. I don't know how it's going to work out.

But I can tell you this. I would not want to miss the blessings God has in store and I would be scared to miss out on them. They were worth everything. They were worth picking up my family, moving everything, going into a new adventure and a new stage of life because I want to see what

God has in store.

I feel God said, "Launch out into the deep and get your nets ready for a catch." I am grateful that, by His grace, I followed His directions.

What is God asking you to do? What does God want you to do? What area of obedience is God looking to you in? Is it to give up drugs? Is it to stop looking at pornography? Is it to love your wife for real? Is it to be honest with your finances? Is it to have integrity? Is it to get rid of your anger? Is it to practice forgiveness?

I don't know what it is, but I know it's between you and God. I hope God is sharing that very issue with you today. I hope God is telling you not to play a prevent defense, not to try and hang on to what you have.

I've seen God's power at work, and I know I need to respond and act accordingly. I hope you do too. I remember going into drug rehab decades ago. When I got out of there, I only wished I had done it sooner. I thought, "Why did I wait so long to do this?" I was so stubborn and so hanging on and fighting every step of the way what was clearly in my best interest.

Us responding to God will be the same way. I believe the only thing we'll say is, "Why didn't we do this sooner?"

I am so thankful that, at fifty-seven years old, God is not done with me. God closed the door on a thirty-one-year chapter of my life in south Florida, but I know I am meant to follow God for the next step. I'm to step out like Abraham and go wherever He leads.

God has a plan for your life as well. We are to fear nothing. We are to walk with Him because that is what really living is. We don't want to miss the abundant blessings God has for us. We don't want to miss the excitement and the joy of seeing Him at work.

God, in His loving way, works in our hearts and His timing to bring us to that point. I pray that it would be the burning desire of your heart to get to the point where you would do whatever you have to do to come closer to God. God says, "When you seek me with all of your heart, you will find me."

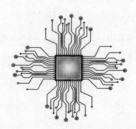

When "Help Me" Is The Only Prayer

Everybody, at some point in their life, needs a good "moving day" story. Here's mine.

We were going to move to Orlando on Friday, September 4, and as of Monday, September 1, we still didn't have a house to move into and I didn't know what mover was moving us.

Remember we only found out we were moving two and a half weeks earlier. All I could do was deal with things minute by minute. I knew the stress was taking a toll on my wife — the stress of the move, the packing, the minute-by-minute uncertainty, not knowing where we're going, who was moving us, where the kids were going to school. It was crushing on her spirit and on mine. I made many trips back and forth to Orlando. We finally got the movers going. We finally rented a house to move into only two days before we went.

I went up Thursday night with a twenty-six-foot U-Haul. On Friday morning, the movers were delivering a semi-trailer that they had loaded Thursday morning before I drove up. My wife and kids were going to hang out and enjoy the last day of school. They were going to go have a party with their friends. We had put them in school for the first month of the year because, obviously, we didn't know we were moving. So that night (Friday) I was expecting them to come up. But they got a late start. They were leaving from south Florida about 7:30 at night. I got a call from Beth about 10:30 that night, and she was crying.

I asked, "Honey, what's the matter?" I had fallen asleep and was waiting for them to call or knock on the door.

She said, "I can't get a cup of coffee."

I told her, "What do you mean you can't get a cup of coffee? You're just coming up the Florida turnpike. There are rest stops every forty-five miles. Pull in somewhere and get a cup of coffee."

She said, "No, no, no. You don't understand." Her Buick Enclave was loaded. She had the dog and the cat in the car, as well as both kids. There wasn't an inch of room in the truck. She figured that somewhere along the way, she'd stop and get a cup of coffee and get some energy. It had been a long day. She didn't realize it was Labor Day, September 4. There was no place to even pull over and park in the rest stop. There were hundreds and hundreds of cars overflowing and jammed in at every rest stop all the way up the turnpike. She was crying, calling me hysterically from mile marker 205.

She had just had it. The weight had crushed her. She was scared. She didn't want to get off one of the exits and go down a road and not know where she was going. She was frustrated and crying and broken down. I was scared that something would happen to her and the kids. I was scared they weren't safe. I was scared that she was freaking out, and she was crying.

She said, "I can't drive anymore. I can't go anymore."

I tried to talk her through to the next rest stop. She talked to me for about ten minutes and then said, "I gotta go. I gotta go," and hung up the phone.

I got on my knees, and prayed, "Oh, God, I need your help right now. God, the thing that matters to me the most, next to you, is my wife and my family, and they're in trouble. I'm worried. I'm sixty miles away, and I only have the U-Haul truck." I kept praying, "God, please protect them. Please just keep them safe, Lord. Please don't let anything happen to them."

As I was on my knees praying to God, I realized everything in my life was worthless, except for God on whom now I was totally dependent to save my family. I knew then that was where God always wants me, every moment of my life. That's what living in the spirit and walking in the spirit and walking with God is all about.

At that moment, I got it. I understood. I understood "die to self." I understood, "He must increase, and we must decrease." I understood dependence on God. I understood submission. I understood surrender. It was the greatest thing in the world. God made it clear to me that, "Jack, this is where I want you and not just when your wife and kids are in trouble and you think the things you love the most might be in jeopardy. Not just when you have no choice but to depend on me because there is absolutely nothing you can do to fix or help the situation. You must depend on me at every moment. That's where I want you every step of the way, the rest of your life, dependent on me. If you do that, you will experience my power. You will experience my Holy Spirit. You will experience my peace that transcends all understanding. You will experience my joy in your life. Then and only then can I use you the way I intend to use you, mightily for the kingdom of God." So I got it.

Let me tell you something about that feeling. You've got to know what you're looking for so you don't miss the feeling. I believe God is saying He wants us dependent on Him. We've got to know what we're looking for, and that's to be dependent on Him. Philippians 4:6 says, "Be anxious for nothing, but in everything, by prayer and petition, with thanksgiving, let your requests be made known to God, and the peace of God, which surpasses all understanding, will guard your hearts and minds through Christ Jesus."

My friend Sean came to get me, and we drove down the turnpike and were able to meet up with my family. We picked up Beth and the kids and drove them back up. They weren't harmed. That was wonderful, a tremendous blessing and I felt great joy and gratitude about that.

We all need to have those moments where we are drawn to our knees, like I was when I thought my wife and kids were in jeopardy. Their lives could have been in danger, and I came to the Lord because He was the only one who could help. We need to be in that exact same spot at every moment, on our knees, dependent on Him every day for the rest of our lives.

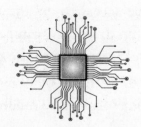

Ending Thoughts

Okay, in the beginning of this book I challenged you to download information about God, to make sure you would have access to it. We talked about the technological age that we live in and how we access and get our information. I trust God has spoken to your heart, that His Holy Spirit has moved in your life as you read this book and God has impressed certain parts of it and certain chapters as being written specifically just for you. That's because they were!

There is something extremely important that remains to be done and perhaps the most valuable thing I could share with you, and that's this... as you well know, it's not enough to download information and have access to it if you don't use it. My prayer is not only did you download the contents of this book in your mind and your heart, but that you will use it and access it. I pray you will not let it get stale, far away, or stored away in some memory storage capacity that you have access to but don't use.

God is alive and wants a loving relationship with you each and every moment, day, week, month, year of your life. Don't bury Him. Don't assume that because you have access to Him you are getting all of the benefits of a relationship with Him. If I have access to an annual pass at Disney or Universal Studios (an example I can easily relate to because I live in Florida) and I never go to the parks, I didn't get the benefits and blessings of what I had access to. Because even though I had access to it, I never used it. Please don't make that tragic mistake with your life and miss the blessings of your relationship with God now and forever in eternity.

I pray that God would be the default setting on the computer of your mind and that every time you open your eyes, your brain would immediately be flooded with thoughts, praise, wonders and communication with God himself, who deposited His Holy Spirit to live inside your heart so you always have access to Him.

It's not like when your electricity is out or when your computer doesn't work and you have no power. God supersedes and transcends all of that so you always have access to Him, His power, His will, His mercy and His grace as God said and promised so clearly, wonderfully and beautifully... "The kingdom of heaven is within you," because that's where God's Holy Spirit lives, inside your heart when you believe in Him. So to God be the glory my friend.

Most of us who have witnessed this computer, informational and technological revolution in our lifetime would say that you would be an idiot not to take advantage of it because it has so many benefits and blessings. I would say the same about missing out on God's blessing and love for your life. Use it, embrace it, explore it, learn all about it, every facet of it. And you will see that just like the computer and technological revolution, it keeps getting better and better. It keeps expanding and compounding. New ways and uses continue to arise, which bring new blessings and new benefits. That is exactly how your relationship with God will continue to explode into new areas, bringing you new benefits and blessings and showing you things you never knew. God says, "You will find me when you seek me with all of your heart." I pray that will be the desire of your heart today and you would miss none of the wonderful life God has in store for you both on Earth and for all eternity in heaven.

That's it. You have the latest technology and equipment (your mind, heart and soul). You have the power source (God Himself)! And most importantly God has gifted you with the know-how and knowledge (the truth about God) and specific instructions of how to access Him and how to get the greatest benefit and blessing out of your relationship with God. Now get to it. And remember one thing about God, you can keep downloading as much as you want forever and ever. He has an inexhaustible, unlimited amount of storage space for you, and He will keep expanding your brain and heart to take as much of Him as you want. No charge! He already paid the price.

All my love,
Jack

PS. Thought you might enjoy this prayer.
I wrote it on Father's Day.

MY
PRAYER
FOR YOU

One last thing Lord, it's all about you. We're going to turn our attention back to the world in another minute and focus on what to eat or what to watch or what to buy, something that's going to be in the trash heap of eternity. Lord, I know there are a lot of people suffering today with individual burdens, with physical sickness, with emotional issues, spiritual issues. I know there are those reading right now who are praying for loved ones, for children, sons and daughters, brothers and sisters, even mothers and fathers and spouses who are far from you, Lord. Father, would you reach into their hearts right now and speak and minister to their spirits? Would you reassure them, Lord, that you are God. You are their fortress and refuge. Would you give them the comfort of the Lord, the peace that transcends all understanding? Would you fill their worry with joy, Lord.

Lord, I know there are many reading today with financial difficulties, crushed by the expectation and burdens of society and demands of keeping up and trying as hard as they can but drowning like a man treading water and running out of air. Lord, would you speak to their hearts and minister to their hearts?

Father, many are caretakers for elderly, or sick children, or those that can't care for themselves. Lord, only you know the burden of that. Would you minister to their hearts, Lord? Would you give them peace, joy, and certainty?

Father, there are so many with so many burdens, some a burden of unforgiveness that are unable to forgive those who have hurt them. Lord, would you minister to their hearts today? Lord, so many have been wronged by others in business, in love. Some have been victims of lack of respect, lack of acknowledgment, lack of achievement that they've earned, Lord, but it's been taken away from them. Lord, would you minister to their hearts?

Lord, so many people are struggling themselves or have family members struggling with addiction. Would you minister to their hearts? Those who are struggling with a specific sin, Lord, would you minister to their hearts? Lord, I pray for repair of families, Lord, those who are separated from their families for physical, emotional, or legal reasons, Lord. I pray that you would minister to their hearts, Lord, that each one, Holy Spirit, would know for certain that you are their refuge and fortress.

Father, I pray that somehow, against all odds, even though we can't see it in the flesh or understand it, you would give them all the joy of the Lord. Today on Father's Day, the present I ask for, Lord, is more joy. You've said to me always, "Jack, you can have as much of my joy as you want. Just come closer to me. I'll come closer to you. Don't run from me. Run to me."

Lord, I just ask that you continue to minister to all those, Lord. It's so easy for us to focus on what's wrong. Sometimes we do that in life, Lord. I'm guilty too. I look at everything I don't have, everything I want, everything that didn't go the way I wanted it to go, or the things I can't see that you've already prepared and taken care of, Lord. You've done it. You've resolved everything. You knew the plan for my life before I was born. You knew me before I was in my mother's womb.

You said, "The plans I have for you are to prosper you and give you a hope and a future, not to harm you," as you promised in Jeremiah 29:11. You said as far as the east is from the west, you've forgiven all of my sins. You said no weapon formed against me will prosper. You said there is no condemnation for those in Jesus Christ. Yet sometimes I'm condemned. Sometimes we're condemned.

Lord, today I pray that, Holy Spirit, you would speak to each reader's heart and that we would focus on what we have, not what we don't have, and we would rejoice in the glory of your kingdom and the riches of our lives with you. Father, we love you. We pray all these things in your precious son Jesus' name.

Thank you for being the greatest Father ever.

DEDICATION

It is with the deepest sorrow and greatest sadness along with extreme joy that I dedicate this book. The sorrow and sadness come from a situation and circumstance my friend and brother in the Lord, **John Rabe, and his wonderful wife Wendy** have found themselves in. This year has seen Wendy heroically fight a battle against cancer. The disease came out of the blue and was a shock to her, John and their beautiful children.

As we live our lives we don't want to think that the unthinkable could happen. An illness could cut our life short, can take away all the joy and beauty that we know, can interrupt the plans that we had for our life, could cut short the time that we have with our loved ones and our time to make an impact here on earth. So that is the sadness and sorrow part, that I know my dear brother and his family are struggling and suffering, and the physical and emotional pain is taking a heavy toll on all of them. Of course, I can only imagine how they feel not having gone through this particular trial myself. My heart breaks for them. I know John has had to face the very real possibility that he may live the rest of his life without his beloved bride, soulmate and best friend by his side. And I know Wendy has had to face the reality that she may be with Jesus in heaven sooner than she had planned. Not to mention the physical battle. The pain, chemo and radiation, the treatment side effects are both painful and torturous. You may ask, where's the joy?

The joy is in watching their faith being tested and tried and being proved genuine. The joy is in knowing that the faith that they are showing is worth more than gold to God. That is the kind of faith and love that God seeks and desires and will reward with blessing for all eternity. The joy is that while it would have been easy to turn away from God, to scream at God, to question God's holiness, His authority, His plans and His actions, that's not what John and Wendy did. They didn't run from God; they ran toward Him! Waving the flag of their faith to each other, to their children, to their friends and family, and coworkers around them, and to a watching world. Never once wavering, never once abandoning the precious love and promises of their Lord and Savior Jesus Christ.

So I dedicate this book to John and Wendy, and thank them for being so transparent as to let me and the world see what they are going through and for living the message that more importantly than their pain and suffering is the certainty of their faith. And that my friends is what I believe being a Christian is all about. So thank you John and Wendy for the inspiration, which came at your own expense. Thank you for the example, and for showing me and everyone else around you, what it means to walk in faith. This is what it's all about, that moment of truth where we realize that we are going to heaven and the certainty that is a blessing and a good thing.

Of course it's sad to think about leaving loved ones and friends and family behind, but if there was ever a time to trust in Jesus Christ, if there was ever a time to be sure of your faith, if there was ever time to make certain your calling and election, this is it. And you know what, they did it! All of them, John, Wendy and their children. And therefore they are my heroes and I dedicate this book to them in love and appreciation.

I am so grateful to John for all the help he's given me on all of my books since the very first one. I salute him for knowing his priorities and for being determined to spend time with his wife and family and walk alongside her through this struggle. For turning down offers and distractions that would get in the way of giving his full attention and priority to the love of his life, his beautiful wife. So for this book he didn't have time to give his editing expertise and strategic opinion and wonderful godly insight and encouragement, but yet his heart and imprint is on every page of this book. Because it's not about what we say it's about what we do, and John and Wendy you guys are doing exactly what God has asked you to do. You're glorifying Him with your lives and actions, trusting Him in all things. I know of no greater purpose or blessing.

We continue to pray for John, Wendy and their family. I've already seen the peace of God which transcends all understanding guard their hearts during this difficult time. I've seen them kneel and place their lives and futures at the feet of the Lord, content with whatever He provides next. Our prayers are always for healing because in our human minds that is what we want and what would seem best. Yet we stand in faith trusting God that He knows best and we will consider ourselves blessed, with whatever outcome God provides. For as the apostle Paul reminded us (so many quote it and sadly don't believe in their hearts), "to live is Christ to die is gain!" We win either way! Thank you Lord for the time you allow us on this earth to live with You and for You and have an impact on the world around us. Thank You for the impact John and Wendy have had with their faithfulness, living their lives so humbly and beautifully for You. I strive and pray that someday the same would be said about me. And that is also my prayer for everyone of you reading this book.

Special Thanks

I thank the wonderful friends around me who poured into this book with their time and effort. **"Downtown" Scotty Brown**, the Pride of Pensacola, who I hope one day will become the Oracle of Orlando and move down here and bring some of that spiritual fire with him. His input and guidance into this project was the first opportunity we've had to work together and came at a much-needed time. With great input, blessing and guidance.

Scott Wolf, whose innovative and awesome cover design is ground breaking, eye-catching and inspirational. Scott, I turned you loose and gave you freedom and out of your design genius came an awesome book cover. Thanks for putting your heart and soul into the book's cover and interior design. I appreciate your friendship and having you in my life more than you can know. It was a joy to be able to work on this project together and I look forward to seeing how God would have us create and deliver more kingdom building projects in the future. Thanks to **Cara, Caleb and Sydney** for letting you devote some time to my projects. You guys are the coolest.

Amanda Brown, whose editing and soulful insight has helped and blessed me tremendously in this book as well as others. I love that you gently suggest when I might be making an ass out of myself...(smile!) and then show me ways to fix it while still keeping my message and points, and the best trick of all is you letting me believe it was my idea to change it... (smile again!) It is a privilege to work with you. Even more than your editing expertise and magic, I believe God has placed us together for a reason as I am deeply inspired by your faith and your courage as you trust God and walk through some situations that would be unimaginable and crushing for most people. Your open-mindedness and willingness to do whatever it takes for the good of your family and for God is not just a sign of your strong faith, but is as inspiration to me and I believe will be to the world as it comes to hear your story. Thank you for working with me and blessing me.

Shaun Smith and his wife Paola who welcomed baby **Josiah** into the world just a few weeks ago. I am so excited to see God bless you abundantly and exceedingly more than you can ask or imagine and the reason I'm so excited to see it is you deserve it. Thank you for your faithfulness to this book and to all my ministry projects. It is a blessing to minister alongside you brother and I am excited to see you go through the doors God is going to open and opportunities he will provide for your joy and your future because of your obedience and faithfulness.

Carl Foster. Another great buddy who has been with me through thick and thin since 2010 when my first book Don't Blow It With God was published. "Foss" I've watched you go through trials and tribulations that I would equate only to what Job must've gone through. And yet no matter how beaten or overmatched you were, you hung tough, you stayed true to God, your faith never wavered as you to trusted him with the outcome of your life and of your future. I know the best is yet to come for you and your family. I am praying for your family, for your marriage, for your children, for your health, ministry and for your business. I am honored and privileged to have a friend like you. God says "there is one a friend who is closer than a brother." It's a great description of you. Thank you for your love, support and loyalty, it means the world to me.

To my brothers at **IronMen of God, Pastor George Cope and my Tuesday morning bible study group in Maitland**, you have no idea how positively you have impacted my life and made it better. Thank you for blessing me.

To **Scott Stevens, "The Outlaw" and Alex Luk, "The Solar King"** my blood brothers, who had been with me every step of the way. Thank God for the D.O.'s! I love you guys and appreciate the opportunity to walk through life with you. You're awesome and deserve all of God's best blessings.

And my brother **Sean LaGasse** who I've had the privilege of working side-by-side with at our church here in Winter Garden. I love you. Working close with you this last year I can honestly say I could never do the things you do and I would never want to, but I am so glad that you do them! It is such a blessing to our church to have a senior pastor like you, who has a true shepherd's heart and who sacrifices himself daily for others, who loves and seeks God with all his heart. I know I don't tell you because it would be extremely sappy (and nobody likes "extreme" sap!) and maybe because we are both so busy, but I am impressed and inspired, excited and ignited about what God is going to do in the future of our church.

We moved up here to Orlando because God was pressing on our hearts to come help you and be a part of this journey. Thank you for giving us the privilege. It is our desire to continue to minister with you for the glory of God. To see the lost come to salvation and believers strengthened, encouraged, motivated and educated as they walk with the Lord, living for Him loving for Him, hopefully stealing a laugh or two along the way. Always remembering and focusing on what the priorities of life are and that is always the priorities of God. So thank you brother for being you and for making sure that the salt-and-pepper is arranged properly in the drawer... Smile!

Last, but certainly not least, I thank my wife **Beth**, for letting me be the weirdo (I mean uniquely talented individual... smile!) I am, for indulging me, for standing beside me, for trusting me to guide the family and for loving me all along the way. I don't know of a luckier man than me in that regard.

My wonderful son **Ricky** and my daughter-in-law **Kristi**. We are so proud of you and excited as you continue to build your lives together. We miss you so much, as we are separated by distance but thank goodness for Southwest Airlines. Thank you for our beautiful granddaughter whose life and future excites us and brings us joy, anticipation and hope each and every day.

To my amazing son **Jackson**, who is not just my son but also a treasured friend and confidant. Getting to watch you grow into a young man is one of the greatest joys I have ever experienced. You are special, unique and amazing. I love you so much.

To my beautiful daughter **Talia**, you are growing up way too quick. I'm not sure I agree with God's timing on that one... Smile!, but it is also an amazingly beautiful thing to see. Your inner beauty, your heart for the Lord, your love for other people, your incredible intelligence and your beautiful smile add up to the most precious package that I have ever received... the gift of a beautiful baby girl.

Beth, I want you and the kids to know my prayers are consumed with your well-being, your joy, your safety, your health, your lives, your futures, and your walk with God. God has blessed me so much with such a wonderful family and I am so lucky to get to see you guys grow and live life. Yet I take the most comfort in knowing that no matter what, that you are protected by God and God is with you and God loves you. God is always there for you and always will be.

Even in the times we don't know it, God knows and it is the truth. So thank you my children for letting me stay young by growing up again with you. That is something I never dreamed possible and didn't even know how amazingly, unbelievably, wonderful it could be. I think God just give me a little glimpse of how great heaven's going to be.

Thank you to all those who take time to read this book. I pray you are inspired and blessed. My wish and prayer for you is you do not miss the beauty of this life and of your time here on earth. I pray that you are not consumed by the issues of the world, that you are not frightened by the passing of time, but instead you embrace each and every phase and time period of your life. Loving it, experiencing it and relishing in it, as if each phase in your life were a new ride at a great theme park, or the beginning of a new season for your favorite sports team, or another chance to see Bruce Springsteen live in concert. You fill in the blanks of what excites you, but you get the point! I pray that joy for you. I pray the certainty of eternity in your heart, head, mind, soul and every fiber of your being. For with that certainty comes life!

All my love.
Jack

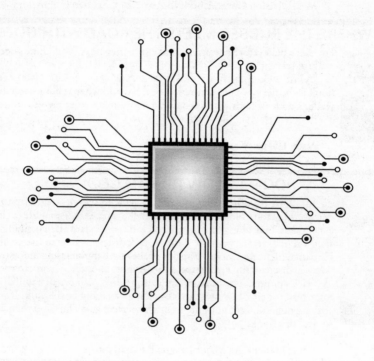

CHECK OUT
JACK'S OTHER BOOKS...

LIVE A LIFE THAT MATTERS FOR GOD

"From a clinical perspective, *Live a Life That Matters for God* has great value as a teaching and therapeutic tool for the soul. From a spiritual perspective it is a direct hit right to the heart of every Christian. This uplifting book will inspire you no matter what chapter you are reading. I love that you can pick up any chapter, anywhere, in any section in the book and be blessed immediately. Jack covers so many different topics that are relevant and critical to our growth as Christians, our happiness and our desire to walk closer with God. Jack's style is straight to the point and laser focused. Jack doesn't just tell you to do it, he shows you how!"

Julie Woodley,
MA, Division Chair American Assoc. of Christian Counselors

WHERE THE RUBBER MEETS THE ROAD WITH GOD

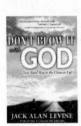

For every believer who wants to make sure they hear "Well done good and faithful servant."

"A knock out punch for Jesus if there ever was one. Jack Alan Levine's book is the heavyweight champion of the world when it comes to Christians walking a life of faith with God. Read it and make certain you will wear the champion's crown of life for Christ."

Nate "Galaxy Warrior" Campbell,
3x Lightweight Champion Of The World

DON'T BLOW IT WITH GOD

In "Don't Blow It With God", Jack Levine reveals his road map to discovering God's blueprint for living the ultimate Christian life each and every day. Come along for the ride as God teaches Jack life-changing lessons that will help you in your life journey. Jack discovers how to live an abundant Christian life experiencing true joy, peace and happiness and along the way you will discover the formula and the insights about how you can too.

"Jack's unique style of communicating God's plan for an abundant life is a must read for all Christians. This book knocks it out of the park. If you've been striking out and want your life to be the perfect game for God then you need to read this book."

Chris Hammond, Major League Baseball pitcher

MY ADDICT YOUR ADDICT

This book is about addiction. Author Jack Levine has counseled thousands of people over the years who have gone through addiction, and knows what a torturous life it can be to be caught up in it. It's an awful thing.

He's experienced addiction in his own life and as a parent, as he watched his son struggle with addiction for years (it started when he was 18).

Whether you are in the throes of addiction yourself or seeing a loved one suffer through it, this book can help you. Jack has results and solutions for real-life situations. Each person's situation is different, but the root is the same for everybody. Through his own story, he can tell you what the choices are, the impacts of those choices, the results of those choices, and what sacrifices you'll have to make to get where you want to be.